Black
Women,
Black
Love

Black Women, Black Love

America's War on
African American Marriage

Dianne M. Stewart

SEAL PRESS

New York

Seal Press
Hachette Book Group
1290 Avenue of the Americas, New York, NY 10104
sealpress.com @sealpress
Printed in the United States of America

First Edition: October 2020

Published by Seal Press, an imprint of Perseus Books, LLC, a subsidiary of Hachette Book Group, Inc. The Seal Press name and logo is a trademark of the Hachette Book Group.

Some names and identifying details have been changed to protect the privacy of individuals.

The Hachette Speakers Bureau provides a wide range of authors for speaking events. To find out more, go to www.hachettespeakersbureau.com or call (866) 376-6591. The publisher is not responsible for websites (or their content) that are not owned by the publisher.

Print book interior design by Amy Quinn

Library of Congress Cataloging-in-Publication Data has been applied for.

ISBNs: 978-1-58005-818-6 (hardcover); 978-1-58005-816-2 (ebook)

LSC-C

10 9 8 7 6 5 4 3 2 1

To all the Black women in the world who desire
and deserve healthy, loving relationships

Contents

Introduction

Marriage is a pervasive and compelling institution—a subject our culture cannot relinquish.[1] From top-grossing films and popular sitcoms to novels, self-help tools, and scholarly studies, the subject of marriage occupies a central place in American life. The archetypal image of standing before the wedding altar with one's perfect soul mate remains irresistible for many, and associations of love, romance, and delight with modern Western marriage continue to captivate.[2] Our relationship worlds revolve within the universe of love and marriage.

Yet it's no secret that marriage is not what it used to be in America. Across the last century, marriage rates declined and divorce rates increased by record numbers, regardless of racial or ethnic background. The beginning of the twenty-first century is already showing similar patterns. But the data pertaining to rates of marriage among Black women register a distinctive social reality. The 2010 US Census, for example, revealed that in 2009, 71 percent of Black women in America were unmarried. Of that group, 71 percent of Black women between the ages of twenty-five and twenty-nine and 54 percent between the ages of thirty and thirty-four had never been married.[3]

These statistics correspond with the decline in marriage among African Americans since 1960. In that year, 61 percent of African Americans over the age of seventeen were married, compared to 74 percent of Whites and 72 percent of Hispanics. By 2010 those percentages had dropped to 30 percent for African Americans, 55 percent for Whites, and 47 percent for Hispanics.[4] Data for the year 2012 continue to show striking disparities. Among forty- to forty-four-year-old women, 88 percent of White women, 83 percent of Hispanic women, and only 62 percent of Black women had married at least once.[5]

Most heterosexual Black women in America today, whether parenting offspring or not, are single by circumstance, not by choice.[6] The trope of the "single Black mother" is much more salient in America's shared imagination than that of the "single Black father" and is often coupled with a different image of the Black male counterpart: "the *absent* Black father."[7] Among policy efforts aimed at single-parent families, the focus on parenting and marriage eclipses the larger problem of absent Black male partners for Black women in general.[8] And despite these decades-long efforts to encourage marriage among single parents, unresolved issues remain.

Perceiving that marriage, especially when healthy, tenders a range of transgenerational rewards for families, communities, and the wider American society, the federal government has launched a series of initiatives designed to increase the rates of marriage among American citizens. The relevant legislation and guidelines for accessing federal resources have always emphasized special incentives for "low-income" women, who often assume primary child-rearing responsibilities, and "at-risk" couples, inclusive of high school adolescents. The African American Healthy Marriage Initiative (AAHMI), a branch of President George W. Bush's Healthy Marriage Initiative (HMI), targeted Black cohabiting couples and single parents specifically and empowered varied organizations and entities to provide culturally competent healthy marriage programs.[9]

Under President Barack Obama's administration, these incentives were reinforced and expanded to encompass official Healthy Marriage and Responsible Fatherhood programs, with the objective of closing the marriage gap and reversing the trend of declension.[10]

Donald Trump put his own spin on past efforts when he unveiled his April 2018 executive order on economic mobility. Among his guidelines for public service agencies is the directive to "promote marriage as a way of escaping poverty."[11]

However, this range of federal initiatives shows that the federal government has miscalculated the problem and its causes. The decoded identity of America's "low-income" mothers, "at-risk" youths, and "irresponsible fathers" is disproportionately Black. And for Black women—the group most likely to check the "never married" survey box—the strategy's deficiencies are all the more evident. By treating the issue as a moral one that demands solutions aimed at socializing poor, "at-risk" (disproportionately Black) women to value marriage, policy makers and implementers have missed the mark.[12] The trouble is not with Black women failing to value marriage; it is the shrinking demographic of those whom Black women want to marry. Instead, federal resources and policy efforts should have moved in the direction of ensuring pathways to financial stability and wealth building, strengthening the range of prosocial kinship networks beyond the nuclear family that remain significant to poor Black women, and increasing the available pool of marriageable Black men.[13]

During my college days in the late 1980s, the perceived social fragility of Black men's existence in the United States compelled me and so many of my Black female counterparts to rehearse the statistic that "for every eligible Black man, there are seven eligible Black women."[14] Black women have never had it as good as other American women when it comes to romantic coupling and marriage. In a pivotal scene from the movie *Sleepless in Seattle*, a male news reporter reminds his female colleagues that "it is easier to be killed by a terrorist after the age of forty than it is to get married."[15] Immediately, Meg Ryan's character, Annie, chimes in, "That is not true; that statistic is not true." However, Rosie O'Donnell's character, Becky, the unmarried, lovelorn spinster, apparently knocking on forty's door, wins the audience's sympathy as she mutters just slightly above her breath, "It's not true, but it feels true."

Watching the scene for the first time, I became acutely aware that the social and emotional distance between Becky and me was measured by the fact that what *felt* true about dating and marriage options for White women actually *was* true about the available pool of Black men. Black men experience the highest mortality, unemployment, and incarceration rates in the country.[16] Thus, for Black women across the age spectrum,[17] the gross imbalance between their personal and professional readiness for marriage and their Black male counterparts' unpreparedness and unavailability could not be *more* true. In some cases Black women lack dating prospects within their socioeconomic group, and in other cases they don't have any dating prospects *at all*!

Growing up Black and navigating my own passage from girlhood to womanhood in North America, I had never expected that the social markers of race and gender would count against me so heavily in the arenas of romantic love and marriage. In obvious public arenas of social mobility—educational and professional attainments—I might have expected racism and sexism to play a role. But even love and marriage are not intrinsically private affairs. They too confer social goods and privileges, and they can also siphon them away.

By the time I entered college, I was awakening to some of the challenges Black women were facing when it came to love and marriage, but I remained a bit of a hopeless romantic. I had latched on to the love story of my great-grandparents Margaret "Mammy" Blissett and Nathaniel "Natty" Brown, whose shared love was so pure that it became my standard for how love should look and feel. Their story stayed with me from girlhood to young womanhood, issuing a strong dose of confidence that enduring love and marriage would never elude me, even if it had eluded so many Black women around me.

Reality proved more difficult. I wedded my first husband one month before I began my doctoral studies in my midtwenties and received my divorce decree one month before I walked across the stage to accept my PhD degree just four years later. The archive of my thirties and early forties stored additional marriage and divorce certificates, each document a story unto itself of shared hopes and disappointments. For much of my adult life, as far as I could see, no Natty of my generation was anywhere to be found in these United States of America. My personal experiences with love and marriage typified another common condition Black women who do fall in love and marry Black men know all too well—early or serial marital dissolution.[18] But I wasn't yet able to see my experience as something collective, shared among many Black women in America.

It was only while researching the topic of love and marriage among heterosexual African Americans for a new course I was developing in the early 2000s that I was able to connect the dots. I began to comprehend not just the gravity of my own and other Black women's unfulfilled romantic desires and hopes for enduring marriage but also the structural nature of our failure to achieve those desires and hopes. The 2004 course, a seminar aptly titled Black Love, addressed diversified themes related to love in the African American experience, with romantic love making up just a small section on the syllabus. However, as I collected materials for the "Black Love and Romance" unit and acknowledged what the sources were telling me—that Black romantic love is deeply entangled with structural power—I developed a different take on the problem. By the end of the course, I could only characterize Black women's lack of options for meaningful love and partnership with Black men as the nation's most hidden and thus neglected civil rights issue to date.

Inspired in part by Black students' intensified racial justice activism both at Emory and nationwide, the 2015–2016 academic year, which seemed to beg for another iteration of my Black Love course, allowed me to explore fresh ways of framing and exposing America's most hidden civil rights issue in preparation for a fall 2016 new and improved Black Love lecture course. While revising the syllabus, I discovered even more materials indicating how systemic the crisis of an undesired single life is among millions of Black women in this nation who either seek love and marriage with Black men or whose marriages to Black men are in peril and often end in divorce. It was soon evident that more needed to be said on this subject from a different angle. Prevailing authors present the problem as a personal hardship or a by-product of socioeconomic, political, and cultural transitions in American life that have impacted Black people disproportionately since the 1960s. *Black Women, Black Love* is my attempt not only to examine what the numbers and narratives tell us about Black women's marital status across four centuries, but also to uncover what historical perspective and cultural patterns reveal about the structural forces that have impacted the quality and assets of Black women's marriages over those four centuries.

The hidden causes of racial and gender disparities in America's marriage market and their compromising effects upon millions of Black women's health and wellness have yet to be fully unveiled. Some point to economic and cultural shifts as well as the myriad social crises afflicting Black communities, including addiction, underresourced schools, and elevated levels of crime that disproportionately impact the lives of Black men and usher them to prison or the grave prematurely at much higher rates than they do Black women.[19] Influential as they are, these factors signal recent developments in the four-century domino effect that has dogged Black people's efforts to surmount the tangible traumas wrought by America's peculiar heritage of racial slavery. The roots of the marriage dilemmas that single Black heterosexual women who desire Black male husbands currently face lie in the soils of slavery, in their ancestors' involuntary presence in these United States.[20]

I can imagine that it's difficult for many Americans to digest this claim. Our country's reigning fictions about its practice of racial enslavement and its enduring effects on racial ascription and stratification today render inaccessible the true underlying causes of Black women's marital dilemmas. The average American's conviction that slavery is long in the past and everything experienced in the present is a matter of individual success or failure precludes them from recognizing how racism consigns Black people to crippling structural disparities totally beyond their control. Those disparities extend to love and marriage when considering the history of Black women in America.

Black women's love odyssey has been interwoven with the nation's political and economic history in ways no other group can lay claim to. State-enforced forbidden love afflicts Black women and the entire Black community, but most people are oblivious to this fact. We know all too well how ideologies of White supremacy and White racism have nurtured batteries of state laws and shared American social norms proscribing romantic and sexual liaisons across Black and White racial lines. The policing and punishing of romantic relationships that transgress the Black-White racial boundary are powerful tropes in America's collective consciousness. My own collegiate experience of witnessing the occasional Black male classmate suffer serious consequences for dating a White female compelled me to broach the subject with my two younger brothers as each was about to begin his college career. I can remember distinctly warning them against developing any sexual or romantic relationships with White women, lest they become accused of sexual assault once a White father got wind that his baby girl was dating a Black boy. My brother Kevin's creamy caramel skin tone and lean, lanky build could possibly temper some White fears generated by his six-foot-three frame, but I was particularly apprehensive about my brother Trevor, who was a handsome, athletic figure with phenotypic deep-brown skin that looked like a silky mixture of the most delectable dark-chocolate fondue. His skin shade was an added liability.[21]

Even in our present century, films such as *Guess Who* (2005), *Something New* (2006), and *Loving* (2016) remind us of the historical and contemporary risks surrounding Black-White coupling and marriage in America. In our haste to associate forbidden love with the taboo of miscegenation, however, we have overlooked something grave in the African American experience. The histories and narratives that fill the pages of this book indicate that we don't have to look beyond the Black community to address the issue of forbidden love. Over the centuries, American rituals of racist sexism have meddled with the love lives of far too many Black women and men, creating a culture that, for all intents and purposes, forbids *intraracial* Black love. In this book, then, I deploy the concept of "forbidden Black love" to reference the manifold structures and systems that make prosocial romantic love, coupling, and marriage difficult, delayed, or impossible for millions of Black people in America. Taking readers from the era of slavery to the era of social media, I study the anatomy of forbidden Black love and argue that this neglected aspect of our shared American heritage is our nation's most unrecognized civil rights issue.

From the early 1500s to the mid-1800s, African men and women were brought against their will to America not for love but for the labor and profit their bodies could produce.[22] Across an epoch of enslavement, even their intimate engagements, whether desired or compulsory, often amounted to a form of sexual labor and capital that delivered more Black bodies into bondage. American slavery could function optimally only if, in conjunction with other tactics of domination, its stakeholders strategically disrupted and even extinguished Black love.[23] It is not overreaching to say that Black love had to steal social, psychological, and physical space to survive the all-consuming pressures of White surveillance and reproductive labor in the slave economy.

After slavery, African descendants confronted the paradox of being emancipated yet unfree and unprotected in civil society. Between the formal abolition of slavery in 1865 and the signing of the Voting Rights Act in 1965, they lived under the incessant threat of death and demise because they were Black in a nation that colored itself

White and authenticated the fabrication of racial difference. This hundred-year reign of terror spawned policies and American customs that continued to annul and desecrate Black marriage and family life as well as "disappear" Black men from their partners, spouses, and loved ones. It provoked several Great Migrations of millions of African descendants who left the South in search of safer environments and viable economic opportunities that could support Black love and Black relationships.

Even when purportedly encouraged by missionaries and federal agents of the Freedmen's Bureau, Black marriages were harmed and undermined. Black people's marital assets remained in jeopardy, as incentives to accommodate Euro-Western marriage customs stripped postenslaved Black women of personal and economic autonomy. With their husbands assuming roles as "head of household," Black Southern wives quickly learned that their spousal status legally fettered them to patriarchal family structures and labor policies. Adding to this injury, marriage rights and privileges did little to protect Black widows of deceased and disabled veterans against federal, state, and municipal governmental powers that frequently denied them spousal pension benefits. And when public servants participated in or turned a blind eye to the lynchings of Black husbands and wives, often for invented crimes they never committed, they were supporting the murder of human beings, but they also were supporting the murder of Black marriage.

Personal testimonies from Black women and children whose lives were touched by federal and state welfare programs, especially during the late 1950s and 1960s, also indicate that Black love and marriage were adversely affected by callous policies that played into racist tropes emphasizing Black women's presumed propensity toward promiscuity, deceitfulness, and inept mothering. Just a few decades later, another strategy of containing Black communities in America was unfolding—mass incarceration. Ballooning almost overnight, the prison industrial complex and its craving for Black male inmates would shine such a bright light on America's heritage of forbidden Black love that even a lazy observer could not miss it. Products of White America's anxiety about Black freedom, the consequences of this nation's not so subtle historical proscription of Black love have reverberated across every dimension of Black people's personal and public lives, from child rearing to wealth building.

But there are other contributing factors to the intolerable state of Black women's inadequate options for marriage. The psychology of beauty and desire in Black communities often reinforces Eurocentric aesthetic values and ideals pertaining to physical characteristics such as skin shade, facial features, and hair texture. Slavery was the petri dish that cultured colorism and phenotypic stratification (CPS)[24] in the American experience. Over time, this psychic inheritance came to dominate the standards of beauty and marriageability upheld by many Black families, individuals, and even organizations. In the twenty-first century, CPS remains potent and decisive, giving light-complexioned women advantages over medium- and dark-skinned women who seek to marry Black men. Those advantages extend to the quality and assets of the mates fair-skinned women are likely to attract because they marry Black men with comparable or superior educational levels and social status at higher rates than their dark-skinned sisters.

Black Women, Black Love amplifies the resonances between these historical realities and the peculiar privation of love and marriage that Black women face today. Each chapter exposes the tangible and intangible forces that have operated systemically across four centuries to preclude far too many Black women in America from enjoying enduring and rewarding romantic love and marriage with Black men. The deliberate focus on heterosexual unions throughout the book in no way seeks to discount sexual diversity as a constant dynamic of the human condition—one that contributes to a repertoire of resourceful coupling and family arrangements beyond that of the heteronormative nuclear family. Moreover, just as some Black women pursue happiness in part through same-sex relationships and marriage, others who identify as heterosexual never aspire to marry; among those who do, not all desire to have children.

Black Women, Black Love aligns with no political or religious agenda in addressing the dilemmas that Black women who *do* desire prosocial coupling and family life with Black men face. Instead, without ignoring that marriage can be a prison under many circumstances, it takes for granted the plethora of global studies showing that marriage secures and promotes institutional, social, and economic assets that enhance individuals' and couples' health, wellness, and sense of satisfaction.[25] Having no viable options to fall in love with Black men might be inconsequential to Black women who don't desire a coupled life with Black men, but a veritable national "sorority" of disappointed and dismayed Black women stands ready to testify to the contrary.

While this volume probes Black women's collective trajectory of love and lovelessness within the US context, it explores as well the contrived circumstances under which millions of Black men have disappeared from the pool of available partners for Black women. The forces behind their steps away from the homes they were expected to forge with Black women have etched into African American history trails of both "calculated disappearance" and "strategic disappearance." Lynchings, false imprisonment, welfare policies, mass incarceration, and other structures of surveillance and social control have engineered the calculated disappearance of Black men in America. And Black men's responses to those forces have required at times their strategic disappearance—leaving their partners and families either temporarily or permanently to circumvent the worst possible outcomes for their loved ones and themselves. We must closely follow both trails to arrive at the roots of why Black women's pursuit of love and marriage has been fraught with so much frustration and tragedy. Thus, in presenting an account of what can only be called America's war on African American marriage through the eyes of Black women, this book provides an account of Black men's experiences across the same rocky terrain.

The tear-stained pages of Black women's collective love tome in this country hold many transgenerational stories of love deferred, held in abeyance, and spoiled. Owing to the centuries-long structural violence against Black persons, the theft of their labor and resources, and the grievous violations of their human and civil rights in this American democracy, Black women's testimonies of stolen love and stolen legacies are legion. However, unearthing the causes of Black women's tragic experiences with forbidden Black love should not silence other historical accounts of their romantic thriving and victories. Portraits of love's revolutionary and sustaining power in Black women's lives allow this book's stories of trauma to be accompanied by stories of hope and resilience.

Attempting to understand those stories, with sensitivity to their personal value for those who lived them as well as what they tell us about patterns in Black life and Black love, requires an extensive network of conversation partners, including social science scholars, and I incorporate a fair amount of statistical and other social science data into my analysis across the chapters. My aim in doing so, however, is not to settle long-standing debates about the socioeconomic forces impinging upon the Black marriage market, especially since the 1960s, the period when African American marriage rates fell dramatically. Coupling social science and statistics with historical research within African American studies scholarship allows us to ask questions about the quality and condition of Black love across the centuries. Even when marriage rates were relatively high, the forces of Jim Crow White supremacy often overwhelmed the limited material and immaterial resources Black couples had to safeguard their love for one another and accrue the expected benefits that marriage supposedly promised.

Echoing W. E. B. Du Bois's 1903 caution to his "Gentle Reader" that "the problem of the Twentieth Century is the problem of the color line," *Black Women, Black Love* shows its courageous readers that, for women of African descent in America, the problem of the twenty-first century remains the problem of forbidden Black love.[26] Once this issue is revealed with candor, we can shift our gaze to see the crisis in Black women's love and marriage outcomes as a public matter of national concern. All Americans, including public servants, policy makers, activists, and religious leaders, have a role to play in establishing new structures and creating optimal environments that foster loving, healthy, and enduring Black couples and communities. By learning to love Black women and Black communities, which I hope this book has the affective capacity to inspire, America can dismantle the structural foundations of forbidden Black love and the unnatural loneliness and heartbreak of so many Black women across our nation.

Jumping the Broom

Racial Slavery and America's Roots of Forbidden Black Love

"*Never marry again in slavery.*" A peculiar piece of advice. Poetic in its brevity and clarity. No other arrangement of five common words could better reveal the contradictions confining enslaved Black women's options for sustained romantic love and marriage during their years of bondage in this country. When twenty-four-year-old Margaret "Peggy" Garner uttered these words to her husband, Robert, on her deathbed, she certainly was not the first among Black women in America to change her mind about the benefits of marriage while legally enslaved.[1]

The institution of marriage assumes a degree of sovereignty for the individuals involved to exercise responsibility for one another and the children they are likely to produce. By her early twenties, however, Margaret Garner had come to know better than any that slavery granted no such liberty. Married bondpersons were mere property in the eyes of the law, and they had no rights over the destinies of their children. They could never know with certainty what the future held for them, their families, and their marriage vows because they answered to the legal authority of their captors. As Margaret came to understand, marriage under the condition of chattel slavery invited only an intensification of the system's most horrific rituals and psychological assaults. And this is what prompted the young bondwoman, moribund from typhoid fever, to forewarn her husband of something he in fact already knew.[2] The privileges and responsibilities of marriage were jeopardized daily by slavery's solicited and unsolicited intimacies.

Endless studies examine racial slavery in America as a reverberating assault upon Black people's historic and contemporary liberties in perhaps every arena of life but one: *romantic love and marriage.* The difficulties Black people, and particularly Black women, face today establishing romantic relationships leading to marriage are explained often without causal reference to slavery. Yet from its very beginnings, the transatlantic trade in human cargo, which set the American institution of African bondage in motion, required the disruption of intimate relationships and marriages. Since the average age range of Africans destined for slave markets was fifteen to thirty, the majority of female captives aboard slave vessels were married with children. "These women were not only daughters and sisters. . . . [T]hey were also wives and mothers leaving husbands and young children behind, or seeing them embark on another ship."[3] In 1669 one such "Angolan" woman, Hagar Blackmore, told the Massachusetts Middlesex County Court how she was "stolen away from her husband and the infant that nursed on her breast"—her enduring trauma of capture punctuated by the dissolution of love and life nurtured through familial bonds.[4]

Blackmore's bondage in America sundered her from more than just her conjugal family. Captivity permanently ruptured her ties to a robust kin group, the source of her social wealth and personal meaning. Marriage would have been the social glue holding together Blackmore's family and clan. Whether polygynous, polyandrous, or monogamous, marriage in Africa was a rite of passage that regulated social life and the care of children and elders. It prescribed rules for inheritance and was the structure through which one's lineage and clan proliferated.

The geography of African marriage was vast during Blackmore's time, as it is today. However, owing to shared cultural orientations across diverse regions of the continent, we can safely assume that Blackmore had many mothers, fathers, and senior and junior siblings, but probably no cousins. She would not have entered into marriage *because of* romantic love and affection, though this is not to say that love and affection were necessarily absent in her conjugal relationship. Seminal as it was for the children it produced, the conjugal union was an aperture to a wider marital arrangement. Blackmore was indeed married to her husband's family members, too; however, her entire identity did not melt into her husband's. Although her culture would have given her permission to tie her wrapper differently around her waist or adorn herself in some way to signal her new social status, Blackmore, whose aboriginal name enslavement erased, would not have relinquished any of her personal names to assume her husband's family name. Nor would marriage terminate her inheritance rights in her biological family lineage or her right and responsibility to participate in the agricultural economy to provide for herself and her family.

Blackmore and her husband had entered marriage because parents and family elders recognized advantages for both kin groups. Their marriage would unify two kin groups to ensure lineage continuity. And Blackmore likely derived a momentous sense of accomplishment and satisfaction when she sacralized her marriage through a series of ceremonies. Involving gifts and other signs of investment, acknowledgment of new kin alliances, pledges, and agreements, not solely or primarily between Blackmore and her husband, but between their kin groups, the rituals involved would have confirmed the sanction of ancestors, elders, and parents. Once married, Blackmore's experience of biological motherhood was further spiritual confirmation that her marriage was "meant to be," and so the calamity of being severed from her family and clan had to have imposed an exile upon her soul that was just as intolerable as the physical disruption and treacherous voyage across the Atlantic. Blackmore's capture and absence also meant that the two kin groups she connected like a linchpin were torn asunder. Thus, she was not the only victim of the transatlantic trade. The people she united through marriage suffered as well and paid a heavy cost because of her capture.[5]

American slavery exploited the marital and familial disruptions that began in Africa for women such as Blackmore, and advanced a host of other intimate intrusions pioneered by the transatlantic slave trade. Slavery's racial logic brought Blackness into existence as a human identity at the same time it brought forbidden Black love to the African captives and their descendants exclusively adorned by its chains and whips. When we examine the status of Black women under the purview of this nation's founding legislative decisions, for example, we find that as early as 1643 the Virginia General Assembly ratified laws that levied taxes on African-descended women's labor, slave or free. Similar taxes were placed on men as heads of their households and on those who worked in agriculture. However, women were not previously taxed until African women alone were identified as a source of revenue for the colonies. The African female labor tax priced many free African descendants out of the marriage market, for if a free Black woman was married, her husband was responsible for paying the tax. It also placed an undue economic burden upon single women of African descent who had to finance the tax without spousal support.[6] Historians might caution that no causal relationship ensues between this practice and the circumstances that have hindered Black women's opportunities to find marriage partners in later centuries. But the larger context of twentieth-century federal and state welfare laws that adversely impacted Black women's marriageability is redolent with seventeenth-century precursors.

Experiences of prohibited love are indeed legion across America's temporal and geographic landscapes of slavery, reminding us that, for nearly 250 years, enslaved African descendants in America, whom Whites bought, sold, mortgaged, gifted, and inherited as movable property, had no legal rights, essentially—and certainly no right to pursue love, coupledom, and marriage based upon their own somatic desires. As disclosed through the accounts of the women's lives examined in this chapter, love for them and their kinfolk was directly or indirectly *forbidden* through the often combined factors of sexual and reproductive violence and control, "misogynoir" jurisprudence and legal transactions, and the domestic slave trade and family separation.[7] In *Bound in Wedlock*, historian Tera Hunter insists, "The character and nature of slave marriages and families depended in large degree on regional, demographic, and temporal shifts in slavery during the antebellum era. . . . And yet there was a great deal of consistency in the challenges slaves faced and the strategies they used to adjust." This chapter's preoccupation is with the "great deal of consistency in the challenges slaves faced," challenges that fostered patterns of prohibition and expectations of fracture regarding love, coupling, and marriage among enslaved African descendants in this country.

Scholars attribute the low rates of heterosexual marriage among Black women and men today to a range of complicated factors that have regulated post-1960s Black life, including shifts in modes of production and socioeconomic institutions as well as mass incarceration and relaxed cultural norms and attitudes about marriage, sex, and divorce. Notwithstanding these explanations, sexual and reproductive violence, "misogynoir" legislation, and separation of families during the slave period have had both a rippling effect and an epiphenomenal impact on Black women's postemancipation episodes with romantic love and marriage in this country. These interlocking pillars of forbidden Black love reappear in the scope of abuses women of African descent have suffered since slavery, whether during Reconstruction, the Great Migration, Black women's entry into the welfare system, or mass incarceration. To understand fully their reappearance and the historical consciousness many Black women today have regarding the circumstances provoking their romantic dilemmas, it is essential to begin our narrative in slavery.

Across two and a half centuries in America, the psychic and emotional trauma married bondpersons endured at the hands of slaveholders and their surrogates was incalculable. What went through the mind of a bondman who had to leave his wife and marriage bed when the slave master or overseer showed up at night? How did married bondpersons manage the threat the domestic slave trade posed to their families or cope with the dissolution of married life when one spouse was sold separately? If granted the privilege of remaining together or in the same vicinity, what did enslaved parents do when the master or his sons began violating their pubescent daughters?

The narratives in this chapter explore each of these questions, illustrating the incompatibility between the sovereignty of slavery and the sovereignty of marriage. Laws and customs designed to uphold and protect slavery trivialized, punished, and forbade Black love and marriage, making it hazardous or impossible for couples in abroad marriages to spend quality time together. Slavery's culture of forbidden Black love likewise deprived individuals of selecting their marriage partners and wedding rituals. The authority of slave owners nullified the authority of the enslaved to protect their spouses and children from the clutches of the domestic slave trade and from sexual, physical, and mental abuse. Even the physical labor enslaved women and girls performed left them vulnerable to sexual advances of any White person with access to their bodies. There was nowhere to hide, practically no way to escape the White gaze, the White penis, and White America's stratification of beauty by phenotype. Categorically, slavery's scale of sexual valuation made Black girls and women of all phenotypes sexual prey in the eyes of their owners.[8] However, Whites' preferential treatment of mixed-race persons created a color-caste system that endured across the centuries and remains influential in today's Black marriage market.

Only by sifting through interviews, letters, poetry, legal documents, and court records of the slave period can we behold the tangled roots of forbidden Black love that nourished these and other conditions of American slavery. The nature and structure of this nation's practice of bondage left Black captives with virtually no weapons to defend themselves against its war on Black love and marriage, and each story to follow illustrates this predicament acutely, penetratingly, horrifyingly, to say the least. The singular message gleaned from the initial 250-year period of Black involuntary presence in this country is that slavery constituted the first battlefield in America's war on African American marriage, making marriage unstable and unworkable for millions of African descendants. This fact must be tempered, however, by testaments of bondpersons' inscrutable capacity to "make a way out of no way."[9] In the thick of their daily battle for love, not all vanquished by slavery succumbed to the forces bent on destroying their bonds of affection. The ensuing accounts of Black love and marriage also feature enslaved persons' aggressive and affective resistance to slavery's encroachment upon their romantic relationships and marital unions. Undeniably, a good number accommodated the spoken and unspoken rules of forbidden Black love. But some fled north to pursue Black love, some chose enslavement over manumission to preserve Black love, others sacrificed their lives for Black love, and some, like Margaret Garner, killed in the name of Black love.

KILLING THEM AT ONCE RATHER THAN BY PIECEMEAL: MARGARET'S STORY

Margaret initially began her northward quest not to kill but to pursue unfettered Black love—self-love, love of her husband, Robert "Simon Jr.," of her family, and of course, of freedom. On January 27, 1856, after fleeing bondage in northern Kentucky, the Garners; their four children; Robert's parents, Simon Sr. and Mary; and nine friends from neighboring farms traversed a frozen Ohio River and separated into smaller units. The three generations of the Garner family remained together and sought refuge at the home of Margaret's uncle Joe Kite.

Within hours, their hopes of securing freedom farther north were thwarted, as slave catchers and US marshals hunted them down and surrounded the house with reinforcements. Robert, however, not only had left Kentucky with his master's horses, but also had taken his gun and used it in the showdown with authorities. Defending his family's liberty, Robert discharged his weapon and wounded one or more of his opponents, while his pregnant wife killed their two-year-old daughter and injured their other children as she attempted to kill them and herself.[10] At this critical crossroads Margaret was forced to choose between surrendering her children to a world of unending horrors or fleeing from it eternally. Although outnumbered and overpowered by their opponents, Margaret achieved a measure of victory in sparing at least one of her children from returning to slavery's stranglehold.

Margaret's Black maternal actions can be understood only through the prism of slave life. One contemporary newspaper reported that Margaret "and the others complain of cruel treatment on the part of their master, and allege that as the cause of their attempted escape."[11] Margaret certainly had revealing scars to this effect. "White man struck me" was all she said in response to inquiries about what had to have been flesh wounds that left such glaring imprints on her left cheek and temple.[12]

Convincing evidence, if not outright proof, also suggests that Margaret endured repeated sexual violation at the hands of her master, Archibald Gaines (or another White man), and her two fair-skinned children were believed to be sired by Gaines, the man with the most access to Margaret, even more than her husband, who lived about a mile away from Gaines's Maplewood farm. Although identified as chestnut brown (Margaret) and a Negro (Robert), their children Mary and Cilla were described as near white in complexion.

That Gaines insisted to deputies dispatched to recover his human property that "no harm whatsoever should be done the little children" conveys an emotional investment in their well-being atypical of a slaveholder with no blood ties to the fugitive children he owned.[13] While we may never know for certain whether Gaines sexually assaulted Margaret, we do know that, with only seconds to act decisively and successfully, Margaret zeroed in on slaughtering her girl child first. Cutting her throat five inches long and three inches deep, from ear to ear, Margaret ensured that two-year-old Mary would not return to the physical, sexual, and reproductive violation awaiting her at the Maplewood farm.[14]

Margaret had apparently attempted to kill all four of her children on that dreadful day of reckoning. After the family was apprehended, her sons, Tommy and Sammy, ages six and four, respectively, were found with knife wounds across their backs and shoulders, and her infant daughter Cilla had sustained a blow to the head from a shovel.[15] However, something telling remains with Margaret's infanticidal wishes and filicidal act concerning her two *girl* children. A local minister, Reverend P. C. Bassett from Cincinnati's Fairmount Theological Seminary, interviewed Margaret after Mary's death, during which she denied any mention that she was temporarily insane.[16] "I was as cool as I now am; and would much rather kill them at once, and thus end their sufferings than have them taken back to slavery and be murdered by piecemeal." According to Bassett, "She then told the story of her wrongs. She spoke of her days of unmitigated toil, of her nights of suffering, while the bitter tears coursed their way down her cheeks."[17] Another curious detail about Margaret's daughters might help answer the question of how Margaret suffered under cover of night. Her two near-white girls and the baby she was carrying at the time of her recapture were conceived during the exact periods when Gaines's wife, Elizabeth, was pregnant and unable to engage in sexual relations with her husband without endangering her and her unborn baby's health.[18]

In the aftermath of the family's recapture, Margaret's remaining daughter, nine-month-old Cilla, would drown during a boat accident while en route to New Orleans. Her master, Archibald Gaines, had shipped the entire family south to avoid having to return Margaret to Ohio to stand trial for the murder and likely secure a more sanguine future with the backing of local sympathetic abolitionists than what he had in store for her on his Maplewood farm. Cilla had been seated on her mother's lap when their steamboat collided with another vessel, and as mother and child rushed overboard, Margaret's hands were actually in cuffs, preventing her from preserving her own life or that of Cilla. When pulled from the water, still in handcuffs, Margaret "exhibited no other feeling than joy at the loss of her child."[19]

Two years after the Garner family's dreadful episode, tuberculosis finally granted Margaret the death she had long preferred to enslavement. She was survived by her husband and two sons.[20] Married bondpersons like Robert and Margaret experienced a peculiar type of spousal abuse at the hands of the slaveocracy, forced to suffer as powerless bystanders at scenes of their wives and husbands being beaten, raped, verbally threatened, and subjected to other unforgettable injuries. In an interview, Robert's mother, Mary, who described herself as a "mother of eight children, most of whom have been separated from her," confessed "that her husband was once separated from her twenty-five years, during which time she did not see him," and "could she have prevented it, she would never have permitted him to return, as she did not wish him to witness her sufferings, or be exposed to the brutal treatment that he would receive." The emasculating shame Simon Sr. and Robert suffered while married to women they could not defend against the humiliating and torturous assaults they witnessed undoubtedly led Robert to the same conclusion his wife expressed: *never marry again in slavery*. When Robert did remarry, it was not until after emancipation.[21]

Birthed by the kind of psychic pain her mother-in-law described, Margaret Garner's 1858 circumspective caution regarding slave marriage is a portal to America's story of forbidden Black love. Slavery tortured and killed Black love, compelling women such as Margaret to kill their own kin in the very name of Black love. During this same period, slavery would force another young bondwoman, close in age to Margaret, to kill in defense of Black love, though in this case someone other than kin would have to die.

"I Struck Him with a Stick Until He Was Dead": Celia's Story

The privilege of autonomy and self-ownership will not allow many readers to imagine how nineteen-year-old bondwoman Celia must have felt when ushered into the Callaway County, Missouri, circuit court on October 10, 1855, to face charges for killing her serial rapist. Perhaps her mind rested upon her first uninvited sexual encounter with Robert Newsom, the then sixty-year-old Virginia transplant and recent widower. Newsom had traveled about a day's distance from his Missouri homestead in Callaway County to Audrain County to purchase her, and already, on the forty-mile ride back to his farm, Newsom raped the fourteen-year-old adolescent. It was the first of many such episodes that would plague her five years of bondage on his estate.

Confronted by accusers in the courtroom, Celia must have centered her thoughts on both her living and her expected offspring, each of whom shared the same blood with her rapist. She was pregnant with her third child, and she could only guess what future her other two children had in store. She probably agonized a thousand times or more about whether it was the act of disposing of her sixty-five-year-old abuser's body by fire that had been her fatal error. Under questioning, she reportedly confessed that "as soon as I struck him the Devil got into me, and I struck him with a stick until he was dead and then rolled him in the fire and burnt him up."[22]

Truth be told, it was Black love that had gotten into her. She had found neither sympathy nor support from the members of the

Newsom family she had approached for help. Following her boy-friend George's refusal to share her with their master, Celia warned Newsom not to force himself upon her anymore. It seems Black love had finally inspired Celia with the courage to resist her rapist's assaults at any cost, including his life and inevitably her own.

To the all-White male jury, her act of self-defense was no different from murder. The fact that she was sick and expecting to bear Newsom's third child when he insisted on violating her for the umpteenth time on that dreadful night of June 23, 1855, mattered not one iota. It was further adjudicated that Celia had no right to defend herself at all. Within a day, twelve citizens of the state of Missouri, many slaveholders themselves, sentenced Celia to be "hanged by the neck until dead on the sixteenth day of November 1855."[23]

Following a November 11 escape from the jail where she awaited her state execution, Celia was returned to state custody several weeks later to face punishment. She was hanged to death in Fulton, Missouri, on the twenty-first day of December 1855 at 2:30 p.m. Her lover, George, was not there to see it; having come under tremendous suspicion of aiding Celia in Newsom's killing and the disposal of his body, he had fled the Newsom estate in the aftermath of Celia's imprisonment.[24]

Celia's story is central to understanding the foundations of forbidden Black love in America. Her experience as a victim of ritual slave rape who acted in self-defense is incomplete without accounting for her true love and desire for George. She was an enslaved Black woman who harbored the ambition to freely choose a Black man as her lover and life partner. Although thwarted by the role the culture and psychology of rape played in American slavery's prohibition and prosecution of Black love, that she decided to eliminate her owner and violator places on record the length to which at least one enslaved Black woman was willing to go in order to experience love and satisfaction with a Black man of her choosing.

"You Had to Court on de Sly in Dat Day en Time"

Most Black women were not as sensationally heroic as Celia or as tragic as Margaret, though almost all suffered sexual and reproductive assaults of some kind, whether physical, psychological, emotional, or verbal. From the dawn of colonial settlement, Black enslaved women were valued for their "increase" potential. Their childbearing bodies fueled the industries and wealth of White slaveholders who conceived short- and long-term investment plans based upon the expectation that natural increase would swell their slaveholdings. This was true even when the slaveholder himself fathered children with his Black female chattel. *Partus sequitur ventrum* (progeny follows the womb) declared all children of enslaved mothers the chattel property of their owners as early as 1662, protecting the right of White slaveholding fathers to keep in bondage the mixed-race children they sired with enslaved Black women and girls.[25]

Ultimately, it didn't matter who impregnated her; the enslaved woman's womb was a "capital asset" that the slaveholder could rely on in his wealth-building plans.[26] Virginia planter William Geddy's 1816 last will and testament discloses the value slave owners placed on bondwomen's fertile wombs and how those wombs actually dictated gender-based patterns of separation among enslaved couples and families:

> I loan to my beloved wife during her natural life, a yellow girl sister and twin to the yellow girl now in the possession of Henry Smith; also a negro man by the name of Charles, a black smith and the smiths tools, also Charles's wife by the name of Eliza and at the death of my wife, said Charles the aforesaid black smith is to go free, but his wife Eliza and her increase to be sold and the money arising from the sales to be equally divided into three parts, my son Edward Geddys children to have one part, and my

daughter Sally Smiths children another part, and Elizabeth Lindsey's children the other part.[27]

Besides the forced work of "increase," enslaved women faced long days of backbreaking labor. As one woman put it, "I had to do everythin' dey was to do on de outside. Work in de field, chop wood, hoe corn, till sometime I feels like my back surely break."[28] Her recollection is no exaggeration. Across centuries of a changing economy Black women in bondage cultivated and processed crops and dairy and tended cattle and other livestock. They also found themselves clearing land of shrubs and bushes, especially during the early days of colonial settlement.[29]

The hoe became the symbol of their attachment to the tobacco, corn, wheat, and rice fields they tilled, and until mechanized milling of rice developed after the mid-eighteenth century, the mortar and pestle also belonged to enslaved women. With this heavy dual-component technology, they engaged their entire bodies—from fingers to toes. Grinding rice in this way was such "a hard and severe operation" that it reportedly "[cost] every planter the lives of several slaves annually."[30]

Scholars have distinguished rice cultivation from other cultivation methods for its reliance on African women's knowledge systems and organizational skills. Lowcountry planters succeeded in harvesting the crop only because women from rice-growing regions of West Africa possessed the expertise to ensure bountiful outcomes. Enslaved women of African descent governed the task system essential to the production of edible rice, often without interference from White planters. Rice cultivation, then, arguably allowed Black women spaces of sovereignty within the suffocating confines of chattel slavery.[31] However, "in the accounting of rice and women's lives, the balance should tip toward misery" because the "work was grueling, the tasks stretched the workday out until well into the night, and the toll that the pounding of rice took on the bodies of the enslaved was so extensive that slaveholders took careful notice of the destruction of their human property."[32]

When they worked inside the homes of their slaveholders, enslaved women also executed physically demanding tasks of laundering, providing child care, preparing food, and cleaning. Across such a wide range of labor assignments, monotonous and exhausting movement choreographed their regimented lives. Pushing, tugging, chopping, lifting, carrying, scrubbing—all these actions positioned enslaved women at risk for further exploitation.

Subjected to these conditions, enslaved black women could never achieve respectable womanhood in the White American imagination. In fact, White people's irreverent views of Black women first took shape when European travelers to Africa discovered that African women cultivated crops, produced food for their families, and marketed their harvests. Since very few European women performed similar work, European travelers, alienated from norms and traditions of the peoples they observed, often described African women as beasts of burdens, oppressed by onerous agricultural labor, even slavishly so under the brutish authority of African men. They likewise submitted commentary about African women's perceived physical abnormalities and assumed ability to bear children and execute arduous agricultural tasks without feeling pain. These fantasies about African women's laboring bodies had circulated across the Atlantic world through an extensive collection of tales and hearsay, and they undoubtedly impacted the crude manner in which African women were subjected to the gang system of labor under the actual slavish authority of White men on America's slaveholding estates.[33] By Euro-Western standards, African women were ontologically and irredeemably unfeminine, and their status as chattel slaves only widened the chasm between them and the White women who owned them.[34]

Although both Northern and Southern standards that defined ideal womanhood accommodated new trends and beliefs across the centuries, some expectations remained constant regarding feminine etiquette and decorum. What women wore, the labor they performed, and the spaces they occupied determined their value as respectable or scandalous women. Associated with domesticity and the privacy of the home, women were expected to be chaste and clothed in public, with very little to no skin exposed. Within this arrangement, Black women embodied the antithesis of everything desirable in a woman.

As they labored in fields, farms, and domestic spaces, enslaved women had to lift or tie up their long skirts and dresses to work efficiently and effectively. The actual labor they performed required them to bend at the waist, kneel on the ground, and spread their legs liberally, to weed fields, pick crops, scrub floors, cook, and wash. Thus, they manipulated the clothes they wore to accommodate the exigencies of work life. By the standards of the day, many enslaved women were inadequately and shabbily clothed, and when they were whipped, they were almost always stripped naked.[35]

Enslaved women lived, worked, and suffered the sting of the whip under watchful eyes. Even domestic bondwomen, laboring in close proximity to their taskmasters, did not escape the rigorous scrutiny of the slaveholding family that micromanaged their every word, gesture, and deed. It is true that some enslaved women were afforded the unsupervised privilege of working and marketing their produce in urban spaces, especially in cities such as Charleston and Savannah.[36] However, the typical surveillance of the slave state made most enslaved women's affairs public.

Perhaps no ritual of exposure was more public for Black bondwomen than slave auctions—a quintessential site of the denuded Black female body.[37] These social gatherings attracted hordes across Southern cities and rural villages, and "when young women were advertised," as one Missouri resident recalled, "'crowds would flock to the court to see the sight.'"[38] What they saw when they gazed at the Black bondwoman on parade, in countless compromised positions, they took as confirmation that Black women were inherently socially unacceptable. Black women, enslaved or free, were assumed to be promiscuous and lecherous, yet unfeminine and grotesque. They remained objects of the White pornographic gaze, which could turn sadistic, especially when peering through the spectacles of medical experimentation and scientific study.[39]

Even as they valued Black "increase," many slaveholders simultaneously circulated myths about Black female promiscuity and sexual deviancy.[40] While stigmatizing Black women for their perceived hypersexuality, Southern slave owners also relied upon and required the Black adolescent girls and women they held in bondage to increase their human holdings. Thus, in best-case scenarios, they allowed and encouraged them to find mates of their choosing. This was not always easy, as the average bondwoman on the US mainland did not find herself on large plantations with hundreds of male counterparts. The majority of enslaved women lived on smaller farms or properties with just a few other enslaved persons. Less than 1 percent of slaveholders in the South held more than one hundred persons in bondage, and by 1860 enslaved persons in the South, on average, lived in groups of ten.[41] For this reason, enslaved women such as Celia were fortunate if they found romantic partners residing on the same properties with them. Like Margaret Garner, most had no choice but to seek romantic companionship with partners living on different estates.

Even on large estates, when bondwomen formed romantic relationships and marriage unions with men enslaved on the same property, agricultural seasons coupled with gendered labor assignments often demanded separate living quarters for husbands and wives. George Washington, America's first president and most prodigious slaveholder in Fairfax County, Virginia, established these kinds of distant living arrangements for close to two-thirds of the enslaved couples working on his twelve-square-mile Mount Vernon estate. Washington saw to it that enslaved laborers lived near their workplaces to avoid losing valuable work hours to the long distances some would have to walk to arrive at their work stations. Consequently, most enslaved fathers at Mount Vernon had infrequent contact with their children, who were raised in the women's quarters.[42] Beyond the inconvenience of physical distance, enslaved women and their consorts could never anticipate how and when decisions from on high would eternally sever the shared intimate bonds they endeavored to preserve. Such an existence under the incessant threat of family fracture could drive thousands of Margarets and Celias to flirt with ideas of escape by surreptitious or violent means.

Among the dozens of bondwomen the Washingtons owned, Ona (a.k.a. Oney) Judge, a personal attendant to Martha Washington, actually absconded from the president's Philadelphia mansion in 1796. Ona's entire existence revolved around waiting on the first lady and fulfilling her every need and comfort. She had no time to even think of pursuing love and coupling until after she made her escape to a life of fugitive freedom. Settling in Portsmouth, New Hampshire, Ona eventually married and had three children with her husband, a free Black man named John Staines. After discovering Ona's calculated absence, the president of the United States stopped at nothing to track her down, even illegally exploiting federal resources to pursue and recapture his property. All of Washington's years-long efforts to recover Ona by persuasion and even by ambush ultimately failed. Staying one step ahead of him, Ona managed to protect her fragile liberty, though not without fear that the Washingtons or other claimants would one day succeed in reenslaving her and her offspring and destroying the marriage and family she had forged as a fugitive from slavery.[43]

Margaret's, Celia's, and Ona's stories illustrate how irreconcilable their Black female slave status was with the social freedom necessary to actualize a truly healthy love and marriage. Many bondwomen knew and dreaded the outcomes they would certainly face if they adopted the strategies of these brazen young women. Instead, they delayed marriage or abandoned the idea altogether, preferring to minimize the wounds of slavery upon their hearts. They knew all too well that they would remain married "until," in the words of a former Georgia governor, "it is the pleasure of their owner to separate them."[44]

To spouses who toiled for different masters, the stress of managing marriage while separated could be overwhelming. Over the smallest infractions, White authorities often scarred their victims for life with brutal beatings that seared bodies and souls. At eighty years old, and approximately seventy years after slavery, Manda Walker of Winnsboro, South Carolina, described one such instance in detail when her father, Jeff, had overstayed his visit with his wife, Phoebe, and their children. Jeff had to become skilled at assessing how long he could stay with his family during visitations, allowing enough time to traverse a creek, which was difficult to navigate when the water rose above the bank, and return to his owner's plantation before his travel pass expired.

On one occasion, Jeff had already struggled to cross the creek and had arrived at Phoebe's cabin "all wet and drenched wid water." When patrollers discovered that Jeff's pass had expired, they "tied him up, pulled down his breeches, and whupped him right befo' mammy and us chillum," even ignoring the pleas of Phoebe's owners to stop since "de crick [sic] was still up and dangerous to cross." The patrollers, Manda recalled, "make pappy git on de mule and follow him down to de crick and watch him swim dat swif' muddly crick to de other side." What seemed most indelible to her, however, was that "low-down white men" were "always . . . doin' de patarollin' and a strippin' de clothes off men, lak pappy, right befo' de wives and chillun and beatin' de blood out of [them]."[45]

The treacherous paths carved by muddy creeks and other prohibitive landscapes, which married bondmen such as Jeff risked to reach the safety of their wives and children, were constant reminders of the equally dangerous penalties slave patrollers meted out to those lacking legitimate visitation permits or those in violation of their time limits. Julia Woodberry of Marion, South Carolina, shared similar recollections, passed down from her mother and others in her community, about the jeopardies traveling spouses confronted:

> De nigger men would want to go to see dey wives en dey would have to get a 'mit [permit] from dey Massa to visit dem. Cose dey wouldn' live together cause dey wives would be here, dere en yonder. It been like dis, sometimes de white folks would sell de wife of one of dey niggers way from dey husband en den another time, dey would sell de husband way from dey wife. Yes, mam, white folks had dese guard, call patroller, all bout de country to catch en whip dem niggers dat been prowl bout widout dat strip from dey Massa.[46]

Selling husbands away from wives and separating families became a common feature of the domestic slave trade in America, especially after the Revolutionary War. As a result, "One third of first marriages were disrupted by the interstate slave trade, and many more were broken apart by temporary loans and long-term hiring out."[47] Julia Brown's uncle, for example, "wus married but he wus owned by one master and his wife wus owned by another." With spousal visitation privileges limited to two weekdays ("the onlist time he could git off"), the unfortunate week finally arrived when he made his typical Wednesday visit, "and when he went back on Saturday his wife had been bought by the speculator and he never did know where she wuz."[48]

Intensifying the grief, couples were given little to no warning that their unions were about to be ruptured. As a son privy to one such instance, an elder William Moore testified decades after his father was sent away during slavery, "My paw is the first picture I got in my mind. I was settin' on maw's lap and paw come in and say Marse Tom loaned him out to work on a dam they's buildin' in Houston and he has to go."[49]

Such hurried separation announcements were usual business for enslaved couples, "incapable of the *civil rights annexed*" to marriage, as the prominent eighteenth-century Maryland slaveholder and lawyer Daniel Dulany put it.[50] But Moore was one of the luckier fatherless children among enslaved communities, for at least he was able to learn of the freak accident that prematurely ended his father's life. "One day word come he was haulin' a load of rocks through the swamps and a low-hangin' grapevine cotched him under the neck and jerked him off the seat and the wagon rolled over him and kilt him dead. They buried him down there somewheres."[51]

In other circumstances, fathers tried to defy the auction block, but inescapably suffered the same undesired result of permanent separation from their wives and children. At eighty-four years old, George Bollinger of Cape, Missouri, described how his father avoided the domestic slave trade but still managed to disappear from his life:

Yes, de' nigger buyers ust'a cum roun' our place. It was sight to see! Dere 'ud be mebbe five 'or six men a'ridin' fine hosses an a-drivin' a whole flock 'er slaves along de rode; jes' like stock, all chained togedder. On time dere wuz Pete Smith, 'Ole Tom Johnson, an' Fred an' Sam Daughery; all niggar buyers—dey wuz at our place an' dey wud all sit dar, an' us slaves had to stan' up in front o' em, an' dey'd bid on us. I 'members I wuz full chested an' dey laid a stick across my chest to see how straight I cud stan'. "Ole Pete" Smith wuz gonna' buy me; but my young folks begged "Massa" not to sell me, 'cause we'd all played togedder—so he didden' sell me. But dey wuz gonna buy my "pappy" an take him way off, but, my "pappy" was smart. He had made baskets at night an' sold 'em when he cud, 'en saved de money—dat night he goes to de fireplace an' lifts up a stone; an' out o' de hole he pulls out a bag a' money an' he runs away. I ain't never seed my "pappy" since.[52]

George's "pappy" apparently fashioned a narrow escape from an explosive interstate trade in human cargo. Fueled in large part by the abolition of the transatlantic slave trade to the United States, the domestic slave trade ensured that roughly 650,000 bondpersons were transported from the Upper South to the Lower South between the 1790s and the 1860s. In addition, more than twice as many were sold in local transactions throughout slaveholding states.[53] The opposite was true for many Northern states that gradually abolished slavery after the Revolutionary War.[54] During the seventeenth and eighteenth centuries, children, especially adolescent boys, were sold away from their parents with some regularity in the New England colonies. And enslaved (and even free) family members could find themselves divided across a variety of households and orphanages—for children of deceased, absent, or destitute parents. Before the war, it was common for New England slaveholders to sell not only enslaved children but also infants. In fact, infants, even unweaned babies, were sometimes advertised as available free of charge to anyone willing to relieve their owners of them.

In the 1740s, Massachusetts newspapers revealed eighteen instances of such sales due to economic distress. A 1774 petition issued by enslaved fathers conveys the emotional turmoil these separations caused them and presumably the enslaved mothers who gave birth to their vendible offspring. "Our children are also taken from us by force and sent maney miles from us wear we seldom or ever see them again there to be made slaves of for Life which sumtimes is very short by Reson of Being dragged from their mothers Breest."[55] With rare exceptions, New England slaveholders, who had little room in their budgets and on their modest farms for additional mouths to feed, found themselves struggling to provide for the offspring of the adults they held in bondage.

The sale of women and girls, especially in the South, commonly invited sexual humiliation and abuse. In the nineteenth-century South, Black female bodies were poked, pulled, and penetrated at every orifice when examined by speculators and slave traders.[56] Even worse, Southern slave traders habitually raped the adolescents and young women they trafficked.[57] No matter the place or time, any moment devoted to the sale of a Black adolescent girl or woman was a likely occasion for sexual violation and humiliation. Auctioneers established a welcoming atmosphere for the sexual gaze of their White male audiences with vulgar jokes and lewd comments that reinforced the wide social gap between White male slaveholders and Black female chattel. Consumers had the right to ensure that their purchased goods were up to standard, and in order to verify that they were free of venereal disease or the commonly experienced pro-lapsed uterus, potential buyers felt no shame in subjecting adolescent girls and women to genital examinations.[58] Indeed, White handlers of Black bondwomen on the slave market exercised all senses—sight, touch, smell, hearing, and taste—to invade the most intimate areas of their bodies normally reserved for spousal access.[59]

Across all slaveholding states, the master and his surrogates assumed the role of husband or patriarch (or both) in the social lives of bondpersons, regardless of whether they were single or married. Slavery, indeed, trumped marriage as the ultimate domestic arrangement, dictating interpersonal relations among bondpersons that satisfied slaveholders' most whimsical desires as well as the bottom line.[60] The disruptions of married life that enslaved African descendants constantly navigated amounted to nothing less than spousal and child abuse, and many who were children during the last decades of slavery would later convey how deeply the injuries of slavery's culture of forbidden Black love wounded them and, especially, their parents. At eighty-five years old, former bondwoman Mary Bell of St. Louis, Missouri, relayed how her parents' forbidden love caused pain and fracture that far outdistanced anything she had experienced:

I so often think of de hard times my parents had in dere slave days, more than I feel my own hard times, because my father was

not allowed to come to see my mother but two nights a week. Dat
was Wednesday and Saturday. So often he came home all bloody
from beatings his old nigger overseer would give him. My mother
would take those bloody clothes off of him, bathe de sore places
and grease them good and wash and iron his clothes, so he could
go back clean.[61]

Yet Bell's memory of her mother's love language also recovers
the healing work slavery assigned to Black love. Under conditions
of bondage, marital intimacies were forged to mitigate not only the
physical and psychic effects of captivity but also the ontological effects. Caring for a captive spouse required mastering discretion not
so much as a quality but as an affective state that made room for
couples to access and transmit their humanity to one another and
others in their communities despite the public degradation they experienced daily as the movable property of others.

This mutual "lovework" was typical of married life among the
majority of enslaved persons who were fortunate enough to select
their mates. In the South, it was not uncommon for some to choose
spouses who lived on a different estate rather than risk marrying
someone who could in actuality be an unknown close relative.[62] In
these cases, couples termed their relationships "abroad marriages."
The uncertainties of slave life also led some to define such marriages as "trial."[63] The terminology alone is enough indication that
slavery and marriage were oxymoronic, for if properly executed, one
social status necessarily annulled the other. Former bondwoman Julia Woodberry from Marion, South Carolina, explained it best in a
1937 Works Progress Administration interview. "No, mam, I ain'
never marry cause you had to court on de sly in dat day en time. I tell
you, I come through de devil day when I come along. I was learned
to work by de old, old slavery way."[64]

Julia's refusal to marry while enslaved echoes Margaret Garner's
perspective. Remaining single certainly came with its emotional

costs, but it likely protected her from emotional entanglements that could have been challenging to negotiate given the precarious environments in which bondwomen lived and worked unprotected against incessant intimate violations. Julia apparently made a deliberate choice not to marry, but others like her were forced to surrender to arranged "marriages" that suited the desires and objectives of slaveholders. In Louisa Everett's case,

> Marce Jim called me and Sam ter him and ordered Sam to pull off his shirt . . . and he said to me: Nor, "do you think you can stand this big nigger?" He had that old bull whip flung acrost his shoulder, and Lawd, that man could hit so hard: So I jes said "yassur, I guess so," and tried to hide my face so I couldn't see Sam's nakedness, but he made me look at him anyhow. Well he told us what we must git busy and do in his presence, and we had to do it. After that we were considered man and wife.

Since Louisa and Sam "was a healthy pair and had fine, big babies," she "never had another man forced on" her. Louisa eventually "learnt to love" Sam on account of his kindness toward her.[65]

Another enslaved woman, Rilla McCullough, was not so fortunate. Although she eventually married the love of her life, it was not before experiencing repeated instances of sexual and reproductive assault on the South Carolinian plantation that held her in bondage. According to her son William McCullough,

> Mother tole me that when she became a woman at the age of sixteen years her marster went to a slave owner near by and got a six-foot nigger man, almost an entire stranger to her, and told her she must marry him. Her marster read a paper to them, told them they were man and wife and told this negro he could take her to a certain cabin and go to bed. This was done without getting her consent or even asking her about it. Grandmother said that

several different men were put to her just about the same as if she had been a cow or sow.[66]

Despite such intimate abuses, Rilla eventually gave her heart to the man of her choosing and married him by her own volition. The sovereignty that her love and marriage union symbolized constituted a radical departure from a slave past of serial sexual intrusion. Thus, the urgency with which Rilla and her husband, Marion, sought to formalize their bond on their own terms was not lost on their son William, who further testified, "Mother said she loved my father before the surrender and just as soon as they were free they married."[67]

For other women such as Mary Gaffney, an exit from arranged slave marriages never materialized after emancipation. "When I married it was just home wedding, fact is, I just hated the man I married but it was what Maser said do." Gaffney describes how her owner planned to "get rich" off of her presumed fecundity. "He put another negro man with my mother, then he put one [Paul Gaffney] with me. I would not let that negro touch me and he told Maser and Maser gave me a real good whipping, so that night I let that negro have his way. . . . Then when slavery was over I just kept on living with that Negro."[68]

"There Was a World of Yellow People Then"

Among enslaved females, rituals of intimate violence marked all the seasons of their wombs and womanhood—puberty, pregnancy, parturition, and child rearing. Beyond the sexual encounters with Black males that slaveholders orchestrated, we can be sure that many enslaved women and girls confronted Black male predatory behavior and sexual assault. However, they were most vulnerable and powerless when the perpetrator was White—especially during adolescent years.

If the pedophilic practices of White men in the style of a Thomas Jefferson, a Robert Newsom, or even a James Henry Hammond had not invaded them before their breasts began to fill out what meager clothing they were rationed, most Black girls, by their adolescent years, would be forced to submit to White male penetration.[69] "No matter whether the slave *girl* be as black as ebony or as fair as her mistress," Harriet Jacobs explained in *Incidents in the Life of a Slave Girl*, "in either case, there is no shadow of law to protect her from insult, from violence, or even from death."[70] Fearing at every turn her master's "whisper of foul words in [her] ear," the average Black girl "learn[ed] to tremble when she hear[d] her master's footfall." After delivering her second child, Jacobs confessed harboring immediate feelings of apprehension over the news of her newborn's female sex. "Slavery is terrible for men; but it is far more terrible for women," she insisted. "Superadded to the burden common to all, they have wrongs, and sufferings, and mortifications peculiarly their own."[71]

Personal correspondence from the pen of a prominent slaveholding sexual abuser provides corroborating evidence for the ordeal Jacobs painfully describes. James Henry Hammond (1804–1864), a South Carolina attorney, planter, and politician whose term in the Senate failed to overshadow his scandalous personal legacy, made concubines of his enslaved female property Sally Johnson and her daughter Louisa at the ages of eighteen and twelve, respectively. In a letter dated February 19, 1856, the future senator bequeathed the pair to his "legitimate" son, Harry, and laid out his wishes for his Black-mixed-raced slaves, both of whom likely mothered several of his children in bondage and one of whom apparently had children with Harry. Hammond's confusion about which children he and his son fathered with the mother-daughter pair is enough indication of the sexual liberties they enjoyed as a bonus for investing in Black female slaves:

My Dear Harry,

In the last Will I made I left to you . . . Sally Johnson the mother of Louisa and all the children of both. Sally says Henderson is my child. It is possible, but I do not believe it. Yet act on her's [sic] rather than my opinion. Louisa's first child may be mine. I think not. Her second I believe is mine. Take care of her and her children who are both of your blood if not of mine & Henderson. . . . I cannot free these people and send them North. It would be cruelty to them. Nor would I like that any but my own blood should own as Slaves my own blood or Louisa. I leave them to your charge, believing that you will best appreciate & most independently carry out my wishes in regard to them. Do not let Louisa or any of my children or possible children be the slaves of Strangers. Slavery in the family will be their happiest earthly condition.

Ever affectionately, J.H.H.[72]

The common Black female predicament of sexual slavery is perhaps why seventy-eight-year-old Josh Miles could tell the bittersweet story of an elderly bondwoman who protested so desperately at the sale of her daughters that her owner decided to let her go with them. When he was still a young boy, Miles's owner had traveled from Virginia to Texas with his entire household, to escape being in "de thick of de war," conveniently selling some of his human chattel at major auction houses along the way. "I seed de old mammy and her two boys and gals sold," Miles recounted in his elder years. "One man buys de boys and old mammy cry, but it don't do no good. 'Nother man bids de two gals and mammy throw such a fit her old massa throws her in, 'cause she too old to be much 'count."[73]

Similar stories of violation and enslaved mothers' efforts to shield their daughters from sexual abuse are less easy to detect in the North. However, they are not totally absent from the written record. Recent scholarship has tied a name that many have come to associate with heroic Black feminism and abolitionism to the sexual abuse bondwomen and girls suffered in the North. Born in 1797, Isabella Van Wagenen (a.k.a. Sojourner Truth) was enslaved in Ulster County, New York, before leaving her slaveholders' home with her baby daughter in tow in late 1826. Since innuendo serves as evidence of sexual impropriety in this case, there is some disagreement among scholars as to the nature of Isabella's sexual encounters with one of her owners. Nell Painter concludes in *Sojourner Truth: A Life, a Symbol* that Sally Dumont, Isabella's fourth owner's wife, was an unexposed sexual violator, explaining that Truth hid Sally's identity from her audiences because she "feared that . . . what happened to her was 'so unaccountable, so unreasonable, and what is usually called so unnatural,' readers who were 'uninitiated' would not believe her." Truth also acknowledged that "her assailant had died, and she did not want to distress the innocent who were still living." At the time that she narrated her story, Sally Dumont, whom Isabella "despised," had passed away, while John Dumont, Sally's widower, was still living.[74]

Since euphemisms can veil documented instances of White men's sexual exploits involving Black bondwomen,[75] unambiguous cases such as Joanna Negro's warrant special scrutiny for what they suggest about White men's lack of boundaries even with Black women they did not own. In 1686 Joanna Negro of Woburn, Massachusetts, revealed in court testimony that her owner's neighbor, a White man named Joseph Carter, had seized upon the opportune absence of his wife to impregnate her, apparently by force:

> He gott her with child in the dyke nere the well and it was when . . . his wife was gon to Reading and as soone as he had dun he bid her laye it to Samson Captain Carters Negro man and about two months after . . . he brought Savin [an abortifacient] to her and said she might take that and it wold kill the child . . . and further he bid her smother the child as soone as it was borne and that she might smother it when she was in extremity. . . . [I]f she layed it to him he wold sett the divel to worke upon her and . . . she should never have a quiet life againe.[76]

Carter's desperate attempts to conceal his crime bring to the surface the possibility that some enslaved women aborted their babies under pressure from Whites who wished to remain anonymous. White men who raped Black women, even enslaved Black women, were not technically above the law in colonial New England,[77] and court records do contain evidence of such exploits. Although he died before his trial, Zebulon Thorp was indicted for the rape of an "Ethiopian" (Black) woman in 1717, and James Studley was the first White man in New England to be tried and convicted of attempted rape of an African-descended woman in 1758. These two cases occurred in Plymouth, Massachusetts, where "justice prevailed" for Black female victims relative to other Northern colonies. In a third 1786 case, this time in Lynn, Massachusetts, Calvin Newhall was whipped twenty times for assaulting a Black woman named Deborah Sarker. While this was no small victory for an eighteenth-century Black female victim, the jury, in fact, ruled lightly, choosing to convict Newhall, a White forty-one-year-old married veteran, of the lesser charge of "assault" rather than "intent to ravish," which was punishable by death.[78]

One aspect of Black women's compounded quandary of love loss, unmarriageability, and marital neglect in the present is a color-caste system that can be traced back to the slave period. Reflecting on the ordinariness of the sexual trauma enslaved girls and women endured during the days of slavery, Rachel Fairley of Little Rock, Arkansas, simultaneously designated *yellowness* as the phenotypic feature that often coded children of White slaveholders and Black enslaved mothers differently than those typically born of two Black parents. "There was a world of yellow people then," she recalled during her Federal Writers' Project interview. "My mother said her sister had two yellow children; they were her master's. I know of plenty of light people who were living at that time."[79]

Mary Reynolds's account of her days of slavery in Louisiana fills in Fairley's sketch of the slavocracy's most open secret: White male paternity was the source of color consciousness among enslaved persons. Reynolds remembers how the "Kilpatrick chillun" made it their duty to warn two fair-skinned bondchildren of the limits of their entitlements on their estate. When the latter attempted to join the Kilpatrick children in the dollhouse where they were playing, they protested, saying, "That's for white chillum." The bondchildren immediately retorted, "We ain't no niggers, 'cause we got the same daddy you has, and he comes to see us near every day and fetches us clothes and things from town. . . . He is our daddy and we call him daddy when he comes to our house to see our mama." Reynolds apparently worked within the slave master's home or in close proximity because she reported that Mrs. Kilpatrick had overheard her children and her husband's chattel children's discussion.

The identity descriptors Reynolds places in the mouth of Mrs. Kilpatrick underscore how phenotypic and social stratification were interwoven. According to Reynolds, Mrs. Kilpatrick was unusually quiet when her husband returned home that evening. When he asked her what was wrong, she responded: "I'm studyin' in my mind 'bout them white young'uns of that yaller nigger wench from Baton Rouge. . . . [T]hey got the same kind of hair and eyes as my chillun and they got a nose looks like yours." Reynolds describes a cool relationship between the couple as time went along, noting that "[Mrs. Kilpatrick] don't never have no more chillun and she ain't so cordial with the massa," while "Margaret, that yellow gal, has more white young'uns, but they don't never go down the hill no more to the big house."

If Margaret had reconciled herself to concubinage or some illicit sexual arrangement with the White man who owned her, Aunt Cheney was just the opposite. Reynolds describes her failed escape attempt, implying that her choice to "run away" when she was "jus' out of bed with a sucklin' baby" was inspired by the trauma of giving birth to "'nother baby of massa's breedin.'" Aunt Cheney couldn't outrun the "nigger hounds" on her trail. "They gits near her and she grabs a limb and tries to hist herself in a tree, but them dogs grab her and pull her down. The men hollers them onto her, and the dogs tore her naked and et the breasts plumb off her body. She got well and lived to be a old woman, but 'nother woman has to suck her baby and she ain't got no sign of breasts no more." Reynold's master seemed to have only one thing on his mind when it came to the black women and girls he owned: breeding children personally or by arrangement. When Reynolds was hired out and had been beaten herself within an inch of her life by "some ornery white trash name of Kidd," she recalled, "Massa looks me over good and says I'll git well, but I'm ruint for breedin' chillum."[80]

Reynolds and Fairley did not have to give birth to "yellow children" personally to know that a range of social privileges often accrued to them within the slave economy. Perhaps this is why Thomas Jefferson (1743–1826), who served as America's third president from 1801 to 1809, selected a racially mixed girl as his concubine. Jefferson's aesthetic valuation of Black and White phenotypic attributes exemplifies the Eurocentric ideological foundations of color stratification not only between Blacks and Whites but also among Blacks of distinguishable skin shades. In his *Notes on the State of Virginia*, Jefferson pondered, "Whether the black of the negro resides in the reticular membrane between the skin and scarf-skin . . . in the scarf-skin itself" or "whether it proceeds from the colour of the blood, the colour of the bile, or from that of some other secretion." African people's "black" skin was none other than a deviant "foundation of a greater or less share of beauty in the two races." "Are not the fine mixtures of red and white, the expressions of every passion by greater or less suffusions of colour in the one," Jefferson fancied, "preferable to that eternal monotony, which reigns in the countenances, that immovable veil of black which covers all the emotions of the other race?"

Yet he did not conclude there. Assuming the authority to register Black people's supposed complicity with the Eurocentric imaginative project of racializing beauty and desire, he persisted: "Add to these, flowing hair, a more elegant symmetry of form, their own judgment in favour of the whites, declared by their preference of them, as uniformly as is the preference of the Oran-utan [orangutan] for the black women over those of his own species."[81] In actuality, Jefferson's preposterous and baseless attempt to animalize Black people places on record his own self-incrimination. It is common knowledge, after all, that Jefferson, like so many of his White male counterparts, acted on his own "preference" for Black females, most famously with Sally Hemings; even though the forty-four-year-old Jefferson commenced a sexual relationship with his Black–racially mixed adolescent possession when she is believed to have been fourteen, we might gracefully decline the invitation to classify him as an orangutan.[82]

Jefferson's notes and reflections illustrate all too clearly how "colorism" and phenotypic stratification are the *afterlife* of White people's impressions of Black people and White men's sexual exploitation of the Black women and girls they held captive during slavery.[83] Despite their insufferable existential condition, the "yellow" children of White slaveholding fathers and Black enslaved mothers, with their light skin shades, straight hair, and European facial features, enjoyed advantages denied most enslaved laborers of darker hues. Even within the confines of their communities, during and after slavery, the stereotypic European features of mixed-race persons conferred upon them undeniable social capital. The rewards light skin and loose tresses afforded some Blacks, along with the repugnance associated with stereotypic African features, had lasting effects on the psychology of beauty and desire in African American culture and the wider American society, coding dark-complexioned Blacks as least desirable for romantic coupling and marriage.

THE ENDURANCE OF REVOLUTIONARY BLACK LOVE

While most spouses would comply, some bondwomen, once overpowered by sexually violent slave owners and overseers, had husbands who were willing to defend them. After Charlotte was raped by her overseer, Coleman, her husband, Alfred, killed him and stood trial in Mississippi for his actions. Alfred's defense fell on deaf ears, as the court ruled, "Adultery with a slave's wife [is] no defense to a charge of murder.—A slave charged with the murder of his overseer cannot introduce as evidence in his defense, the fact that the deceased, a few hours, before the killing had forced the prisoner's wife to submit to sexual intercourse with him, and that this had been communicated to him before the killing." For his crime, Alfred was sentenced to death by hanging in 1859.[84]

The internal anguish that enslaved men could experience when the institution of slavery violated the institution of marriage in the most personal dimensions of their lives was rarely expressed in their own words. In 1861, however, the *Weekly Anglo-African* got wind of a bondman's untimely end, publishing a revealing poem he authored under the most agonizing circumstances. Vulnerable and haunted by his own pending doom, Mingo's poem offered prescriptions for self-appreciation and self-repossession despite the hopelessness of bondage. If the cruelties of slavery that dissected families upon a whim meant he could no longer touch and see his beloved spouse, Mingo would keep their flame of love and connection alive through texts that were devised to reach not just his wife's hands but also her heart. While imprisoned and awaiting sale away from his family, Mingo scratched the following verses on a beam within the walls of his cell:

> *Good God! and must I leave them now,*
> *My wife, my children, in their woe?*
> *'Tis mockery to say I'm sold!*
> *But I forget these chains so cold,*
> *Which goad my bleeding limbs; though high*
> *My reason mounts above the sky.*
> *Dear wife, they cannot sell the rose*
> *Of love that in my bosom glows.*
> *Remember, as your tears may start,*
> *They cannot sell the immortal part.*[85]

After archiving these thoughts, Mingo took his chances and mustered an escape from his slave prison cell. He was tracked down by slave catchers and mangled so badly by their bloodhounds that he succumbed to his wounds without knowing whether his wife would ever read his enduring confession of love.

A dictated letter from the last days of slavery also reveals the emotional turmoil that plagued husbands and fathers who yearned to no avail for reunification with their wives and children. James Tate's correspondence to his "dear Wife" portrays the infrangible emotional ligatures that survive physical separation. Tate's family had been owned by a different master and had been sent over 250 miles away from West Point, Georgia, where he still lived, to Mobile, Alabama. In his letter dated February 4, 1863, he insisted his "dear wife . . . must kiss Jimmie and little Mary Olivia for me and tell them their Papa would give any thing he had in this world to see them both." Tate also assured her that, contrary to the wishes of his owner, he "would be a very unhappy man to be married to another woman and to always be thinking and studying about *my dear wife* and *dear little children* that are in *Mobiel*." However, after pining over the loss of physical connection with his family and devising unworkable plans to see his wife and children, Tate eventually seemed less convinced that he would *never* marry again, as his master had encouraged him to do soon after his wife's departure. Signing his letter with, "Your devoted husband. James Tate," he confessed, "If I ever do take a notion to marry again my dear wife I shall write and let you know all about it but I do not think I shall ever take such a notion again directly not if I always feel like I do now, for I can not think of any other woman nor love any other but *you* my dear wife."[86]

Sharing the same depth of love and loyalty for his wife that James Tate possessed, Stephen Lytle, a former Tennessee bondman, preferred to be *reenslaved* if enslavement was the only means of keeping his family together. After purchasing his and his wife's freedom from two different slave owners, Lytle was informed that unless "they shall immediately remove from the State of Tennessee," "the Second Section of the act of 1831, Session acts, page 121.2 prohibits his emancipation & that of his wife & child." Lytle, who had toiled long hours to purchase not just the flesh he repossessed and the flesh he loved but also the land upon which they would establish a homestead, was unwilling to abandon "the spot where he . . . lived, for nearly fifty years." Even if he could turn his back on Tennessee "by promising that he would never return," Lytle had "no hope that for his wife and his child he could get such security" and "believe[d]" they were "wholly unable to do it." Instead, he successfully petitioned the Tennessee General Assembly to guarantee their freedom and right to remain in the state, declaring in no uncertain terms, "Before he would leave the State and separate himself from his wife & child, dear as liberty is to him, and galling as are the chains of bondage, he would remain a slave."[87]

As a preponderance of laws was passed during the 1850s to control the presence and movement of free Blacks across slaveholding states, "voluntary slavery" became a legal option for free persons attempting to circumvent expulsion laws that would separate them from their spouses and children. Free persons with enslaved consorts forced to move to a distant location could also enter or reenter a life of bondage so as to remain connected with their families. In 1862 C. A. Featherston filed a petition in Gaston County, North Carolina, on behalf of a free man seeking such an arrangement: "A free negro boy [*sic*] named Wyat about 35 years of age tired out of being buffeted about from place to place with no settled home has made application to me to become my slave. The said Boy had taken up with my negro girl and lived with me several years in South Carolina unmolested." When Featherston moved his family and enslaved property to North Carolina, Wyat "came with me not knowing it was contrary to law." Once Featherston became aware that he "violated the law in bringing [Wyat] hither," he "sent him back to South Carolina." Featherston conveyed, however, that "the Said boy prefer[ed] a life of slavery with the master of his choice & with the woman he had taken up with & his children to the life of a free negro" and requested "your Honorable Body to take the matter into consideration & allow me to own the said negro and make me a bona fide Deed for the same."[88]

If some free persons in mixed-status marriages and relationships were willing to forgo their circumscribed liberty for love under bondage, others already in bondage would risk their lives for love and marriage in freedom. The astounding psychological and physical deaths resulting from the incompatible institutions of marriage and slavery gave some bondpersons the courage to flee their condition. And some even lived to write about it.

William and Ellen Craft's narrative of their 1848 escape from slavery indicates just how determined this couple was to avoid the added torture that marriage in bondage would undoubtedly introduce. As William explains, freedom from bondage was a necessary condition for the couple's desired marriage. The victim of mother-child separation during her childhood years, and a witness to "so many other children separated from their parents in this cruel manner," Ellen was determined not to marry "under the wretched system of American slavery."

Sensitive to her trauma, and no stranger to family separation himself, William initially decided to delay the idea of marriage until after he and Ellen could devise a strategy to deliver themselves from slavery. Nothing they conceived at the time, however, was worth the risk. The Crafts considered numerous options, but "all seemed crowded with insurmountable difficulties," including the threat of "professional slave-hunters" capturing and sending them back to a fate of sure separation, grueling labor assignments, or even torturous executions "in order to strike terror into the hearts of others, and thereby prevent them from even attempting to escape from their cruel taskmasters."[89] The two reconciled themselves to marrying while in slavery but revisited the idea of fugitive freedom for fear that their future offspring would be parted from them one way or another. Following a risky and circuitous escape from slavery, the Crafts made their way from Georgia to Massachusetts, but they had to flee to England before they experienced any reliable sense of security for the life they had hoped to build as a wedded couple.

JUMPING THE BROOM BY FORCE AND BY CHOICE

If the Crafts had waited to hold their nuptials in the North as originally planned, they would have succeeded in exchanging their vows without the presence of White slave owners. Despite slavery's power to impede Black love and marriage, one would expect the wedding ceremony itself to have provided enslaved couples a space of refuge and momentary triumph over the despair that separation and subordination caused them daily. But the stark truth is we still don't know enough about enslaved couples' matrimonial rites, and many have incorrectly presumed a generic African heritage as the source of the one ritual most have come to associate with enslaved weddings—"jumping the broom." Since the airing of the 1977 television miniseries *Roots*, which featured Kunta Kinte and Belle's broomstick wedding in episode two, African Americans have attached sentimental value to the ritual, considering it a dignifying African tradition that their ancestors preserved to sanctify their nuptials.

A good number of enslaved persons, when permitted to marry, did indeed submit to jumping the broom with pledges of everlasting love until slave owner–induced separation would tear them asunder. In doing so, however, they were upholding European rather than African customs.[90] Pre-Christian Roma and Celtic communities in the British Isles were notorious for jumping the broom to seal their wedding vows.[91] Accounts from the 1880s describe multiple instances among these groups in which jumping over a broomstick was the central legitimating act in the marriage ceremony.[92] Rural Anglo-Saxons were known to embrace the practice as well. The

Welsh, in particular, sustained the ritual at least until the 1840s and likely carried the tradition to the American South, where so many of them settled throughout the slave period. In fact, the United States is the only region beyond the British Isles with a preponderance of analogous broomstick marriage customs.[93]

Some former bondpersons' memories of this wedding ritual unveil the less salutary intentions of White slave owners who could impose the foreign custom upon couples desiring symbolic "documentation" of their marriage ceremonies as the next best thing to an official wedding. At times, they "used the broomstick not merely to mark slave marriage as transitory and unimportant but also to assert authority over black households."[94] Other recollections of slave weddings suggest that enslaved communities often did exhibit control and agency over their varied wedding ceremonies, including those involving the broomstick ritual.[95] In fact, slaveholders, who supported the marriage requests of their enslaved laborers, generally consented to encourage reproduction and deter desertion.[96] Some even took enough interest in Black marriage ceremonies to publish accounts of them in local newspapers. One such 1860 report describing a Georgia ceremony was republished by outlets in the South and the North.[97]

For some African Americans, it is of little significance whether jumping the broom was imposed to remind those present of the slave owner's authority over any degree of sovereignty the ceremony might have inspired as enslaved couples took vows of responsibility for and fidelity to one another. Nor does it matter if the slave owner intended to trivialize the marriage ceremonies of their human property or found amusement in the use of an old pagan custom to acknowledge marriages of enslaved African descendants.[98] Inspired by *Roots*, jumping the broom resurfaced in the marriage ceremonies of countless African American couples over the past half century. The ritual has become a source of pride and connection to what many Blacks believe is an ancestral custom that honors their enslaved foreparents. For others, any evidence of belittlement from slaveholders and the mere fact that the ritual's origins have been traced to Europe rather than Africa will be unsettling.

Given the historical association of the broomstick ritual with marginalized groups and lower classes in Europe and the United States, it's not surprising to learn that some bondpersons willingly adopted the practice from the poor Whites who surrounded them and adapted the ritual to suit their needs. Class dynamics among enslaved communities might have played a role in such decisions because, as one bondman summed it up, "De fiel' han's am willin' t' jump de broomstick, but when de house sarvans gwine t' marry, dey wants a white preacher."[99] Aware of the social stigma matrimonial broomsticks elicited, some apparently expressed disdain for the practice or preference for a "real" or "true" wedding, and though not always by choice, they lined up by the hundreds to have their marriages or renewed vows officially registered by licensed ministers and government agents in the aftermath of slavery.

Marital and Familial Reunification

As the Civil War came to a close in 1865, the federal government encouraged and even mandated newly emancipated couples, whether previously married during slavery or not, to present themselves before an approved authority for their official exchange of marriage vows. To do so, thousands would have to locate their spouses, lovers, and children who were separated from them during slavery. Such efforts were widespread from the immediate aftermath of slavery to the first decade of the twentieth century.[100] When the professor and poet George Marion McClellan lauded Charles Chestnut as "the best delineator of Negro life and character," he referenced the fiction writer's attention to African Americans' postemancipation preoccupation with finding lost family members and poignantly asked: "Who has not sat at some time in a Negro church and heard read the pitiful inquiry for a mother, or a child, or a father, husband or wife, all lost in the sales and separations of slavery times—loved ones as completely swallowed up in the past (yet in this life they still live) as if the grave had received them."[101]

Fortunately, for Nettie Henry, the grave did not receive her father, who was plucked from her family during the Civil War and could return to his loved ones only when he was freed from bondage. "My pappy didn' go wid us to Mer-ree-dian. He b'longed to one set o' white people, you see, an' my mammy b'longed to another. He'd come to see us till de War started, den his folks jus'kinda went to Texas . . . an' took my pappy wid'em. But after de War he come back to us, walked mos' all de way frum Texas."[102]

Nettie's "pappy" was not alone. Numerous other emancipated women and men walked hundreds of miles, faced the elements, swallowed their hunger, and confronted obstacle after obstacle to reclaim loved ones lost in slavery. In one case a former bondwoman, Marie Johnson, received transportation from the Raleigh, North Carolina, Freedmen's Bureau to travel the remaining distance of just two counties after an exhausting trip across several Southern states in search of her long-lost husband. The power of enduring love that motivated Johnson's sojourn must have touched the agent on site in some measure: "This woman states that about fifteen years before the War she was living with her husband at Tarboro NC. Each were the property of a different slaveholder. The one that she belonged to moved to Miss. She states that her husband is living in Tarboro that she has walked, worked and scuffled from West Point, Miss to this city and has now neither strength nor means to go further." After explaining her story of marital separation and her desperate struggle to reunite with her spouse, the bureau granted Johnson's wish and paid the minimal fare for her remaining journey.[103]

African Americans also used the press to advertise their search for lost spouses and family members, sometimes decades after their separations had occurred.[104] In rarer cases the press published astonishing stories of reunification, as in the 1891 case of Alexander Foley, a bondman from Natchez, Mississippi, who returned to his old owner in Carrollton, Kentucky, to inquire after the whereabouts of his wife. Surprisingly, she was still residing in Carrollton, and the couple was soon reunited after decades of separation.

The Foleys' reunification demonstrates that Black love and marriage could prevail against the odds.[105] But for every marital reunification such as this one, many more former bondwomen died without seeing the faces and financial support of the spouses they lost to slavery. The pension petitions of Black widows of Civil War veterans tell this story well, and the story of love and marriage after Reconstruction will illustrate that freedom from enslavement did not necessarily guarantee Black women the freedom to enjoy the comforts and benefits associated with love and marriage.

Still, slavery had a lasting effect on Black love. The testimonies, letters, and wider records of the slave period suggest that very few bondwomen had the good fortune of remaining with their spouses for the duration of their married lives. Practically none could have been as lucky as Aunon, an enslaved Kalabari woman who, in her bad fortune of exile from her West African homeland to French Guiana, was accompanied by her husband, Quambon. Their love and union withstood the Middle Passage, the auction block, and the horrors of enslavement, for they remained married while condemned to work on the Remire estate in Cayenne (the modern-day capital of French Guiana). Estate manager Jean Groupy des Marets recorded them as having the same forty-two years of age in 1690 and, referencing Aunon, remarked, "She came, was bought and sold with her husband, and has never left him up to the present day."[106]

Slavery delivered a very different romantic outcome for so many of Aunon's sisters in North America and their daughters across the generations. Undeniably, powerful legacies tie the impoverished options for love, coupling, and marriage among African American women to factors dating back to the 1960s.[107] However, if we rely on statistical data alone, we apprehend only a fraction of what historical narratives and other contextual sources reveal about what can only be described as America's heritage of oppressing and terrorizing Black people *and* Black love. Such oppression and terrorism have thrived through intersecting socioeconomic and cultural structures that were designed to protect White supremacy, structures that have either directly or resultantly impacted African American hearts and romantic affections beginning more than three centuries ago. Celia knew it. Margaret Garner knew it. And that is why her marriage advice transcended her own experience and spoke to African Americans collectively.

"*Never marry again in slavery.*" Garner's words were the opening line of a public epistle to the nation about Black women's unspeakable collective experience with love and marriage in America, an epistle that this book will continue to read out loud.

CHAPTER 2

Slow Violence and White America's Reign of Terror

The end of slavery spelled new troubles for Black love, coincid-
ing with a four-year civil war that sowed chaos throughout a
divided nation. As fugitives from slavery and legally free Black men
enlisted in the Union army, many of their wives and children trailed
behind, following them to the very camps that housed them. They
were not always welcomed. The sheer numbers of roaming black
bodies in search of family stability, sustenance, and protection ob-
structed traffic on public roads, disrupted military operations, and
challenged the resources of even the most sympathetic federal officers, who worried about maintaining public health and safety in and
around their encampments. Many officials made no pretense of even
trying to help the masses of Black women and children who came
seeking rescue. They simply expelled them from campgrounds, at
times even denouncing the Black wives of their fugitive recruits as
prostitutes and loose women.

Beyond the bounds of the camps, conditions were unforgiving.
Malnutrition, insufficient clothing, disease, and emotional turmoil
accompanied Black wives and their children into the frigid tempera-
tures of bitter winter landscapes, where they often wasted away and

died.[1] Yet most still preferred taking their chances in the wild to returning to the properties of their owners.

Dire consequences awaited those who returned to the plantations, and awful punishments were visited on those who stayed behind. Spiteful slaveholders saddled deserters' wives with their absent spouses' arduous tasks, physically torturing them as the next best option to punishing the fugitive men now out of their reach and even promising to "kill every woman [with] a husband in the [Union] army."[2] In one case, a Louisiana bondwoman named Arana was transported more than ten miles from her home for this express purpose. Her husband, George Johnson, "a regularly enlisted man," learned that, in his absence, "four whitemen . . . came to [his wife's] residence . . . and kidnapped her. carried her down to the plantation of Dr T. B. Merritt. Eleven miles down the Mexican Gulf Rail Road. and there subjected her to the most cruel and unmerciful treatment." The April 3, 1863, complaint describing Arana's sufferings captures the contempt defenders of the Confederacy had for bondpersons who claimed their right to life and liberty during the last days of slavery:

> The Overseer of the plantation. whose name is Stamply. beat her unmercifully with a Stick. he afterward turned her clothes over her head, and Struck fifty two lashes. at the time he was thus punishing her. the Driver. remarked. Mr Stamply. if you don't be careful. you will Kill that woman. thereupon, Stamply drew his Revolver. and pointing it at the Driver; Said, God damn you, if you Say another word. I'll blow your brains out. the Yankee's have turned all you Niggers fools. and I intend to Kill all the niggers I can.[3]

Kentucky bondwoman Patsy Leach's account of her ordeal after her husband enlisted in the Union army and died on the battlefield exposes even more precisely the depravity governing the hearts of vengeful slaveholders. On multiple occasions, Leach reported, "my master [Warren Wiley] whipped me for no other cause than my husband having enlisted." Leach knew Wiley's reasons for abusing her because his verbal assaults were as stinging and rancorous as his whip. "He treated me more cruelly than ever," Leach revealed,

> whipping me frequently . . . and insulting me on every occasion. About three weeks after my husband enlisted, a Company of Colored Soldiers passed our house and I . . . looked at them [likely searching for her husband's face in the crowd] as they passed. My master had been watching me and when the soldiers had gone I went into the kitchen. My master followed me and knocked me to the floor senseless saying as he did so, "You have been looking at them darned Nigger Soldiers[.]" When I recovered my senses he beat me with a cowhide[.] When my husband was Killed my master whipped me severely saying my husband had gone into the army to fight against white folks and he my master would let me know that I was foolish to let my husband go[;] he would "take it out of my back," he would "Kill me by piecemeal."

With her infant child fastened to her hip, Leach managed to flee Wiley's fury. But in March 1865, she would seek government support to recover the four children she was forced to leave under Wiley's control during her desperate escape. At the time of her petition, Leach's wounded flesh, which displayed "still visible" marks "on my back," evoked her sufferings at least as vividly as her pen.[4]

Meanwhile, the reenslavement business was booming. At contraband camps, intruders regularly seized on the wives, children, and parents of Black soldiers and sold them to the highest bidders. A medical officer reporting on the state of affairs at northeastern Louisiana "contraband family camps," situated "on the right bank of the Mississippi," had encountered "about ten thousand women and children, who, having left their plantations, were roving about without adequate support or protection." Many were vulnerable prey for "some of the quasi agents of the government [who] have an understanding with the [Confederate] guerillas to supply them with negroes at the following rates. A male $300, a female $200, a likely child $100."[5]

Slavery was dying a bitter, painful death, and its end hinted at the new dimensions of suffering and trauma that would follow emancipation over the course of the hundred-year reign of terror still to come.

Across the South, the instability of social existence during America's Civil War determined what was possible for Black love and marriage. Tethered to the notion of ideal citizenship, monogamous marriage in America had long been predicated on the English patriarchal doctrine of coverture, which deprived wives of economic independence and established husbands' legal authority over acquisition of property and any other contractual negotiations involving their wives.[6] With cultural norms of their own for mating and marrying and alienation from property ownership, postenslaved African Americans had to be initiated into these long-standing White American marriage-citizenship rites of passage that were foreign to their customary stages of courtship and coupledom. "Sweethearting," "taking up," "trial marriages," and "abroad marriages" would soon be supplanted by registered monogamous marriages.[7] It was just the beginning of what would be a new chapter in America's long history of interference with Black love.

Reconstructing Black Marriage and Family Formation

The friction between Black love and patriarchal, state-orchestrated matrimony began before the war was even over. Federal and ecclesial authorities charged with supervising or assisting "contraband" camps took great interest in Black marriage and family arrangements, and not always with noble intentions.[8] Their efforts were frequently motivated by a desire not to secure Black families and romantic relationships but to ease the burden they feared indigent Black women and children would place on the state.

This mission was solidified in March 1865, when Congress established the Bureau of Refugees, Freedmen, and Abandoned Lands (usually known as the Freedmen's Bureau) to oversee relief efforts for former bondpersons and poor Whites as well as the general reconstruction of social institutions in the South. Under this recovery plan, bureau agents were assigned responsibility for marrying Black couples and influencing them to embrace monogamy and the gender roles expected of wives and husbands. In effect, the government sought to prepare postenslaved African descendants for compliant citizenship through the institutions of heterosexual marriage and the patriarchal family.[9] By May 30, 1865, the bureau commissioner issued a circular ordering agents deployed across the South to register marriages. Noting, "Registrations made by US Officers will be carefully preserved," the circular included provisions for the peculiar status of former bondpersons:

> In places where the local statutes make no provisions for the marriage of persons of color, the Asst. Commissioners are authorized to designate Officers who shall keep a record of marriages, which may be solemnized by any ordained minister of the gospel, who shall make a return of the same, with such items as may be required for registration at places designated by the Asst. Commissioners.[10]

The circular also promised, "The unity of families and all the rights of the family relations will be carefully guarded." But this was a promise the bureau could not keep.

Some relationships deviated from the customs associated with monogamous marriage and included plural marriages, or alternative courtship and marital arrangements. Bureau agents believed any arrangement at variance with monogamy contaminated the sanctity of marriage and positioned women and children to become dependent upon the state. One agent spoke for many federal authorities who, with no regard for the intricate polygamous unions slavery had designed for a great number of African Americans, insensitively imposed monogamous marriage upon former bondpersons and to the detriment of Black women. "Whenever a negro appears before me with 2 or 3 wives who have equal claim upon him," he explained, "I marry him to the woman who has the greatest number of helpless children who otherwise would become a charge on the Bureau."[11]

Though patriarchal monogamy may have been intended to guarantee stability and protection for women and children, it was an open question what was to be done for the unrecognized and dismissed wives and children of slavery's shattered polygamous marriages and family arrangements. This predicament was no incidental issue in the recollections of former bondwomen such as Hannah Jones. "The niggers had three or four wifes before de war, as many as dey could bear chillum by," she explained. "But after de war dey had to take one woman and marry her. My mother had three chillum by him [an unnamed consort] and de odder wifes had three and four chillum too."[12]

Perhaps Jones's memories stretched back to breeding liaisons coordinated by slave owners because her comment relayed nothing of the enduring emotional bonds and unabandoned love expressed in the 1869 letter Laura Spicer's husband sent to her when four years of searching finally disclosed his whereabouts. Even after having married another woman whom he loved dearly, his adoration for his first wife and their children endured. "Send me some of the children's hair in a separate paper with their names on the paper," he wrote. But the desire for pieces of his children that they could painlessly sacrifice was more than a powerful indication that "they have a good father and one that cares for them and one that thinks about them every day," as he asked Laura to tell them. His specific instruction to distinguish each lock of hair by name signals a determination to channel his paternal affection into spiritually protective power. From a distance, this father could at least access African religious rituals to ensure the safety and thriving of his children that unpreventable circumstances deterred him from providing them.

Addressing his first wife, Laura, directly, he insisted that she "please git married, as long as I am married," reminding her that "it never was our wishes to be separated from each other, and it never was our fault." Laura's husband freely confessed that he could not place his love for his second wife, Anna, above his love for her and closed his letter with copious declarations of unadulterated love for the wife slavery deprived him of loving and caring for in the flesh.

Repeating Laura's name like a mantra, he ensured her that the special passion they shared in the flesh had never been extinguished: "The woman is not born that feels as near to me as you do. You feel this day like myself. Laura . . . I thinks of you and my children every day of my life. Laura I do love you the same. My love to you never have failed. Laura, truly, I have go[t] another wife, and I am very sorry, that I am. You feels and seems to me as much like my dear loving wife, as you ever did Laura."[13]

THE COMPLICATIONS THAT UNRAVELED FOR Black married couples after the Civil War were largely inherited from the culture of forbidden Black love that took shape during slavery. Unexpected love triangles and other prickly scenarios presented themselves in the immediate postwar years for many. In some instances, Black women resolved such surprises by choosing to remain married to the same man, not necessarily as cowives but as comothers. After "months making her way" from Alabama to South Carolina to reunite with her husband and some of her children lost to her through the domestic slave trade, Dorcas Cooper was satisfied to remain in a polygamous relationship when she recognized how well her husband's new wife had taken care of her children. Cooper, in fact, "liked" her husband's second wife, Jenny, "and would not let anybody say anything against her." The two women resided comfortably "in the same house" with their spouse until Cooper passed away.[14]

Federal and state authorities sought to recognize slave marriages from the previous era regardless of whether former bondpersons actually desired to remain married to the partners their masters had selected for them.[15] By so doing, former slaveholders and state and federal authorities could alleviate themselves of caring for indigent and destitute Black populations. Married Black men would then assume such responsibilities as "heads" of their households. They would have to sort out how to put food on the table for their children, wives, and parents, as well as sick, disabled, and elder relatives.

Not only did states compel African Americans to register their marriages, but they also penalized them when their marital arrangements violated statutory definitions of a legitimate marriage or when they refused to register their marriages at all. In 1866 General Clinton Bowen Fisk, the Freedmen's Bureau assistant commissioner for Kentucky and Tennessee and founder of Fisk University in Nashville, Tennessee, published sixteen lectures under the title *Plain Counsels for Freedmen*. In his seventh lecture, "To Married Folks," he used his authority to place Black coupling arrangements that emerged during slavery beyond the purview of respectable marriage. "When you were slaves you 'took up' with each other, and were not taught what a bad thing it was to break God's law of marriage," Fisk declared. "But now you can only be sorry for the past, and begin life anew, and on a pure foundation. You who have been and are now living together as husband and wife, and have had children born to you, should be married according to law, as soon as possible."[16] Fisk's lectures appeared at a time when common-law marriages among Whites were not rare. However, even if slaveholders recognized the marriages of their human property, the very fact that enslaved persons were property and not citizens by law rendered their marriages ineligible for common-law status.[17]

Fisk was not a lone voice in the wilderness of Reconstruction determined to free postenslaved Blacks from their scandalous violations of "God's law of marriage." *The Freedman's Spelling-Book*, published by the American Tract Society and distributed to postenslaved persons around 1866, offered advice comparable to Fisk's. Lesson 252, "The Family," specifically instructed former bondpersons to adopt what were presented as sacred and inviolable marital and familial roles: "The fam-i-ly re-la-tion was or-dained by God in the garden of E-den, when he cre-a-ted Eve from one of Ad-am's ribs, and brought her to him to be his wife." Quoting from the book of Ephesians in the Christian Bible, the lesson continues, "The Bi-ble con-tains ma-ny di-rec-tions to hus-bands, wives, par-ents, and chil-dren, as to their du-ties to-ward each oth-er. Child-ren, o-bey your par-ents in the Lord, for this is right. Hus-bands, love your wives, e-ven as Christ al-so loved the church. Wives, sub-mit your-selves un-to your own hus-bands. Fa-thers, pro-voke not your chil-dren to wrath; but bring them up in the nur-ture and ad-mo-ni-tion of the Lord.—Eph.v. 22, 25; vi. 1, 4."[18]

Both documents were influential ideological devices designed to train postenslaved individuals for the "proper" roles and responsibilities associated with an inflexible vision of married life. They established Christian boundaries of moral behavior for husbands, wives, and children and located the nuclear, patriarchal family within a heterosexual "household" structure—the only legitimate basis for extended kinship networks. All previous arrangements that deviated from this model of Christian marriage and family would not be tolerated.

But while in some quarters postenslaved couples were lectured about the illegitimate status of their marriages and unions forged under slavery, in other quarters individual states found it expedient to rethink this determination. The state of North Carolina, for instance, quickly legalized Black unions formed during slavery. In 1865 its constitutional convention was sure to extend legal recognition of

Black relationships retroactively, declaring lawful the unions of all emancipated Blacks who "now cohabit together in relation of husband and wife" beginning with "the time of commencement of such cohabitation." Deliberate calculation went into writing the act this way to ensure that support for children born prior to emancipation would remain with parents rather than the state.[19]

The Georgia General Assembly approved a similar act on March 9, 1866, with penalties for men and women participating in polygamous unions. The "Act to prescribe and regulate the relation of Husbands and Wives between persons of color" stipulated "that persons of color, now living together as husband and wife, are hereby declared to sustain that legal relation to each other, unless a man shall have two or more reputed wives, or a woman two or more reputed husbands." The act went on to specify a remedy for postenslaved men and women in plural marriages: "In such event, the man, immediately after the passage of this Act by the General assembly, shall select one of his reputed wives, with her consent; or the woman one of her reputed husbands, with his consent; and the ceremony of marriage between these two shall be performed." With no regard for complicated situations that might have called for flexible marital arrangements, the act listed the range of criminal offenses noncompliance would invite. "If such man, thus living with more than one woman, or such woman living with more than one man, shall fail or refuse, to comply with the provisions of this section, he or she shall be prosecuted for the offence of fornication, or fornication or adultery, or, fornication and adultery, and punished accordingly."[20]

State marriage laws such as these rested on patriarchal foundations that had the effect of placing Black men under scrutiny as the so-called heads of their households. Not only in Georgia but across former slaveholding states, Black men were monitored and adulterers arrested. Some states such as North Carolina and Florida established a limited window during which cohabiting couples could marry or face criminal prosecution for adultery and fornication.[21]

Couples often paid fees to marry, at times presenting nothing more than "'six eggs' or a 'quart of strawberries.'"[22]

Contemporary Americans, even African Americans, can hardly imagine how deeply the double-edged sword of the civil right to patriarchal monogamous marriage pierced the lives of postenslaved Blacks. When alienated husbands and wives, sold away during slavery, returned to spouses who had remarried, charges of bigamy often followed along with legal prosecution and penalties.[23] Aiming to simultaneously shore up slaveholders' free labor supply while solving the problem of indigent children, local judges followed up these bigamy charges by simply ordering the removal of Black children from their families, placing them with former slaveholders under the guise of providing them adequate care. State apprenticeship laws allowed this practice of child reenslavement to explode for two years after emancipation as parent protests went unheard. Only an 1867 Supreme Court ruling arrested the practice.[24]

Black Widows or Fraudulent Wives?

The precariousness of marriages during slavery was a harbinger of the new bureaucratic universe that would engulf African descendants in the years to come. Although Congress passed the general law pension system act on July 14, 1862, only in July 1864 did Congress stipulate eligibility criteria for "colored" widows seeking pension benefits with no legal proof of marriage to a service-related deceased or disabled veteran.[25] Most problematic for Black women and Blacks as a whole, the federal government's pension administration tended to view them as frauds and schemers who deserved added layers of scrutiny and policing that White petitioners generally did not face. Nearly two decades after the national pension plan was put into effect, in 1881 the United States Pension Bureau issued *General Instructions to Special Examiners of the United States Pension Office*, which prescribed guidelines for handling the cases of "colored claimants, widows and dependent relatives."[26]

The document offers a window into the minds of bureau agents examining and making decisions about petitioners. It reveals an assumption that Black widows were prone to fabricating evidence and concocting fictive dependents to bolster their cases and forced them to go to extra lengths to prove the validity of their petitions under intense bureaucratic scrutiny. The *General Instructions* even gave the bureau "examiner" the authority to invalidate the parentage of a couple's dependent children by assessing whether the complexion of the child matched those of the claimant and spouse. "The Examiner . . . should see all the children for whom pension is claimed; their color may sometimes indicate whether they are the children of the soldier and the claimant." If a petitioner "resides . . . at a great distance from the place where she resided when the soldier was living," the examiner was instructed to "inquire into the case, so far as he can" and forward the case file to the bureau so that "a Special Examiner in that part of the country where the parties formerly resided" could pursue witnesses and other required evidence.[27] Nowhere did the *General Instructions* encourage sympathy for and patience with postenslaved claimants, due to impeding factors such as structural illiteracy, undocumented births and marriages, and "the inconsistency of surnames on military documents."[28]

In North Carolina, for example, Black widows were swindled out of their pensions by White agents hired to prepare petitions and handle negotiations on their behalf. Others were interrogated extensively about their sexual histories and made to account for disruptions in marriages they could not have avoided while living in bondage. The stories of claimants such as Ann Blackley and Maria Ann Counts offer telling insight into these inner workings of the system. The Pension Bureau approved Blackley's widow's pension application in 1869 and issued her "a check for more than one thousand dollars of accrued benefits." However, Blackley's agent, Seth Carpenter, denied receiving the funds. Later, when Carpenter was investigated for fraud due to numerous complaints, Special Agent

George Ragsdale described him as "a pension crook," and, because Blackley had remarried during the process, Ragsdale reported that he "was convinced that Carpenter planned to cash Ann Blackley's check himself when she 'remarried' or if she 'died.'"[29] For her part, claimant Maria Ann Counts was forced to disclose how sexual violation resulted in the birth of a daughter and a son during slavery. When a bureau official inquired about the paternity of her children Caroline and Census, both born before her marriage to Caesar Counts, she named William Green, her "master's uncle," as the father. Even this public exposure of her past humiliation and trauma was not enough to win a pension in her lifetime. By the time her case was finally approved, Maria Counts had already passed away.[30]

This bureaucratic procedure was not merely a Southern phenomenon, as Black widows from the North faced similar Pension Bureau investigations as well. In 1878, Ohio resident Emily Carrick's pension benefits were terminated when the special agent overseeing her case determined that she "had married Thomas Fike in Buffalo, New York, two years earlier," and although the laws of Ohio stated that "'cohabitation or the practice of living together as man and wife' did not constitute marriage," Carrick was disqualified nonetheless "on grounds of marriage by cohabitation."[31] Elizabeth Sible's pension benefits were also discontinued on questionable grounds because no credible evidence could prove that she had violated bureau policies. Despite the bureau examiner's suspicion that the New York resident "had lived as the wife of Charles Haight for a period of two years" with communal acknowledgment of the couple's marital status, the investigation "failed to uncover proof of formal marriage." Still, expunging her from the rolls, the examiner took the liberty to interpret her living arrangement to be consistent with the definition of marriage under New York State law.[32]

Sible's case was terminated in 1881, just a year before the federal government would pass a law revoking the benefits of widows who were fortunate enough to find love and companionship following the death of a veteran spouse. On August 7, 1882, federal law declared that any widow receiving pension benefits found cohabiting or having engaged in "illicit sexual relations with a man since her husband's death" would be disqualified from collecting future benefits.[33] Although not targeting African American beneficiaries directly, the act placed an undue burden on Black widows, many of whom had already undergone extensive special investigations to receive approval at all.

Though a considerable number of Black widows' petitions were ultimately approved, many were also denied. Out of a sample 1,946 African American women who filed claims for pension benefits, one researcher found that 843 (44 percent) were not approved.[34] But what is also important to remember is how protracted and invasive the pension process was for Black widows (and Black veteran beneficiaries overall), whether they were successful or not.[35] When comparing cases of poor White and Black widows, a distinct pattern emerged. Quite often, Black widows were required to undergo special examinations to prove their purported marriages to war veterans were legal.[36] A similar study comparing the rate of approval for Black and White widows in 350 pension applications found that 40 percent of Black widows (117 out of 298) were denied pension benefits compared to 16 percent of their White counterparts (41 out of 252).[37] Even when the cases of Black widows were approved, the scrutiny did not end, as the eventual termination of benefits for widows such as Emily Carrick and Elizabeth Sible illustrates.

No fewer than 186,000 Black men from slave states served in the Union army, and more than 50 percent of them or their dependents petitioned the US government for pension benefits.[38] The flow of applications for pension benefits from Black widows would increase exponentially after the Dependent Pension Act of 1890, which removed the condition of death or disability of a veteran spouse. Beginning in 1890 all veterans and dependents were eligible for benefits based on a veteran's service and honorable discharge.

Historian Tiffany Player underscores, "By eliminating the burden of proving a service-related injury, the 1890 Act provided new economic protections and articulated long-term obligations to veterans as they advanced in age and their earning capacity diminished."[39] Even though the administration and determination of benefits were rife with racial disparities, the 1890 act was a positive step forward that widened the door for Black and other beneficiaries to pursue their entitlements.

Roughly 40,000 Black soldiers died in the Civil War, most from infection and disease, leaving a greater number of honorably discharged Black veterans, disabled or not, with the prospect of supporting their families through federal pension funds, as of the last decade of the nineteenth century. For those who had died, surviving widows still had the right to claim pension benefits. However, if limited regional figures are any indication of what was true nationally, close to half of the Black widows who filed for pension benefits were unsuccessful. Though inclusive of all Black and White pension applicants nationally, not solely widows, calculations for the year 1889 disclose a more disturbing disparity: out of 6,035 Black applicants, 1,217 became pensioners, a 20 percent success rate that paled in comparison to the 67 percent success rate of White applicants.[40] The sizable number of denials Black widows confronted illustrates the liminal place Black marriage occupied in America during and after Reconstruction.

Legally recognized marriage was a central portal to citizenship rights and responsibilities. Consequently, African Americans' admission into free society was conditioned on acceptance of an inflexible patriarchal family structure and gendered divisions of labor and space. Questions about Black women's marital status also provided state and federal authorities an outlet for disparaging Black widows' reputations, branding them as frauds and liars, meddling in their private lives, and even invalidating their marriage claims altogether.

Even as some Black widows were able to secure pension benefits, allowing them to mourn their deceased loved ones while receiving financial relief from the government, a growing number of Black widows were losing their spouses not to war but to lynching, a crime that brought no financial restitution. During the last quarter of the nineteenth century, lynching replaced the whip in the wide repertoire of punitive technologies White Americans had designed to desecrate Black bodies while enforcing the customs of White-supremacist democracy. It is no accident, for example, that the first documented institution inspiring the murder of thousands across Southern states was the Southern Democratic machine itself, which, between 1868 and 1871, engineered the disfranchisement of Blacks (not to mention some White Republicans).[41] The most effective tactics in this campaign strategy would be mob lynchings, burnings, and massacres of Black citizens. Beyond arenas and times devoted to electoral politics, lynching crept into American quotidian life as a means of controlling postenslaved Blacks, trampling on their civil rights, including the right to love, marry, and transmit humanity to their posterity.

Murdered with a Black Family's History in Her Womb: Mary Turner's Lynching

Between 1877 and 1950, at least 4,075 "racial terror lynchings" were committed against Black persons across twelve Southern states alone[42]—a number that reflects only the documented cases of Black people illegally killed by a group of at least three persons. And while most Black victims of lynching were male, the gendered landscape of lynching was not by any means monolithic. By 1922 the National Association for the Advancement of Colored People (NAACP) had documented 66 Black female victims since the year 1889.[43] One of those victims was the pregnant Mary Turner. Her death during the high season of lynching in America illustrates the boundless powers White Americans had to injure and kill Black citizens at will.

Thirty-three-year-old Mary and her husband, Hazel "Hayes" Turner, were residents of Brooks County, Georgia, living in conditions that mirrored what slave existence had been for their ancestors on Georgia farms sixty years prior.[44] Both Turners worked for Claude Hampton Smith. The twenty-five-year-old White farmer regularly purchased cheap and exploitable labor at the local jail by paying fines for Black convicts.[45] Subsequently, the parolee would be forced to work on Smith's farm to reimburse him.

Like thousands of other White farmers in the South, Smith had become masterful at practically reenslaving Black people through Georgia's peonage system. And like many other Southern states, Georgia openly defied the congressional law prohibiting debt peonage in 1867. Smith's way of life was a public testimony to this fact.[46] At one point, in 1917, Smith had beaten Mary Turner, and when her husband fired back with threats, he was placed on a chain gang, only to be released back into Smith's abusive employ at the end of his sentence.

Since Black people's verbal warnings and threats had no authority to arrest White violence, it is no wonder a plot eventually developed among Smith's neo-enslaved Black laborers to kill the White boss before he killed them. The spring 1918 plot was supposedly conceived at Hayes and Mary Turner's home. On May 16, the day of the ambush, the perpetrators positioned themselves outside the Smith home and fired a shot through the dining room window while Smith and his wife, Leila, were eating dinner. The bullet struck Smith, killing him instantly. In a panic, his wife immediately fled the home and fell into the hands of the assailants. During a scuffle she was wounded in the chest by gunshot, but she was not raped, as widely rumored. His wife survived the attack and identified her assailants as Sidney Johnson and Julius Jones, two Black men who indeed worked on her deceased husband's farm. In the days leading up to his death, Smith had actually beaten Johnson mercilessly for attempting to take a one-day sick release from work, and it was later reported that Johnson was the chief conspirator of the plot against Smith.[47]

A six-day rampage of mob lynchings ensued, and no fewer than five hundred Blacks fled Georgia's Brooks and Lowndes Counties. Unfortunately, Hayes Turner was not among them. His immediate May 18 arrest for purportedly contributing to the murderous plot left him vulnerable to the mob's clutches. While being transported from the Brooks County jail in Quitman, Georgia, to another facility, Turner was lynched and his corpse left hanging at an intersection for two hot spring days.

The South had long ago proven that words of defiance uttered by Black tongues could be death sentences. Mary only voiced her outrage over her husband's gruesome murder and her intention to bring the forty-plus masked perpetrators to justice should she ever uncover the participants' identities, but it was enough to seal her fate. The following day, the irate mob hunted her down and desecrated her body with heinous cruelty. Mary was hung upside down from a tree limb, feet tied like a hog, dowsed with oil and gasoline, and set ablaze while still alive enough to feel a hog-splitting knife slicing her womb so that her unborn baby, one-month shy of a natural birth, would be delivered into hell. When Mary and Hayes's legacy plunged into the dust, a mobster lifted his boot and smashed the infant's head. The orgy climaxed with the raging crowd riddling Mary's body with hundreds of bullets. Just days later, one participant reveled in Mary's agony when he told NAACP assistant secretary Walter White, "You ought to've heard the nigger wench howl!"[48]

With the lynching of the Turners, the South and the governments that empowered it murdered more than just three Black family members. It symbolically murdered Black love and marriage, depriving the two surviving Turner children of parental nurturance and refuge. Perhaps they could at least take comfort in discovering that their mother lost her life in defense of Black love, in defense of her husband—their father—whose innocence of any wrongdoing related to Claude Hampton Smith's death she steadily upheld until her last breath.[49]

Mary Turner's marriage never had a fighting chance to take root in the intimate joys and sorrows of a wedded life, to grow old and strong like the trunks, limbs, and leaves that bore the weight of lynched Black bodies across the South *and* the North. And the death of Black marriage through such horrendous acts was not a singular event. Other Black women and communities subjected to the mayhem of American race riots and massacres would experience the same loss. Whether wounded or destroyed, Black love and marriage would pay a tremendous price for America's "White rage" and its ritualized violence.[50] Such violence at times went far beyond snuffing out individuals and families, ravaging and scattering whole Black communities in its thirst to demolish any sign of Black flourishing.

BURNING AND LOOTING BLACK LOVE

The year was 1912 and the state was Georgia, though it could have been Oklahoma, Louisiana, North Carolina, Illinois, Tennessee, Mississippi, Arkansas, Pennsylvania, and Georgia *again*, six years prior. News that several Black males had raped and savagely beaten a young White woman had circulated through town soon after eighteen-year-old Mae Crow was found clinging to life in the Oscarville community's surrounding woods the evening of September 9. Ernest Knox, a local motherless-fatherless child who had lived hand to mouth for most of his young life in Forsyth County, confessed to the attack under the duress of a "mock lynching." The White man who first questioned the vulnerable orphan while tying a rope around his neck had intimidated the teenager into confessing exactly what he wanted to hear—that Knox was the perpetrator of the crime.[51]

Knox was now most certainly marked for death. But seeing the vengeful hordes swelling in numbers outside his window, the sheriff acted quickly to outmaneuver them. Under a judge's order, he moved Knox from his Gainesville jail to Atlanta's Fulton County jail to evade the seething mob's death grip. Knox's inquisitor had rushed him to the Gainesville jail, just over the Chattahoochee River in neighboring Hall County, to escape the mob that was ready to lynch the adolescent prisoner if he had been taken to the Cumming jail.[52] With Knox now out of the mob's reach, the entire town of Cumming, the seat of the county, and neighboring Forsyth citizens were whipped into a fury. Forsyth and other nearby Georgia counties had been soaked with black blood of the slaughtered for decades, and just four days prior to Mae Crow's attack, another White woman, Ellen Grice, was reportedly "awakened by the presence of a negro man in her bed."[53] The insinuation was that she had been raped. Forsyth sheriff William Reid and his deputy Mitchell Gay Lummus immediately arrested five suspects with no evidence to justify their detention. Another Black man, a well-respected preacher's son and a part-time preacher himself, was whipped nearly to death by a mob of three hundred for comments he made about the unnecessary trouble that had befallen one of the suspects "on account of 'a sorry white woman.'"[54] Rescued by officers of the law before he could be lynched, he too had been taken into custody. The mob was enraged that its prey had been ushered to secure locations for their safety until trial.

The now two thousand–strong vigilante group would not be deprived this time around. Taking advantage of rumors tying one of Knox's acquaintances, Robert Edwards, to the crime involving Mae Crow, the vigilantes quickly seized the opportunity. On September 10, the day after Crow's attack, Edwards became the first lynched victim related to her case. A month later, a shoddy trial found Ernest Knox and another fragile Black teenager, Oscar Daniel, guilty of Crow's assault, and an audience of about five thousand assembled to view their execution by hanging on October 25, 1912. Swift justice by any measure of the word.

Killing Knox and Daniel wasn't enough for the White mob of Cumming, Georgia. Mobsters actually wanted to rid Forsyth

County of all Black presence. Just days after the Crow incident, White men began to gather during the evenings, systematically threatening Black communities with terroristic violence if they did not pack up and leave the county. The purge only intensified when White residents feared Black retaliation. The same night of Robert Edwards's savage killing and display on a telephone pole near the Cumming, Georgia, courthouse, a mysterious fire broke out, consuming the storehouse of a local White man named Will Buice. The White citizens of Cumming took the fire as a sign of Black retribution for Edwards's lynching. They had long feared that Cumming's Black citizens would someday retaliate for the centuries of mistreatment of enslaved and postenslaved Black communities and saw the fire as a signal that it was time to escalate their terror campaign and demands for a Black exodus. To be sure Black citizens knew they were serious, their terrorism went beyond stoning Black residences and firing warning shots at front doors. They also burned Black churches and properties. With neither homes nor Black institutions to return to, Forsyth's Black refugees would have to find new places to settle and start over.[55]

Driving the pandemonium even further was the fact that, despite her doctor's prediction that she would recover from her injuries, Mae Crow had contracted pneumonia while in a coma and died a few weeks after the attack. One Atlanta headline read, "Enraged White People Are Driving Blacks from County." Another announced, "Negroes Flee from Forsyth."[56] An involuntary exodus of eleven hundred people cleansed the county of Black presence within the space of two months, spelling incalculable losses of property, spouses, and other life investments. Garrett and Josie Cook, for example, were not spared even a day to figure out where to run or how to part with their immovable wealth—twenty-seven acres of land. The morning after Mae Crow's funeral, George Jordan, a sympathetic White farmer, had gone to check on the Cooks, only to find sheer mayhem. The Cook home "had been shot so full of holes that all the legs on the tables, chairs, and bed had been shot off."

Fortunately, Josie and Garrett took cover in the woods, but after the attack on their home they immediately fled Forsyth County, never to return. So did every other Black person in the area. According to George's daughter Ruth Jordan, night riders paraded in the streets "every night until no colored was left."[57] Another local White resident, Joel Whitt, recalled that, over time, "certain men would go to a black person's home with sticks tied up in a little bundle [and] leave'em at the door." When such lynching props were placed "outside the cabin of some last, proud black farmer, by sunup he and his whole family would be gone."[58]

The exodus severed families as well. Byrd Oliver literally lost his wife and three of his seven children while fleeing Forsyth County with about seventy-five other Black residents. "They would walk so far and then count [everyone in the group]. Just before they got to the river, three of [Byrd's] relatives were missing. But you couldn't turn back to look for them," Byrd's daughter Dorothy explained. She knew from memory the story of how her father's first wife, Delia, and their three eldest daughters were nowhere to be found among Forsyth County's group of Black exiles who made their way along an eleven-mile route to Gainesville, Georgia. Byrd resettled there with his four boys and remarried Beulah Rucker, the woman who would give birth to Dorothy. However, not knowing the fate of his first wife and three daughters was a psychic wound that never healed.[59] We can only speculate about the spontaneous decisions Byrd and Delia were forced to make about their family's unknown future, struggling to exit Forsyth County without stumbling into the hands of night riders. What we know for certain, though, is that local White terrorism drove them out, severed their union, and destroyed the wealth and assets of their love.[60]

THIS SEVERING OF BLACK FAMILIES and the destruction of their property and investments through racially motivated massacres intensified across the nation as Black people gained independence, launched enterprises that competed with local White businesses, and acquired coveted jobs.[61] On February 22, 1898, Lavinia and Frazier Baker's home burned for this reason alone. The perpetrators destroyed not just property and persons. They deprived survivors of Black love—the comforts and security that the marriage dyad provides children and a wider kin group. An unwelcomed outsider in a predominantly White settlement, Frazier Baker, the upwardly mobile Lake City, South Carolina, postmaster had been targeted before. He was wounded by gunshot shortly after accepting his new appointment and relocating to his assigned office in Lake City.

The first attack was definitely more than a warning. The outcome of the second attack, however, was devastating because after the Bakers and their children's unsuccessful attempts to smother the fire, they fled their residence for the shelter of the streets, only to have a mob of White men open fire on them. But the shots were lethal even before they could unlatch the front door. The youngest family member, baby Julia, was the first to fall. Lavinia had sought to shield the twenty-three-month-old under her arm in hope of dashing to safety in the nearby woods. But then a bullet entered Lavinia's hand and ripped through Julia's skin, killing the infant instantly. With a blazing fire consuming his home and no place left to hide from the random shots penetrating the house, Frazier quickly opened the door and withstood several bullets before collapsing in a lifeless heap. Even in death, Frazier extended protection to his baby, for Julia's body had been sheltered from additional gunfire under cover of her father's corpse. The three eldest Baker children were terribly wounded by continuing gunfire as they made their escape. Left to her own resources, Lavinia scrambled to the woods to collect and comfort the three who had been wounded along with the two who had fled unharmed from the atrocity.

In the aftermath, benevolent White community members offered support to the Baker survivors, but it was the Black community that most immediately wrapped its arms around what was left of the severed and severely wounded Baker family, providing sanctuary to Lavinia and her five remaining children.[62]

By the first decade of the twentieth century, new waves of terrorist mobs had joined lynch mobs to become the chief coconspirators in White America's assaults on its Black citizens.[63] Massacres and pogroms in Wilmington, North Carolina (1898); Atlanta (1906); Springfield, Illinois (1908); and East St. Louis, Illinois (1917), seemed harbingers of the fateful "Red Summer" of 1919, when twenty-six "race riots" erupted in different American cities throughout both the South and the North.

What would be described as the most brutal of all these terrorist campaigns during World War I occurred in East St. Louis, Illinois. In 1917 the city was home to a series of racially motivated violent outbreaks that targeted Blacks, but the month of July was most horrific. Enraged by the rise in Black employment within local factories, White laborers roamed the streets and murdered Blacks upon sight, sparing no women or children. With the assistance of police and soldiers, White women and children even joined in the pogrom, attacking hundreds of local Blacks and displacing, by conservative estimates, more than six thousand people. One twenty-four-year-old victim, Lula Suggs, took shelter in a cellar with nearly a hundred women and children while attackers incinerated the School for Negroes. Suggs witnessed White terrorists throwing Black children into one of the raging fires they had set, and another victim, Beatrice Deshong, saw Whites of all age groups, even girls and boys, perpetrating crimes against humanity. The White gangs were unrelenting in their feverish pursuit and ambush of even the most vulnerable Black infants.[64]

Gunnar Myrdal preferred to call such savage bursts of White "collective effervescence" "massacres" or "mass lynchings."[65] In no uncertain terms, these so-called race riots offered large public stages upon which America's purveyors of White rage could play out their rituals of burning and looting the valuables of Black families and businesses. Their rampages resulted in the destruction of not only revenue and capital investments but also investments of the heart and the emotional and social capital of Black love and marriage. White marauders burned and looted Black love and its assets as much as they did Black businesses and households, forcing husbands and wives to scramble for cover, unable to protect each other from the onslaught. Such was the sad story of Sarah and Haywood Carrier, victims of the 1923 Rosewood, Florida, massacre. Haywood was away hunting when the killing spree and destruction occurred. Returning home to the carnage and discovering his wife, Sarah, murdered along with their two sons, Haywood Carrier "died just a year later, and family members said it was grief that killed him."[66]

Sarah Carrier and her sons were among the 3,446 Blacks known to be lynched in America between 1882 and 1968, certainly an undercounted figure since so many racially motivated Black deaths at the hands of Whites went unreported.[67] Scrutinizing the figures of the lynching era's preliminary decades alone, we find that Southerners could count on at least one Black person being lynched every four days between 1889 and 1929.[68] Whether killed during high or low lynching seasons, every Black life matters, and the loss of Sarah Carrier to racially motivated violence is already one spouse too many. The fate of her husband, Haywood, is all the more a tangible sign that the incremental effects of the burning, killing, and raiding took a toll on Black love, marriage, and family relationships across the life of our nation.

In some regions, White terrorists went so far as to target Black love and marriage directly. During the infamous two-day 1921 Tulsa, Oklahoma (Greenwood District), riots, White marauders demolished a central site of Black love and romantic life. An *Ebony* article on the destruction of what became known as Tulsa's "Black Wall Street" described the Black-owned Williams Confectionery as "the most popular hang out for the young." It was common knowledge that "more proposals for marriage . . . happened at the [confectionery's] popular soda fountain than any other place in the city."[69] Depriving Black couples of community-owned intimate spaces to court and delight in the pleasures of romantic love was ruthless enough. However, robbing Black victims postmortem of the bodily sovereignty and integrity that death can be said to grant those most degraded in life constituted a theft of unspeakable proportions.

STRANGE, SEDUCTIVE FRUIT AND THE UNJUST ENRICHMENT OF WHITE LOVE

The South's geography is thick with landmarks to forbidden Black love, many located in the state of Georgia. At Moore's Ford Bridge, the July 25, 1946, lynching of two Black couples—George and Mae Murray Dorsey and Roger and Dorothy Dorsey Malcolm—was reportedly accompanied by moments of each husband and wife screaming for the other. Like Mary Turner, Dorothy Malcolm was (seven months) pregnant.[70] What is also underemphasized about this case is that two of the victims, George and Dorothy, were actually siblings, and so the deaths of these four individuals and their unborn progeny blighted the branches of two connected family trees. Moreover, a peculiar though not uncommon detail about their fate in death unveils a psychosocial dimension of America's war on Black love and marriage.

A young White Navy veteran, Donald Garrett, admitted that he "went to Moore's Ford Bridge the day after the killings, eventually leaving with a human tooth pulled from a pool of blood at the site." Garrett gave the tooth to a local politician's daughter, "who, he recalled, wore it as a charm on a bracelet around her wrist."[71] It's hard to miss the religious and romantic overtones in the sacrificial slaughtering that yielded not just the material Black body for White souvenir collectors who cleaned up after strange fruit was left swinging from trees and poles. In Garrett's case, the death of Black love served to kindle White love.

One way to make sense of the tooth gift is to see it as confirmation of what many philosophers and social scientists have theorized, that Black identity was necessary to make White identity possible. What this means is that there is no way to enshrine in a nation's consciousness the fiction of a superior race without devising its opposing counterpart. So, perhaps, it should not be surprising that collecting the fragments of Black lynched bodies was the surest means of memorializing and revisiting a peculiar ecstasy experienced during lynchings and other celebrations of White power. And perhaps, too, those who so desperately need that ecstasy in order to define themselves as White are likely to associate that same feeling with the ecstasy of White love.[72] Undoubtedly, the transfer of the tooth is a transfer of White power status. It is a gift that grants White female membership in the cult of White supremacy. However, it also tells us something else—that White-inflicted Black death is a romantic affair for Whites, that extinguishing Black love and marriage yields Black bodily materials that enhance White love.

White males' fixation on Black male genitalia both during and after lynchings also contributes to this perverse interplay between Black bodies and White love.[73] White Americans have long conceived the Black male penis as a threat to White female chastity and White male dominance. Mythologized as oversize and dangerous, Black male genitalia constitutes a site of power to be conquered, and numerous reports from the lynching era document White men's obsession with either possessing the penises of their lynched Black victims or dispossessing Black male penises of their virility. White men repeatedly castrated their lynched Black male victims, preserved their penises in jars of formaldehyde, and displayed them as trophies for public viewing. They were also known to stuff their victims' mouths with their dismembered "manhood," the ultimate display of White male sovereignty over the greatest threat to their masculinity.

In the psychosocial universe where lynching rituals such as these unfolded, the retrieved tooth carried a phallic symbolism. The gifted phallus conveys virility, fertile affection, romantic love, and even blessings for a charmed White life. Whether acknowledged or not, it has sacred significance for White love. Sacrifices and gifts are essential ingredients in the making of any religious culture. And so in America's twisted national love story, we have to confront the disturbing reality that the gifting of Black bodies has simultaneously destroyed Black love and served as fodder for White thriving and expressions of passion.[74] Thinking through the implications of this interlocking dance between death and love within the larger story of White-perpetrated Black lynchings surfaces a tension between love and labor.

HISTORICALLY, THE FEAR OF THE so-called Black male rapist and accusations of rape led White citizens to rid their communities of Black men either by murder or intimidation. Doing so, however, vexed those Whites who depended on cheap neo-slave labor to work fields, wash, clean, cook, and take care of White children. If they were killed off and forced out of town, *who* was going to do the *work?*

In the aftermath of Mae Crow's untimely death on September 23, 1912, Forsyth County's landowners and upper-class citizens struggled to resolve this quandary. When women in the Strickland family complained to their patriarch, Ansel, that their Black female domestics disappeared almost overnight, he used the reach of the *North Georgian* to disseminate a public response with advice for neighbors and friends:

> The Negro is gone from Forsyth county and you had as well roll up your sleeves and follow me. For the last 33 years I have always hired my wife's washing done by negroes . . . but on the morning of October 22, 1912, my negro washwoman informed me that she was going to leave my washing for my wife to do [because] . . . the people did not give the negro proper protection. I told her . . . that

if I had to sell my daughter's virtue to negro boys in order to retain her as a wash woman, she could *get* [depart].[75]

Most White Southerners couldn't live with Blacks, and they couldn't live without them. Labor protection for Blacks in the employ of Whites left White love unprotected. Yet by killing the Black body, White perpetrators' psychic and sexual satisfaction increased exponentially. Even in death, they raided Blackness for additional unjust enrichment. White supremacy and White love feasted on Black tissue, blood, bone, and other severed materials of the Black body.[76]

Of course, the opposite was true for Blacks. Every lynching, every calculated disappearance of a Black person, including those whose corpses were never recovered, caused profound affliction for surviving spouses and family members. To say that lynchings, racial cleansings, and massacres killed Black love and marriage and scattered Black families is to state the obvious. But while discussions about these forms of terrorist violence most often focus on the swift violence of the impetuous mobs that perpetrate such assaults, there was also a slow violence of daily harassment, segregation, social control strategies, and the collateral damage suffered as a result of mob violence that served to turn Black love into something forbidden.

With the constant possibility of death by terror regulating Black life during and after Reconstruction and the economic exploitation and impoverishment African Americans faced across the South, millions left and, in so doing, accommodated living arrangements that approximated slavery's conventions of abroad marriages and dispersed family life, partitioned now by the Mason-Dixon line and Jim Crow border states. Surprisingly, most migrant marriages remained intact during this period. However, too many marriages sustained wounds that never healed. Whether punctuated with the finality of divorce or not, others unraveled under the pressures of structurally induced isolation, separation, and White rage. Inez Starling's marriage was one of them.

Escaping the Reign of Terror

During the Second World War, the government recruited most able-bodied laborers for service, which meant that the workers of Eustice, Florida, for once had the upper hand. In 1944 a group of fruit pickers struggled for higher pay. The White foreman wanted to pay laborers fifteen cents per box, but George Starling and two of his close comrades, Mud and Sam, pushed their coworkers to fight for greater compensation. One day they mobilized the workers to return home rather than pick tangerines for ten cents less per box than what they demanded. This time George had attracted the direct attention of the grove owner himself. The grove owner confronted the strikers, brandishing a pistol that he threatened to use if they abandoned the grove. Unimpressed, George coached his band of terrified laborers to stand their ground.

This was the last straw. Fearful that George and his conspirators would make circumstances much more difficult, a group of grove owners schemed about ways they might eliminate the radical element among the pack. Word got back to George about their plans for his lynching, and he reckoned it was a sign he ought to leave the South permanently. When she heard the news from her husband, Inez Starling's heart sank. Would her newfound life partner reach his destination safely? Would she be able to join him? If only he had remained satisfied with their weekly allotment of meager pennies for the kind of work that could tire an ox by day's end, they could have weathered the same stable instability in their own pursuit of happiness, at least within the limits of what the Jim Crow South could offer.

Before the grove owners leveled their threats at George, the couple had high hopes for their future. George had lofty ambitions of completing college, and Inez's dream was to exchange the mop and the toilet brush for the hot comb and the blow dryer at the Angelo Beauty College, where she would train as a professional hairdresser. Aiming to finance Inez's dream, George made every effort to supplement the pennies from the boxes of picked fruit he earned at his main gig. He doubled as a makeshift insurance salesman and taxi cab driver on most nights and weekends and, during a brief stint of employment in Detroit, faced down a major race riot fueled by rumors of White infractions upon Blacks as much as by Black infractions upon Whites. All of these sacrificial labors, this deliberate planning, finally allowed Inez to begin attending beauty college— not to mention that moment of pride as he paid in full the $300 bill for the furniture Inez had reluctantly picked out at his urging once he decided it was time to leave his father's home and branch out on their own.

As of April 1945, none of those dreams mattered anymore. George found himself suddenly confronting the same crossroads that hundreds of other Black men in Georgia, Alabama, Texas, Mississippi, Virginia, and Louisiana, indeed all over the South, had confronted. He could remain in the South and die or escape to the North to try to eke out a new life there. And so, like many before and after him, George Starling hopped a train to Harlem, where he would join some family members already settled in a city bustling with Black presence and possibility. Inez would stay behind until he could send for her.[77]

That Black families emerged resilient from centuries of slavery, terror, and what can be described only as "domestic refugeeism" is remarkable. Early theories of African American kinship held that Southern Black migrants' mating habits corrupted Black urban coupling and marriage patterns in the North. However, contrary to what towering Black scholars such as W. E. B. Du Bois and E. Franklin Frazier concluded about destructive Black marriage and kinship arrangements developed during slavery and transported north during the Great Migration, newer studies are revealing that Black migrant marriages in the North were actually less likely to end in divorce than their Black counterparts native to the region.[78] Other studies clarify that, across diverse global contexts, migrant families generally demonstrate greater resilience when confronted with social and economic strife than native-born nationals. In addition, some scholars underscore that a significant proportion of migrants were actually single men who did not leave nuclear families to pursue new dreams in Northern urbanscapes.[79] At the same time, a rare study treating the subject of divorce in Washington, DC, and Virginia between 1865 and 1930 identified the Great Migration as a contributing factor to African American divorce cases.[80]

It is nearly impossible to say now whether, had divorce not been so stigmatized between the 1860s and 1930s, the Black community would have witnessed higher rates of marital dissolution, given its subjugation to historic and contemporary trauma and oppression. Even if migrant marriages did not terminate with legal divorce, marriage could become another Northern landscape of unwelcomed adversities, including betrayal for some Black women whose husbands indulged in outside affairs. Bessie Smith's 1925 recording of "St. Louis Blues" exposed the infidelity and consequent internal deliberations some women experienced during the Great Migration. "St. Louis Blues" easily could have been titled "Harlem Blues," "Detroit Blues," or "Philadelphia Blues" for its testimony that migration offered many roads to the hearts of Northern mistresses:

> *I hate to see the evening sun go down*
> *I hate to see the evening sun go down*
> *It makes me think, I'm on my last go 'round*
>
> *Feelin' tomorrow like I feel today*
> *Feelin' tomorrow like I feel today*
> *I'll pack my grip and make my getaway*
>
> *St. Louis woman wears her diamond ring*
> *Pulls my man around by her apron strings*
> *Wasn't for powder and this store-bought hair*
> *The man I love wouldn't go nowhere, nowhere*

I got them St. Louis blues, just as blue as I can be
He's got a heart like a rock cast in the sea
Or else he would not go so far from me.[81]

"So far from me" is what many Black women reckoning with a third party to their marriages felt about the disloyal husbands they loved. Whether Black wives waited in the South for a ticket north to join their spouses or already resided with their life partners in cramped apartments of Black metropolises, this final lamentation of "St. Louis Blues" conveys not so much physical distance as much as the emotional distance of broken vows and alienation. However, beyond the interior webs of disappointments and violations afflicting any vulnerable Black marriage, external structural forces from Reconstruction up through the Great Migration sustained a culture of forbidden Black love that had either direct or delayed impact upon the emotional and financial resources and wealth-building capacity of Black marriages and families.

As the narratives examined thus far reveal, throughout slavery and after, Black love and marriage remained under attack in this country, either directly or indirectly. During slavery the disruptions and prohibitions impacting enslaved Black couples were so visibly unapologetic and gruesome, it could be said that American slavery was waging a full-scale war on Black love and marriage. And when the control of the slave estate ceased, the nation-state and White vigilantes stepped in to take its place. Over the course of centuries, through slavery, Reconstruction, and Jim Crow, Black love and marriage faced American aggression on multiple fronts.

Between 1865 and the early 1960s, the war on Black love raged on mostly via terrorist tactics that targeted legally free Black people. Black love and marriage might not have been the direct target, but the effect was still the same. The phenomenon of forbidden Black love that began with slavery continued during the reign of terror, albeit through different institutional measures. Certainly, this was a time when the increasing rates of Black marriage could lead many to presume that forbidden Black love simply disappeared after slavery—that America's war on Black love and marriage ended with the Civil War—but nothing could be further from the truth.

For nearly a century after the Civil War, Black love and marriage sustained the impact of what Rob Nixon calls "slow violence."[82] While aggressive and macabre in its rage toward "free" Black persons, America's accumulated bursts of frenzied physical violence and paternalistic ideological violence, across ten decades, taxed Black love and marriage. Gradually but steadily, the first hundred years after emancipation allowed the slow violence of forbidden Black love to wage a new war whose effects are arguably still being felt in Black America today. Because of how it works, slow violence can go undetected, leaving most at a loss for addressing its effects.

Legal historian Annette Gordon-Reed argues something similar, calling the actions of President Andrew Johnson, under whose leadership states' rights ruled the South, a "slow-motion genocide." Johnson essentially gave Whites permission to commit any atrocity they wished against Blacks. His presidency enabled the powerful legal and political machinery of states' rights to actually protect White criminals and terrorists of all stripes, including one who confessed with no sense of shame that he killed a Black man because he "wanted to thin out the niggers a little."[83] The era of lynching and race massacres certainly aided the "thinning out" process, and the Great Migration only confirmed that a "slow-motion genocide" was indeed in place. The slow violence of forbidden Black love worked similarly and concomitantly across a century's expanse, operationalized through the psychic trauma that shattered Black lives for generations within families forced to cope with lynched and disappeared mothers and fathers, wives and husbands.

In a telling scene from the episode "Into the Fire," covering the first thirty years of the reign of terror, the *African Americans: Many Rivers to Cross* documentary series host Henry Louis Gates asks in sheer bewilderment, "How could [Black people] survive every day and have hope, build a family and fall in love?"[84] Somehow they did. Yet, even in love, the parameters for intimacy and familial formation were being redefined for those just emerging from slavery.

The exercise of Black love and power took on new gendered dimensions as postenslaved African descendants adopted Euro-American norms and ideologies pertaining to marriage and family life. As a result, since the earliest days of Reconstruction, millions of postenslaved African Americans have suffered another consequence of America's slow violence of forbidden Black love. Ironically, that violence—the uninterrogated normative ideologies of patriarchal marriage—has penetrated the heart of Black marital arrangements and expectations for a century and a half. Given Black people's tumultuous love story in this country, it is worthwhile, though, to ask whether patriarchal marriage is what the Black community really needs. In fact, we might inquire further whether patriarchal marriage has actually harmed the Black community and sabotaged Black women's options for achieving stable and fulfilling marital partnerships with Black men.

RECONSIDERING PATRIARCHAL MARRIAGE

Whether denied and unrecognized, encouraged and compelled, or belittled and mocked, the institution of marriage was and remains for Black people a burdened American legacy. Despite what many may think, Black heterosexual marriage has never been a straightforwardly private affair, and the structures governing American civil society never privileged the independent wishes and agency of Black women and men to love and marry one another and to pursue happiness with the same degree of liberty allowed White heterosexual couples.

Even with the havoc that the imposition of patriarchal monogamy wreaked upon Black people's civil right to love and enjoy the benefits of American democracy after 1865, thousands upon thousands of emancipated African descendants married, remarried, or registered their preemancipation marriages with the Freedman's Bureau. In fact, Herbert Gutman's well-known 1976 study of African American marriage patterns and customs during slavery and the reign of terror revealed the prevalence of two-parent Black families across both periods.[85] Because he was focused on debunking the Moynihan Report's harmful and inaccurate portrait of the Black family that played into racist stereotypes, Gutman's study understandably did not emphasize disruptions to family life during slavery. Although two-parent nuclear families were certainly prevalent, the "problem was that most of them could not be sustained through slavery, displacement, and war." The patterns and seasons of slave life made "the most enduring family form . . . the matrifocal unit, often created out of the remnants left behind when families were sundered or turned into saleable units put on the auction block."[86]

With this said, it might be tempting to celebrate the fact that Black marriages and nuclear families increased in the decades after slavery and triumphed by the turn of the twentieth century. A married couple was present, for example, within 80 percent of African American families as early as 1880.[87] However, if studies were available to measure the stress Black marriages absorbed from White terroristic violence and furtive assaults on Black liberty and love, as well as the virtual health of those marriages, the picture might not look so rosy.

Some scholars contest the enduring perception of marriage as a benign institution that secured citizenship advantages for Black Americans across the centuries. The "Reconstruction period did not feature happy black brides and grooms so much as fragile black unions too often forged through trickery, government coercion and punishment," writes law professor Robin Lenhardt, and her point is not driven by pessimism.[88] There are certainly good reasons to be cautious about viewing the high rate of marriage among Blacks during the last decades of the nineteenth century as a self-sustaining achievement. Black marriages exhibited signs of distress during and after this period, as couples navigated social and cultural challenges in new urbanscapes across the nation.[89] Thus, "even though the majority had married and created stable families," the social and economic burdens associated with Reconstruction and the reign of terror "left marriages and families vulnerable to the assault of massive stresses in the last half of the 20th century."[90]

Other findings also complicate our perception of marriage stability and quality among African Americans during earlier historical periods. Tera Hunter identifies the 1940s as a critical moment when a significant disparity between Black and White marriage rates began to surface. She explains how racist practices at the state and municipal levels prevented Blacks from accessing the bountiful range of benefits that accrued to Whites through the Selective Service Readjustment Act of 1944 (commonly known as the GI Bill of Rights). The bill provided veterans employment opportunities as well as funds and subsidies to pay for a college education or a home. It also encouraged marriage by extending additional benefits to wedded veterans.[91] A 2015 study amplifies this point. Researchers examined marriage statistics over the twentieth and early twenty-first centuries, concluding that the gap in marriage rates between Blacks and Whites began decades earlier than the mid-1960s when considering ever-married women who remained married with a coresident husband by midlife (early forties). The study showed a noticeable disparity between the 69 percent of Black women and 88 percent of White women meeting these criteria. But even before the 1940s, when divorce was uncommon in the early 1900s, Black women underwent marital separation twice as much as White women.[92]

When Black marriages failed to reward couples with the happiness and support they imagined for themselves, how much of that failure could be traced not only to tangible external stressors but also to harmful and unrealistic expectations of the elite White American patriarchal nuclear family that Black people increasingly adopted in the aftermath of slavery?[93] Since the 1860s, patriarchal marriage, I would argue, has set Black people up for failure in love and relationships, and we need more discussions about why this is so. Allowing that patriarchal marriage might be defended as desirable in some circles, collectively speaking, Black men were never in any historical position to leverage resources, power, and authority to "govern" over their families, especially as sole breadwinners and providers.

If we could return to March 26, 1944, when six Mississippi White men were party to the lynching of Reverend Isaac Simmons, we would ponder how well even benevolent patriarchy was working for Black men and their families in the Jim Crow South. Simmons was a Black man doing every legal thing possible to ensure that official documentation was in place for his land to remain in his family's possession. He was up against a man named Nobel Ryder, a local White farmer intent on stealing Simmons's unmovable wealth. Simmons's family had been the legal custodians of 278 acres of a particularly coveted swathe of Amite County land since 1895, his father having purchased the first plot as early as 1887. Also coveted by neighboring White farmers was Simmons's secret remedy for curing sick animals. When inaccurate news circulated of oil-rich land on Simmons's estate, a dispute broke out about the extent of the property, and the sixty-six-year-old did what any benevolent patriarch would do. Safeguarding his family's future, he consulted an attorney to settle his disagreement with Ryder and coconspirator Vaughn Lee.

But Simmons's assertion of his patriarchal right to protect his family violated the Southern system of patriarchal belonging and exclusion. It was a system that empowered White men to remind Black men such as Simmons that they were "boys," not men, and certainly not land-owning patriarchs. Simmons's refusal to submit cost him his life.

Enraged at the "'smart niggers' for going to see a lawyer," Ryder and his posse gave Simmons's son Emmett, an earwitness to his father's murder by gunshots, just over a week to clear the remaining family members off the property. It was later discovered that the Ryder posse also cut out Reverend Simmons's tongue, perhaps to remind Emmett Simmons to calculate his family's losses in dead silence, since Ryder had warned the younger Simmons that "if this comes up again you had better not know anything about it."[94]

During the early twentieth century, Black men across the South knew perfectly well that "'signs of prosperity' could attract 'nightriders' who would drive [them] from [their] land." As a result, they could be nothing more than beggars at the table of White patriarchal privilege. Their entire existence revolved around socioeconomic liminality—Black men "better not accumulate much, no matter how hard and honest [they] work[ed] for it" because they couldn't "enjoy it," a Black Georgia farmer explained. In some places across the South, Whites laid off Black sharecroppers for several weekdays just to impede their intentions of securing even modest financial reserves. Ned Cobb, an ambitious sharecropper and lumber hauler, explained, "Whenever the colored man prospered too fast in this country under the old rulins, they worked every figure to cut you down, cut your britches off you." So debilitating was this arrangement that Ned's brother Peter resolved to put minimum effort into his work because "it weren't no use in climbin too fast; weren't no use in climin slow, neither, if they was goin to take everything you worked for when you got too high."[95]

Over time, America's violent structural exclusion of Black men from patriarchy has served unfortunately and unfairly to illuminate their widely perceived inadequacies as men, husbands, and fathers.[96] In this way, patriarchy and patriarchal marriage injure heterosexual Black men (and queer Black men to be sure), the women they love, and the children they bring into the world.

Yet patriarchy also strips Black women of their independence, authority, and decision-making power over their labor, their lives, and their love. During the earliest decades of freedom from White bondage, Black Southern women confronting the patriarchal inter-section of agricultural labor contracts and marital contracts recog-nized immediately how their independence was slipping away from them under legal parameters they had never known in slavery. In regions where tenant farming was prevalent, Black women had vir-tually no avenues to economic stability unless they were married.[97] White proprietors insisted on negotiating tenancy contracts with husbands—in their eyes, legitimate "heads of households" tasked with organizing and controlling the labor of their wives and chil-dren. Such patriarchal labor arrangements incentivized Black women to marry early, but they also led some to later abandon or legally terminate their marriages in protest of the legally sanctioned gender subordination they experienced.

Across most Southern states, Black women were emancipated from slavery only to discover that Euro-Western marriage was yet another long-standing institution of legal bondage, that marriage deprived them of economic rights they never imagined they would have to surrender to their husbands. Emancipation established gender-based inequality in Black marriages and families.[98] With the legal authority to control not only their own but also their wives' labor contracts, earnings, personal belongings, and immovable prop-erty, black husbands exercised a new form of gender sovereignty, while Black wives experienced a new type of gender subjugation. This *loss* of autonomy and independence was simply untenable for a good number of *freedwomen*, and it is important for Black women, men, and children today to grasp the significance of their foremothers' self-advocacy when they defended their civil right to self-governance, rejecting the Euro-Western coverture doctrine and patriarchal traditions that rendered them subordinates to their hus-bands. The subordination that many White women had been so-cialized to embrace within the confines of patriarchal marriage was utterly foreign to Black freedwomen, some of whom would not accept this war on their cultural values and their rights as women, laborers, and wives.[99] Even leading up to emancipation, Black women went further than just rejecting patriarchy. Among antislavery activists, Black women, most of whom had never experienced spousal subordination, led the campaign for a woman's right to self-ownership and self-determination.[100]

The Euro-Western concept of coverture is intrinsically linked to patriarchal notions of protection. However, Black foremothers, fresh out of slavery, knew more than 150 years ago that there is no husbandly "protection" that Black women need when it comes to decisions about their personal or marital lives. What Black women and men should do to manage their shared lives is *partner*, not control or be controlled by another. In support of this vision of marriage, a 1999 study showed that collaborative decision-making, friendship, and partnership were the most important characteristics in stable and satisfying African American marriages.[101] Recent research found similar results, including a study published in 2013 that identified links between husbands' conservative attitudes toward gender roles and inadequate levels of marital love. On the other hand, couples that embraced egalitarian divisions of household labor also reported more fulfilling and stable marital love.[102] Judging from their history in this nation, Black couples would do well to *de*couple notions of the ideal husband from patriarchal conceptions of masculinity and manhood as well as notions of the ideal wife from patriarchal conceptions of femininity and womanhood.

The Black community now more than ever needs to revisit the historical roots of the patriarchal expectations of marriage that continue to strangle Black love and destroy opportunities for enduring marital unions. The climate for redefining what it means to be a "wife" and a "husband," or perhaps even better—a spouse—is pregnant with ideas in a national environment where Black lesbian, gay, bisexual, transgender, and queer community members are leading the way in disrupting many of the essentialist and binary assumptions upon which patriarchal marriage rests, and the entire Black community could benefit from a sustained conversation about gendered identities, gender roles, and marriage involving heterosexual and LGBTQ persons.

The new conversations about Black love and partnership unfolding in the twenty-first century should not lose sight of the therapeutic manner in which Black women and men in love and marriage relationships have attended to one another's embodied pain. Across the centuries, they have treated one another's racist-sexist wounds, sometimes through the unspoken energy of being in the moment, shared tears, and healing touch. There are particular "protections" that Black men have provided Black women in the face of misogynoir assaults. And there are particular "protections" Black women have provided Black men when they have confronted "misandrynoir" assaults in this American experience, and not solely as romantically involved couples (though romantic love and marriage remain my focus here).

We might recall from Chapter 1 the moving testimony about the enslaved wife and mother who found herself in the predicament of an "abroad marriage." During weekly visits with his family, her husband often bore the physical marks of his torturous overseer. Yet her love for her husband's bruised and violated body bled deeper than any of the wounds she routinely dressed. The care and affection she showed her husband remained life lessons for their daughter, who witnessed the healing power of her mother's love when she would "take those bloody clothes off of him, bathe de sore places and grease them good and wash and iron his clothes, so he could go back clean."[103] Such protective ways of loving and sanctifying Blackness are ennobling assertions of Black human dignity. And they are not reducible to White patriarchal norms, even when they might seem to mimic patriarchal demonstrations of protection. They are what I can only call *restorative ontological protections* that people who endure the experience and legacies of the Middle Passage and racial slavery give to and receive from one another.[104]

My criticisms of patriarchal protection, particularly among married heterosexual couples, have nothing to do with these protections. Rather, they are intended to interrogate and oppose the exertion of a husband's power that actually serves to *control* his wife and curtail her agency and authority as an individual and a partner in marriage. Whether in particular instances or through accumulated effect, the social capital that patriarchal protection invests into marital relations and wider implicit social contracts that govern heterosexual coupling guarantees wifely submission while prohibiting spousal partnering and power sharing. Studying America's episodes of slow-motion genocide as well as the slow violence of forbidden Black love during the wider reign of terror unveils the trap that patriarchal protection and patriarchal marriage, in general, actually was and remains for Black couples. Acknowledging the historical harms of patriarchy, then, gives the national Black community and the nation at large an opportunity to reflect upon the devastation they have caused Black families and Black love, especially since the postemancipation period.[105]

BLACK LOVE AND MARRIAGE IN THE ERA OF FREEDOM

It is not easy to assess the outcomes of the stops and starts that afflicted and purportedly encouraged Black marriage between 1865 and the early 1960s. Black marriages did proliferate over this period. However, looking longitudinally, Black marriages did not escape the slow-violence effects of White American patriarchy, Jim Crow, and terroristic assault. In the century after slavery, Black love and marriage experienced a "violence that occur[ed] gradually and out of sight, a violence of delayed destruction that [was] dispersed across time and space, an attritional violence that is typically not viewed as violence at all." The "slow-motion toxicity" that infected Black love and marriage during Reconstruction and the reign of terror plundered the hopes and dreams of peace and liberty Black couples harbored in the land of the free and the brave, especially in the South.[106] "Since Reconstruction times," General Robert Smalls declared in 1895, "53,000 [Negroes] have been killed in the South, and not more than three white men have been convicted and hung for these crimes."[107] Smalls, a venerated Black congressman, revealed this shameful figure to those assembled at the South Carolina Constitutional Convention, proving that, three decades after slavery, Blacks actually were not free at all—certainly not free from culturally sanctioned systemic terror.

The probability that torture and death would strike suddenly and unexpectedly haunted Black couples and families well into the twentieth century. "Every Negro in the South knows that he is under a kind of sentence of death," John Dollard aptly explained in his 1937 study, *Caste and Class in a Southern Town*. "He does not know when his turn will come, it may never come, but it may also be at any time. . . . If he loves his family, this love itself is a barrier against any open attempt to change his status."[108]

As we've seen throughout this chapter, beyond open defiance of White power, random accusations of conspiracy against Whites also shattered Black marriages well into the twentieth century. Such was the fate of Atlanta, Georgia, resident Carolyn Gilbert, who lost her forty-two-year-old husband, Henry, to a police-inflicted White terrorist lynching in 1947. Married for twenty-two years, the Gilberts had miraculously devised a way to actualize their ambition for a better life in the Jim Crow South. They labored together as sharecroppers and subsequently leased a parcel of land for seventeen years before accumulating enough savings to purchase a 111-acre farm to finally settle their longest marital dream.

Henry's purported offense was assisting a "young black troublemaker who had shot and killed a white man because the man was beating him with a stick." After his arrest for "helping the murderer escape by letting him hide on his farm," Henry had been transferred from one facility to another, and Carolyn did her best to track his whereabouts but never laid eyes on her husband after the county sheriff and two accompanying police officers first courted him off to jail. The dreaded day that countless Black wives faced with desolation and outrage came for Henry's wife, too. A week and a half after she and her three daughters last had contact with their husband and father, Carolyn "was told to come down to a funeral parlor and claim her husband's battered body." She would later report that "when she held Henry's head in her hands and kissed him she could feel 'the broken pieces of bone under the skin.'" A county cop had shot Henry and defended his actions, claiming the "deacon and treasurer at his small Baptist church 'drew a chair on me.'" The undertaker's observations, however, told a different story. Henry "was riddled by five bullets fired at close range." His "skull was crushed to a pulp both in front and the rear. One leg and one arm were broken. All the ribs on one side were smashed into splinters."[109] With the death of Henry, much more was smashed than his ribs. Also smashed were the Gilberts' marriage, wealth-building prospects, and potential to secure and finance the capacious farm they had long saved to purchase and develop with their three daughters.

Whether Blacks encountered White terror directly or indirectly, the stress caused by the ubiquitous tension of expecting, avoiding, and experiencing terror is what drove Southern Blacks to flee north, west, and in some cases farther south and southeast to regions of Central America and the Caribbean during and even long before the periods known as the First (1910–1940) and Second (1940–1970) Great Migrations. Some even went "back" to Africa for what was viewed as the most secure escape from White terror. [110] In the artful prose of W. E. B. Du Bois, Black Americans "still [sought] the freedom of life and limb, the freedom to work and think, the freedom to love and aspire," and so they had to be brave in their search for new landscapes of life without the "smell of burning flesh."[111]

BLACK LOVE AND MARRIAGE REMAINED resilient during the long Great Migration, but the leitmotif of anguish over couples' separation is unmistakable in the memories and the music of the time. Bessie Smith, for example, sang Black women's love blues better than any with her 1923 recording of "Chicago Bound Blues." Characterizing the heartbreak of Great Migration separation as a deathblow to a Black woman in love, Smith placed in the record the regret, bitterness, and despair her sisters, suspended in the limbo of the South, could and did feel about their husbands and romantic partners' departure for Northern promises of a better life and better jobs.

Late last night, I stole away and cried
Late last night, I stole away and cried
Had the blues for Chicago, and I just can't be satisfied

Blues on my brain, my tongue refused to talk
Blues on my brain, my tongue refused to talk
I was followin' my daddy but my feet refuses to walk

Mean old fireman, cruel old engineer
Lord, mean old fireman, cruel old engineer
You took my man away and left his mama standin' here

Big red headline, tomorrow Defender *news*
Big red headline, tomorrow Defender *news*
Woman dead down home, with old Chicago blues
I said blues.[112]

These Chicago blues resembled Inez Starling's blues in Harlem. She indeed discovered, with every work assignment George accepted in the North, that migration and displacement took a toll on their marriage's intimacy and loyalty. The healthy, inspiring love she had desired now seemed out of reach. The move north was just a passageway to additional separation, as George accepted a job as a railroad attendant that required his travel and long stays away from Inez and their two children. Eventually, the effects of the alienation crept into the marriage, and the stress of raising children with an absentee husband and father would ultimately poison the futures of both children.

Inez and George's only daughter, Sonya, who became pregnant at the tender age of thirteen while spending her summer vacation at her parents' Florida hometown, delivered a baby boy just months before George's mistress delivered their son, Kenny. The twofold devastation destroyed Inez. Adding to this unbearable load was the news she would learn of her beloved son's drug addiction that first came to light when Inez's niece had come up north to stay with the Starlings after her mother's death. Gerard was only twelve at the time, and already the tentacles of urban despair had begun to hold him hostage. His life would reflect what anyone would expect of a heroin addict—robbing his parents of whatever valuables he could pilfer, witnessing friends die from drug overdoses, and getting clean, only to fall back into his demon's clutches. Inez died of breast cancer in 1978 and did not live to see whether her first-born child would be restored to a sober and independent life.[113]

Although Inez and George found gainful employment in the North, and stayed together physically while growing apart emotionally, their willingness to support the same household made welfare a mute subject in their home. This was not the case for other Black female migrants from the South who were fleeing similar conditions that Inez and George escaped. And the government's policing of Black widowed pension beneficiaries—officially in 1882, and unofficially before—was a dress rehearsal for invasive misogynoir practices of the welfare state, beginning in the mid-twentieth century.

CHAPTER 3

Love and Welfare

*Johnnie Tillmon and the Struggle to
Preserve Poor Black Families*

Many Americans have been taught that the federal government's largesse toward Black "welfare queens" has gotten out of control. A great many undeserving mothers, we are told, prefer to milk the system rather than provide for their children. As enticing as this tale is to the multitudes who believe it, a long paper trail exists to tell a very different story. That story endorses activist Johnnie Tillmon's assessment of "welfare fraud" as a rationale that *policy makers* have seized on in order to control poor and vulnerable Black women forced to depend on federal and state support for their basic family needs.[1]

Ever since the establishment of welfare programs during the early twentieth century, Black women who qualified for public assistance have elicited little sympathy from the nation that, for two and a half centuries, had literally and figuratively milked their enslaved foremothers from sunup to sundown. In 1939 one Southern Welfare Program field supervisor captured the shared antipathy White powerbrokers showed Black women applying for public assistance programs: "The number of Negro cases is few due to the unanimous feeling on the part of the staff and board that there were more work opportunities for Negro women and to their intense desire not to interfere with local labor conditions. The attitude that 'they always have gotten along,' and that 'all they'll do is have more children' is definite."[2]

Not surprisingly, Black women were initially excluded from participating in state and federal welfare programs. In 1931 only 3 percent of Black women were recipients of state-run mothers' pensions programs after twenty years of operation,[3] and the probability of racism tainting the execution of the program was of no concern to lawmakers when Aid to Dependent Children (ADC, renamed Aid to Families with Dependent Children [AFDC] in 1962) was established under Title IV of the 1935 Social Security Act. Prior to its passing, the US Congress held hearings at which representatives of the NAACP and the Federal Council of Churches testified, urging that specific measures be included to prevent racial discrimination against Blacks, especially at the state level. Their petitions, however, fell on deaf ears. The Social Security Act, which governed ADC, gave no deliberate attention to protecting Black and other citizens of color against racially motivated inequities and their potential systemic manifestations.

The federal ADC program would work in conjunction with state legislatures to supplement and ultimately replace mothers' pension programs that had long positioned White mothers and their children as deserving recipients. Though states were required to at least partially fund their public assistance programs, federal policy allowed them tremendous administrative freedom when determining eligibility criteria and payment allotments.[4] The net result of this federal-state partnership was a powerful expression of White supremacy that from the very beginning treated Black women and their children with suspicion and hostility. From the 1930s to the 1970s and beyond, everywhere we turn, we find state hands dispensing insufficient public assistance checks only grudgingly to America's Black mothers and children.

The story of Las Vegas welfare-rights activist Rosie Seals is a case in point. During the 1960s, Seals had worked alongside other AFDC recipients at a local laundry but discovered the discrepancy between the size of her government check and that of a White co-worker only when the latter asked her how much welfare she received. After Seals revealed the amount, her coworker responded, "Hell, *I* get more than you get and *you* got more children than I got." Seals describes feeling at that moment "like someone gave me an electric shock" and goes on to say that it "pissed me off enough that I finally did something."[5]

Whether most were aware of the inequities defining their participation in federal and state welfare programs or not, the number of Black women ADC recipients did increase over time. From 1937 to 1940, Black participation in ADC teetered between 14 percent and 17 percent, and it was standard practice across the nation for Black children—though more impoverished generally than White children—to receive smaller financial allotments for their care.[6] As the economy shifted in the postwar era, Black women had no other option but to seek welfare benefits to compensate for the gross inequities between their meager salaries relative to those earned by Black males, White females, or White males.[7] By the 1950s, faced with a Hobson's choice of feeding their babies or preserving their pride, Black women began enrolling in the ADC program in high numbers out of necessity.

Within ten years, Blacks were disproportionately represented across sixteen surveyed states, constituting nearly 40 percent of ADC's recipients "of color."[8] Not surprisingly, as the face of welfare darkened, federal and state legislators implemented more aggressive policies to ensure behavior modification that would curtail Black women's presumed promiscuity and indolence. These "man-in-the-house," "suitable home," and "substitute father" policies, which penalized Black women and Black families if men were present in their homes, monitored and punished Black love, sending the rates of Black marriage into sharp decline throughout the 1960s and 1970s.[9]

Perhaps nothing broadcast more clearly the scrutiny of home and heart that Black women on welfare suffered at the hands of AFDC social workers than the 1974 film *Claudine*.[10] Starring Diahann Carroll, James Earl Jones, and a cast of other talented young actors, *Claudine* depicted the structural obstacles welfare posed to Black love and marriage and the stark reality that for millions of Black women in America at the time, choosing marital fulfillment (as the main character Claudine eventually does) meant losing welfare benefits. The most gripping scene occurs when Miss Kabak, a young White female social worker, makes a surprise visit to Claudine Price's apartment to ensure that she is suitably impoverished for her monthly welfare allotment. Luckily, Claudine's son, Paul, always on the lookout, spots Miss Kabak early enough to warn his mother of her approaching steps. Anything shiny, new, or relatively expensive could signal the support of a hidden husband or male consort. Claudine and her six children hustle to conceal every possible sign of upward mobility, every sign of support from Claudine's clandestine job or her boyfriend, Rupert.

The scene is truly painful to watch. The accompanying song, playing not so softly in the background, "Mr. Welfare Man," mirrors the steps the family must take to try to outsmart Miss Kabak as she sneaks up the stoop, hoping to catch Claudine unawares in her presumed web of lies. The song continues to play as Miss Kabak enters the apartment and begins peppering Claudine with questions about the most intimate dimensions of her life, underlining the scene with allusions to the emotional anguish imposed upon Black female welfare recipients by the abusive interrogations of White caseworkers.

Distressing and to the point, *Claudine* exposed yet another debilitating chapter in the history of forbidden Black love: the surveillance of Black women and their romantic relationships under a system of welfare that did at least as much to undermine Black female recipients and their families as it did to support them. As Gladys Night sang it in "Mr. Welfare Man," love was *not* a luxury to be sacrificed. It was a necessary human right:

Keep away from me, Mr. Welfare.
They just keep on saying I'm a lazy woman,
Don't love my children and I'm mentally unfit.
I must divorce him, cut all my ties with him
'Cause his ways they make me say,
It's a hard sacrifice (hard sacrifice)
Not having me a loving man.
Society gave us no choice
Tried to silence my voice
Pushing me on the welfare.
I'm so tired, I'm so tired
Of trying to prove my equal rights.
Though I've made some mistakes for goodness sakes,
Why should they help mess up my life?
Ooh, so keep away from me, Mr. Welfare.
Did you hear me? Keep away from me, Mr. Welfare.

Holding me back, using your tact
To make me live against my will, (hard sacrifice).
If that's how it goes, child, I don't know.
I can't concede my life's for real,
It's like a private eye for the FBI,
Just as envious as the Ku Klux Klan.
Though I'm of pleasant fate it's hard to relate,
I'll do the very best I can.
Ooh, so keep away from me, ooh, ooh Mr. Welfare.
No, no, did you hear me? (Keep away from me)
Don't come near me, stay away, Mr. Welfare . . .[11]

These two stanzas alone convey, in no uncertain terms, the quandary that welfare was for poor Black women. It provided insufficient financial support while at the same time taking their pride, their dignity, their ambition, *and* their husbands. Whatever meager dollar amount the welfare system doled out, there's no exaggeration in songwriter Curtis Mayfield's pairing of the American government's heartless "envy" of Black women's ambition and prosperity with the Ku Klux Klan's same sentiments toward "uppity niggers," especially ambitious and business-savvy Black men. Understandably, some Black women chose to "do the very best they could" rather than accept the humiliation and abandonment that were sure to come with a government welfare check, for as "Mr. Welfare Man" poignantly captures, the strategic disappearing acts that Black men married to Black women on welfare were forced to perform during this period seem now as unsubtly rehearsed as a Stepin Fetchit film.[12] Mayfield's portrayal of the welfare system and the realities depicted in *Claudine* provide an important analytical lens for examining forbidden Black love and its impact upon many Black women through the public assistance of Aid to Families with Dependent Children.

JOHNNIE TILLMON'S PATH TO AFDC

Though fictional, *Claudine* struck a chord with hundreds of "Claudines" across the United States who knew that "A.F.D.C. [was] like a supersexist marriage," where women "trade[d] in a man for *the* man," as Johnnie Tillmon observed in her 1972 *Ms. Magazine* article, "Welfare Is a Women's Issue."[13] Tillmon understood personally the outcome of the "man-in-the-house" regulation, having reluctantly enrolled in the AFDC program after a treacherous bout of tonsillitis kept the chronic arthritis sufferer hospitalized for a month. Living in Los Angeles at the time, she had been attempting to raise five children while her brother and his wife cared for her newborn in Richmond, California, with whom she had no other choice than to part. Though poor, she was also a proud working woman who had no one to watch her baby girl while she was pressing 150 shirts per hour at a local Compton laundry.[14] Her arthritic condition and long hospitalization, however, forced her to quit her laundry job and apply for public assistance.

Once a welfare recipient, the thirty-six-year-old's life radically changed, as she and other women from Nickerson Gardens, the low-income housing project in the Watts neighborhood where they resided, contended with "*the* man" behind AFDC. With every welfare check the state of California issued, Tillmon's private life and financial decision-making came under increasing scrutiny. Caseworkers chastised her for investing in a television and surveyed her refrigerator while handing her a preplanned budget to guide her monthly spending.

Tillmon soon developed a newfound appreciation for the independence and autonomy she had enjoyed before enrolling in AFDC. "When I left my job in the evening," she reflected, "I was through until the next morning. And on the weekend I didn't have no one peeping and peering, telling me what to do or what I couldn't do. . . . When I was working everyday [*sic*], if I wanted to have male company, then I had male company. But when you're on welfare, you can't have too much male company."[15]

At the time she recorded these words, Tillmon had spent nearly a decade on the front lines as a welfare recipient turned reform activist, and her advocacy would continue until she took ill in her midsixties. Her journey from Southern sharecropper to Northern shareholder in a movement designed to halt the crippling effects of forbidden Black love is a story that illuminates the struggles of so many similarly situated poor Black women. Like Tillmon, a significant number of them fled the constraints and terrors of the South for the promises of the North, only to fall victim to a double-edged welfare system that surveilled their every move, infantilized them, and punished them for pursuing romantic love and companionship.

Prior to her enrolling in AFDC, Tillmon's neighbors had fore-warned her about the program's invasive policies that targeted recipients' affairs of the heart.

I was around women who were on welfare long before I was. . . . and they were always talking about social work-ers. . . . They were afraid . . . to have boyfriends, because usually the husband had to leave, or they were afraid because sometimes the husband would have to slip in. They didn't want to separate, but in order for the family to survive, he would have to say that he left the house. They used to come in at midnight, and they would look all in the clothes closets, even empty the dirty clothes out of the washing machine because a lot of times . . . people used to put things in the washing machines to store'em away. They used to pull those things out, empty the clothes hamper . . . looking for men and men's clothing . . . and if they were to find anything, those recipients wouldn't get a check the next month, and they had once-a-month payments in those days.[16]

In 1962, just one year before Tillmon enrolled in AFDC, such rou-tine searches were formalized under Governor Ronald Reagan's administration. First launched in Kern County, California, the "Op-eration Weekend" program of late-night searches and raids spread like wildfire as county after county adopted it.

Johnnie Tillmon was not about to put up with this kind of abuse. A Black woman from the Deep South with enough courage to give a White man a beatdown if he was fool enough to call her a racial epithet did not hesitate to take on the welfare establishment after finding herself victim to its policies. "I was forty-six years old and in the nation's capital before I was ever called a nigger," she relayed in an interview with Brian Lanker a decade after the event. After hear-ing the vulgar epithet personalized for her by a complete stranger, as it had been for countless Blacks throughout American history,

"I politely took off my coat," Tillmon recalled, "handed my bag to my attorney, and went and had me a fist city on the man's head. He didn't hit me back or nothin', but he ran. Never had been called that by a white person out of all the thirty-five years I lived in Little Rock and Arkansas. But many years ago I had decided that's what I was going to do."[17]

We can only imagine the range of experiences that would compel a person to prepare for an inevitable encounter with White hate speech the way Tillmon did—the way only Black people might have to in our American democracy. Perhaps she had witnessed some gross theft of Black dignity in the cotton fields of rural Arkansas where she secured her first job at seven years old. Given her vulnerable position in a racially divided world, it was only natural that Tillmon had rehearsed in her head how her own "nigger" incident would one day play out.[18] Race relations in Arkansas would have taught her to prepare, the different options for responding as clear as their implications: save your life and lose your dignity, or lose your life and save your dignity. Somehow Tillmon walked away from the incident with both her life *and* her dignity intact. No matter how penetrating and effective the psychological colonization of a people under siege might be, there will always be some who refuse to settle for the material and immaterial indignities defining their subordination. Johnnie Tillmon was one such woman.

Tillmon took her first breath on April 10, 1926, and was named Johnnie Lee Percy after her daddy, John Percy. Born to poor and industrious sharecropping parents in Scott, Arkansas, Johnnie and her two brothers followed them from farm to farm, seeking employment wherever opportunities arose. She also learned very early the value of self-reliance and inventive "making a way out of no way" strategies from her parents, including a stepmother who replaced her natural mother, Gussie Danforth, after she died in childbirth when Johnnie was only five years old. Her father kept the memory of the family's African heritage alive, sharing details of his mother's arrival in America with the "last slaves on the ship that docked in South Carolina."[19]

Family heritage narratives such as young Johnnie's had more power than most imagined, disrupting America's mythologies of race that naturalized Blacks as innate slaves with no identity beyond those bestowed upon them on the shores of America. Knowing that her grandmother had been born in Africa and forced into slavery against her will emboldened Johnnie's intrepid spirit with a sense of *somebody-ness* that disputed America's long history of chattelizing Black flesh. Her sense of belonging to a heritage that had nothing to do with American slavery or the White settlers who established it derived specifically from personal knowledge of her grandmother's not-so-distant past. Her father's mother was a tangible source of actual, genetic rather than generic or symbolic connection to Africa, and Johnnie would later confess that she found this rare and treasured detail about their lineage "quite unusual, 'cause most dark people never talked about their African inheritance to their children."[20]

In 1944, as she reached her late teen years, Johnnie moved to her aunt's home in Little Rock to attend high school. Working at nights and during the summers to support herself, she eventually quit school to work full-time in the laundry industry. By 1948 the twenty-two-year-old wedded James Tillmon and moved out of her aunt's home. Her life with her husband was short-lived, however, and the couple divorced in 1952. While working and mothering her expanding family, Tillmon proved a dutiful daughter, caring as well for her aging father, who resided with her until his death in 1960.[21]

After her father passed away, Tillmon headed for California, where her two younger brothers already resided and where she might find better opportunities to support her five children and expected sixth child. Upon settling in Los Angeles, Tillmon secured employment as a laundress and busied herself with the tasks of child rearing. Although her specific reasons for seeking public assistance hinged on a bout of compromised health that put her out of work for a period along with the need to continue caring for her children, there were, in fact, a million and one reasons Tillmon and other poor Black women had for enrolling in AFDC. In her case, she would discover from neighbors that, beyond the financial deficit she was facing, there were personal reasons that required her vigilant presence at home. Her fourteen-year-old daughter had begun to skip school and apparently needed parental supervision to keep her on the right track. AFDC support would allow Tillmon to remain home and supervise her children when they needed it most.

Tillmon felt no shame in demanding access to what were, for all intents and purposes, compensatory resources for the stolen entitlements and opportunities a democratic America had funneled away from her people. "I will never accept that I got a free ride," Tillmon would say. "It wasn't free at all. My ancestors were brought here against their will. They were made to work and help build this country."[22] Add to this that she had long paid taxes to support Social Security programs such as AFDC before, during, and after receiving welfare benefits. As an elder Tillmon bluntly put it, "I worked in the cotton fields from the age of seven. I worked in the laundry for twenty-three years. I just retired from city government after twelve-and-a-half years."[23] Tillmon had actually labored and contributed to the American economy for thirty years before requesting AFDC benefits in 1963.

Trading Black Men for "the Man": Welfare Policies and the Punishment of Black Love

Tillmon was no different from many Black women, traveling with their children in tow from sharecropping farms to Northern cities, only to find a new life of urban poverty and deprivation revolving around the local welfare department. Their love lives spoke of struggle, cooperation, and ambition paired with tension, separation, and alienation. As single women they had only to convince the officials controlling the checkbook that they were somehow managing to lead faultlessly chaste lives that would pose no threat to their children's moral development. But no dimension of the new arrangement was nearly so destructive as its attendant prohibition of Black love. "There used to be a time when they would look in your dirty clothes hamper for men's clothes," Tillmon recalled in a feature interview for the book *I Dream a World*. "They used to come to your house at midnight and they used to pump the kids, 'Where's your daddy?' If your kids look clean or your house looks clean, then you must be doing something fraudulent because they understand that you really shouldn't be able to do what you do with the money you get."[24]

Not only in the North, but across the entire nation, states adopted the AFDC criterion of ensuring that enrolled single mothers provide a "suitable home" for their children, effectively prohibiting them from developing intimate relationships of any kind while receiving public assistance. As Tillmon succinctly explained, "On A.F.D.C., you're not supposed to have any sex at all. You give up control of your own body. It's a condition of aid. You may even have to agree to get your tubes tied so you can never have more children just to avoid being cut off welfare."[25]

By 1960 suitable home and other coordinative policies were enforced so brutally across half of the United States as to disqualify unwed mothers and those deemed promiscuous, who were disproportionately Black. In Louisiana, Mississippi, Tennessee, and Georgia, laws were even passed to render children born out of wedlock ineligible for AFDC benefits.[26] These supposedly race-neutral laws targeted Black women with the vengeance of a previous century. Among the 6,000 families accounting for 22,500 children that Louisiana alone purged from its welfare rolls 5,700 (95 percent) were Black families.[27]

Social workers often had the freedom to stretch the limits of AFDC regulations to address the specific circumstances they encountered as they monitored the mothers assigned to them. In one instance, a social worker who disapproved of a Wayne County,

Detroit, "mother's conduct with men" actually went as far as requiring her to sign the following affidavit:

> I . . . do hereby promise and agree that until such time as the following agreement is rescinded, I will not have any male callers coming to my home nor meeting me elsewhere under improper conditions. I also agree to raise my children to the best of my ability and will not knowingly contribute or be a contributing factor to their being shamed for my conduct. I understand that should I violate this agreement, the children will be taken from me.[28]

Even if pledges of this sort were not compulsory across states, by 1962 nearly half of the United States had implemented patriarchal policies that placed upon even a brand-new suitor or love interest the financial burden of caring for the holder of his affection and her children if they were AFDC recipients. Whether it was day one of their relationship or day one hundred, if he was able-bodied and visible during a caseworker's impromptu visit, his presence constituted a violation of the "man-in-the-house" or "substitute-father" regulations.[29] It's not surprising, then, that when asked by the US Commission on Civil Rights if "there were ways in which welfare payments could be supplemented," Mrs. Alyce Friels from Gary, Indiana, replied:

> If you have a boyfriend . . . he might be able to give you some money, but no man wants to take on the responsibility of a whole family. So they are very hesitant about it. It's very hard, I'd say, to find somebody to marry because when you already have a family, most men in this area, if they were willing to marry a woman that's on AFDC, they don't make enough money to take care of her themselves . . . without some kind of assistance . . . because many people here make less than $2,000, less than a thousand a year."[30]

Black women had nowhere to turn to cushion the blow welfare posed to their love lives, and neither did Black men. For Black women, loving a man and acting on that love were construed as criminal behavior since Black women had to cheat on "*the* Man" in order to "steal" love and the comforts of companionship they needed and deserved. Meanwhile, Black men were framed as criminal accomplices in the eyes of the welfare state. In order to qualify for welfare, mothers had to be single and unemployed with underage children to support. If a recipient developed a romantic relationship with a man or got married, her male consort or husband had to assume full financial responsibility for her and her children's care and well-being; thus, she would no longer qualify for public assistance. Because most poor Black men (by and large the demographic Black mothers on welfare would be dating or marrying) were underemployed and victimized by structural poverty as exploited sharecroppers, new migrants to Northern cities, or unskilled job seekers with limited educational attainment, their socioeconomic lives, too, were designed to reinforce the structures of forbidden Black love. The discrimination low-skilled Black men faced in the labor market rendered most incapable of providing the Black women they loved the financial wherewithal to forgo AFDC program benefits.[31] Within such an unforgiving welfare structure, low-skilled Black men also had to forgo building healthy, sustained relationships with the Black women they loved.

Between the 1950s and the 1970s, poor Black men, essentially bereft of resources and opportunities, confronted the quandary of being damned if they stayed with the women and children they loved and damned if they left. The Anglo-American conception of the family situated a male figurehead as the proper breadwinner and financial caretaker of his wife and children. But if with one hand AFDC advanced this patriarchal model of the family as the normative and respectable ideal that welfare recipients were expected to embrace, with the other it prohibited it. Having a man in the house meant no assistance for either gender.

Nor was it enough for a Black woman to be without a husband—unmarried mothers who dated or gave birth to children out of wedlock were also deemed unable to provide "suitable homes" for their offspring, and for a time many were purged from welfare rolls as a result.[32] Some of the most ruthless regulations appeared to have been instituted specifically to sabotage the innocence and welfare of the defenseless children most in need of public assistance. The Washington, DC, Department of Public Welfare exemplified this approach with insufferable directives that policed its recipients' domestic and nondomestic partnerships during the early 1960s:

> Children are ineligible whose mother associates with a man in a relationship similar to that of husband and wife and the man continues a relationship with the children similar to that of father and children regardless of whether such man lives in the home. . . . Children are ineligible whose mother associates with a man in a relationship similar to that of husband and wife and the mother, her children, and such man live in a family setting regardless of whether such man is the father of the children.[33]

Black love was ensnared in a paradox. While patriarchal marriage might protect the reputations of mothers seeking public assistance, the very presence of an able-bodied husband and father in the home immediately disqualified them and their children from AFDC programs. With trenchant legacies of racism and White privilege having left most Black men on the lowest economic and social rungs of a stratified American society, when employed in unskilled positions, they could expect to earn substantially less money than their White male counterparts earned for completing the same duties. When seeking jobs, they regularly faced competition or technological advances that in a changing economy had virtually outpaced them. Inevitable racial discrimination only further reduced their chances of winning the most prized jobs and, should they have been hired, limited their mobility and earning potential within those positions. This was true even for educated and credentialed Black men, many of whom were forced to hold jobs for which they were overqualified.

In most cases, AFDC officials stringently upheld man-in-the-house and substitute-father policies, turning deaf ears to women whose husbands were out of work or earned hardly enough to provide for their families' basic needs. Even the most destitute and economically crippled Black men, if married to women enrolled in AFDC, had to accept full responsibility for feeding and sustaining their wives and children.[34] State agencies, it seemed, couldn't wait to eliminate as many Black families as possible from receiving welfare benefits. Under the substitute-father regulation in Alabama alone, Black women and children accounted for 97 percent of those purged from welfare rolls in a sampling of seven counties.[35]

Naturally, many mothers who were not single faced the dilemma of what to do about their husbands or male partners whose very presence in the household disqualified them from receiving welfare. Chicago migrant Ruby Daniels confronted this very problem after the birth of her last of eight children in 1961. Luther, the father of four of her children, proved an obstacle to the $246 public assistance check she desperately needed in order to care for her family. Insisting that since he wasn't in any public assistance program, "he didn't have to dodge anybody," he had refused to stay away from the apartment he shared with her on Saturdays when the caseworkers were likely to appear, expecting to find a man on the premises who nullified Ruby's eligibility for welfare. Sure enough, one Saturday, two social workers made a surprise visit to Ruby's residence. After finding Luther, scrutinizing his identification, and discovering his razor in the bathroom, they told him, "Luther Haynes, we've been looking for you. You have children to support. We could assess you for back payments, but we won't. Support your children from now on."[36]

Thus warned that her checks would be "cut off," Ruby and Luther moved out of their apartment to a "slummier place," and, with several underage children to mind, Ruby found a cleaning job that required her to work from 6:00 p.m. to 2:00 a.m. Fortunately, she received one final check that had already been processed and mailed before the social workers uncovered her relationship with Luther. But Luther's unwillingness to play cat and mouse with welfare officials meant that Ruby's welfare well had run dry, and she would now have to take her chances in leaving her children unattended in order to feed and clothe them on her meager salary.[37]

Disconnected from her kin network in Mississippi, the new arrangement would prove challenging for Ruby, who had envisioned the North as a region of possibilities unimaginable in the South. Before migrating to Chicago, Ruby's Clarksdale, Mississippi, universe of labor opportunities and wage earnings was an endless field of cotton waiting to be harvested. She had spent most of her young life picking clouds of small dreams for inadequate pay, despite the fact that she was among the most efficient pickers around. When she wasn't in the field, she worked as a domestic, but the meager $2.50 per week couldn't compete with the nearly $4.00 per day she made as a wartime sharecropper. By the time she decided to make Chicago her permanent home away from Clarksdale, Ruby anticipated a life enhanced by wages that the South could not top. But with welfare authorities disrupting her family, and playing their own cat-and-mouse games with her monthly allotment, Northern existence was at times as transient as the sharecropping world she had left behind.[38]

The monthly aid that Ruby and other Black mothers lined up for was specifically earmarked for "deserving"—which is to say White—children who, by way of unfortunate circumstances, had lost the presence and support of their "legitimate" fathers. In many cases, however, the welfare system *was* the unfortunate circumstance that caused Black children to lose the presence and support of their "legitimate" fathers. In other words, some married couples had to make the painful decision to separate just to have access to the funds to feed their children. Jacquelyn Williams confronted this predicament as a young child, when her family was preparing to transition from the unfit slums of St. Louis, Missouri, to the newly constructed Pruitt-Igoe housing project in the 1950s. "Before we moved into Pruitt-Igoe," Williams recalled, "the welfare department came to our home. They talked with my mother about moving into the housing project, but the stipulation was that my father could not be with us. They would put us into the housing project only if he left the state. My mother and father discussed it, and they decided that it was best for the 12 children, for the father to leave the home, and that's how we got into the projects."[39]

When husbands did not leave, the consequences for concealing ties with a spouse (or fiancé) could go beyond mere dismissal from ADC/AFDC. In 1961 Tressie Neal Shirley found herself on trial and subsequently convicted of "grand theft under an indictment charging that she unlawfully took $1,811 of funds of Tulare County between October 1, 1958 and April 30, 1959." Her crime, however, amounted to nothing more than living with her future husband, for it was after his identity became known that the state of California found reason to press charges against Ms. Neal Shirley.

When a social worker visited Ms. Neal (not yet Shirley) on April 11, 1959, and "found a Mr. Shirley there, fully clothed but wearing bedroom slippers," the welfare department asked investigators from the district attorney's office to make further inquiries at Ms. Neal's home. Arriving a few days later at 2:30 a.m., they discovered the same Mr. Shirley in bed in Ms. Neal's bedroom. Ms. Neal acknowledged that Mr. Shirley had been living with her for six months and had made weekly contributions of $30 toward household expenses. When Ms. Neal informed the welfare department on April 23, 1959, that she had married Mr. Shirley on April 22, the department calculated that she had been overpaid by $1,811 due to the support provided by Mr. Shirley. It was determined that Ms. Neal Shirley had "made false representations of fact with intent to defraud" and that "welfare payments were made in reliance upon the false representations and that the county was defrauded." Ms. Neal Shirley was granted probation and her appeal for a new trial denied.[40]

Although most women were not criminally indicted when caught accepting welfare while also presuming to claim a full emotional life for themselves, they suffered severe and demeaning consequences nonetheless, most conspicuously in the fracturing of their families. Sociologist Joyce Ladner did research among St. Louis's Pruitt-Igoe residents as a young graduate student and vividly recalls encountering countless mothers who, despite their best efforts, found themselves deeply embedded in poverty because, apart from the measly welfare checks they collected monthly, AFDC man-in-the-house regulations cut off other critical sources of financial and emotional support. Ladner maintains that she "never saw the people in Pruitt-Igoe as that different from the lives of poor people I had grown up with in Mississippi, except for one thing: The strong, tightly knit communities and families in which I grew up had begun to shatter around the people who were displaced in a Northern city with few supports."[41]

AFDC policies and regulations undoubtedly contributed to the shattering of the Black families Ladner met at the Pruitt-Igoe housing project. As she describes it, the housing project itself—a 1950s urban renewal answer to the city's slums—nearly doubled as an AFDC headquarters:

> The welfare department had a rule that no able-bodied man could be in the house if a woman received aid for dependent children. If a man lost his job, he's looking for work; he still had to leave the home. And there was even a night staff of men who worked for the welfare department whose job was to go to the homes of the welfare recipients [in Pruitt-Igoe], and they searched to find if there was a man in the home. Sometimes men came back at night to be with their families. Some were found in the closet hiding.[42]

To avoid detection, mothers had their children rehearse prepared answers like lines of an Easter play, anticipating the inevitable moment that caseworkers might descend on their offspring unawares and riddle them with questions about their fathers. Columnist Sylvester Brown, who grew up in Pruitt-Igoe, had his prepared "no-man-in-the-house" script committed to memory and performed it when necessary before White AFDC interrogators.

> I remember, vividly, my mother telling us, if White people come to the house and ask you guys questions, tell them that your father is not here; tell them that your father has never been here; you have not seen your father." I trusted her. I knew that there was a reason that we had to . . . do this charade, and I participated in the charade. I sat there and looked those people in the eye and told them . . . with pure earnestness, no, I have not seen my father, and no, my daddy does not live here. . . . But I knew I was lying, and that made me wonder, who are these people, and how did they have the power to make my mother lie.[43]

"They"—the machinery of the state—had the power to do a lot more than *that* to poor Black women. As welfare recipients, Black women and their children lived at the mercy of the state, which at times went much further than controlling the flow of male traffic and merchandise through their homes. In one of the most egregious cases of 1968, the state of North Carolina went through perfectly legal channels to sponsor the unfathomable—the sterilization of fourteen-year-old Elaine Riddick, without her knowledge simply because the vulnerable teen, who had been impregnated through rape, happened to be a dependent within her grandmother's AFDC-supported home. Riddick's pregnancy was discovered during a routine visit from an AFDC social worker who threatened to ship the adolescent off to an orphanage if her grandmother did not sign a sterilization consent form.[44]

Not content to police black marriage, in the latter half of the twentieth century the state deployed sterilization as a tactic for suppressing Black female reproduction itself. With the goal of reducing the number of dependents and thus what the state presumed would be the sizes of welfare checks, Black girls and women in North Carolina were surreptitiously targeted for sterilization. According to John Railey and Kevin Begos, North Carolina's "biannual eugenics board report for 1966 to 1968 [the year of Riddick's sterilization] shows that 99 percent of the operations were performed on women; [and] 64 percent of those . . . on black women."[45]

Riddick's case illustrates all too clearly what happens when the state consolidates its resources to strip Black women of their right to love and the pursuit of happiness. When North Carolina's AFDC program and eugenics board joined hands to impose sterilization upon the still developing adolescent, they helped consign her to a life of loneliness and heartbreak, with several marriages dissolving as a result of her infertility. Riddick's first husband, in particular, became bitter, calling her "barren and fruitless."[46] Having discovered her infertility only after one year of marriage and failed attempts to have a child with her spouse, she was left with only the offspring of her rapist. Although a proud grandmother today, Riddick still lives with the stinging pain of what was taken from her.

TILLMON'S FIGHT FOR WELFARE RIGHTS

All over the United States, Black mothers on welfare were under assault until the most fearless among them, women such as Johnnie Tillmon, encouraged them to refuse the intrusion and humiliation through organized resistance. Tillmon testified that most in her community, during the 1960s, were fearful of confronting caseworkers or reporting their indignities to supervisors:

> The women who lived around me had experienced the hardship of waiting a long time [to complete the AFDC enrollment

process]—not having a person to call a supervisor's office. . . . A lot of times social workers mistreated them highly, and they didn't know anyone else to go to. They wouldn't dare go to a supervisor . . . and the people around me were always crying and complaining and so I said if you don't like it you can do something about it.[47]

Labor and community organizer that she was, Tillmon convinced a group of mostly Black mothers in Nickerson Gardens and other housing projects in the Watts area of Los Angeles to resist such federal- and state-sponsored harassment and abuse. In 1963 they began by founding an organization called Aid to Needy Children–Mothers Anonymous and established its office headquarters in Watts. Among other things, ANC-MA prepped its members for potentially tense exchanges with welfare officials and assisted women who had been expunged from welfare rolls or denied grocery orders and monthly checks, often without warning, to access the requisite funds and resources.[48]

Tillmon's first attempt at local welfare-rights organizing met its share of challenges. Welfare departments kept the identities of their recipients confidential, and many women were reluctant to reveal their welfare status to avoid the stigma associated with the program. Tillmon managed to circumvent this roadblock by surreptitiously obtaining a list of AFDC recipients during a visit to her local welfare office. But it would take some persuading before some women joined the cause.

One coresident of the Nickerson Gardens housing project, Dee Johnson, actually hid her AFDC enrollment status from Tillmon when she showed up at her door to invite Johnson to a welfare-rights meeting. "I didn't want to be associated with the welfare department. . . . I didn't want my friends to know I was getting welfare."[49] Tillmon herself confessed to having suffered initially from shame and thus attempting to conceal any signs of her participation in

AFDC. She "used to hear older [White and Black] women . . . who worked" and "called themselves homeowners" discussing "welfare mothers" while traveling on the bus to work. "They spoke of them in general as . . . lazy, shiftless women. . . . They complained about their high taxes, and how that money was being used for women who had babies just to get another welfare check."[50]

Though its first meeting attracted more than three hundred women from Nickerson Gardens alone, the ANC-MA initially protected its members' anonymity and "stayed underground for about 18 months." To capitalize on the experience and knowledge in the room, the ANC-MA founders conducted interviews with each of the women. For three days, participants aired their grievances and began to discern the fledgling organization's main priorities.

The group subsequently targeted AFDC recipients in neighboring communities, adding members from the fairly large Imperial Courts housing project and smaller housing projects such as Hacienda Village and Avalon Gardens. "As an organization . . . we were always involved . . . and I was always personally involved in the political process. . . . We got to know the head of the [welfare] department . . . and some of his deputies. . . . And we . . . began to work on individual caseloads early back in '64." ANC-MA would address grievances by going over social workers' heads and negotiating directly with welfare supervisors to solve its clients' problems. "The social workers used to hate us," Tillmon explained. "They felt that . . . we had gotten too big for our britches . . . but we never got in no argument with them because the social workers would talk to their bosses, and their bosses would get on their behinds when we made telephone calls."[51]

Tillmon's activities grew to include personal involvement with political campaigns for the state legislature. But she never imagined, when her speaking appearance at the April 1966 Citizens Crusade Against Poverty meeting in Washington, DC, caught the attention of Dr. George Wiley, a former member of the Congress of Racial

Equality and poverty rights activist, that she would be catapulted to the center of a new movement. Months later, in August 1966, ANC-MA nominated her to represent the group at a Chicago meeting of welfare-rights activists across the nation, where she encountered Wiley again along with about twelve women activists from varied states, all of whom would eventually help to forge the National Welfare Rights Organization in August 1967. By then, Tillmon had been elected and served eight months as the first president for the state of California's newly formed Welfare Rights Organization.

Tillmon soon found herself engaged in welfare-rights agendas on all levels, for she remained actively engaged with her local ANC-MA organization while presiding over the state of California's welfare coalition and holding an official leadership position in the NWRO. One year after its founding, the NWRO had attracted a membership of thirty thousand and elected Tillmon to chair its national coordinating committee. Under Tillmon's coleadership with Wiley and a team of paid organizers, NWRO ensured that local welfare departments complied with their own guidelines and regulations, pushed (unsuccessfully) for a minimum financial allotment for welfare recipients, and through negotiations with department stores helped open lines of credit for them. They also met with welfare officials, released policy statements, and worked with attorneys to change harmful policies.[52]

With a complex understanding of race, gender, and class stratification within the institution of marriage and other American social institutions, Tillmon brought a distinct vision of intersectional politics to her leadership role in the NWRO. She privileged women's independence, defended motherhood and family planning as important rights and responsibilities, and decoupled Blackness and welfare. Her commitment to these three ideological positions and their important outcomes for poor mothers on public assistance meant at times defending single motherhood, especially in the face of patriarchal marital conventions that harmed women and their children.

It also involved disabusing most people of the common assumption that "lazy" and "shiftless" Blacks constituted the majority of women on welfare. As Tillmon constantly reminded opponents, "There's six white women to every black one on AFDC . . . in this country. But nobody never talks about that."[53]

Her stance on birth control, a controversial issue in the 1970s, illustrates how she moved beyond one-dimensional thinking to grapple with the layered and competing dynamics of poverty versus responsibility, autonomy versus regulation. "Nobody realizes more than poor women that all women should have the right to control their own reproduction," she argued. "But we know how easily the lobby for birth control can be perverted into a weapon against poor women. The word is choice. Birth control is a right, not an obligation. A personal decision, not a condition of a welfare check."[54] One year after making this statement, Tillmon put her views to work, coissuing a 1973 statement with the executive director of the Association for Voluntary Sterilization, Charles Fanueff. The pair denounced the compulsory sterilization of welfare recipients, a practice many welfare departments had been guilty of enforcing with virtually no legal consequences to deter them.[55]

Even a cursory examination of Tillmon and other NWRO activists' efforts dismantles persistent myths painting Black welfare recipients with one brush as conniving grifters with no ambition to achieve financial self-sufficiency. The sophisticated and comprehensive tactics Tillmon and her comrades deployed to meet the diverse predicaments and ambitions of such women expose their wide-ranging objectives and intentions as mothers who desired for their children outcomes similar to those that many mothers untouched by welfare desired. Establishing child-care centers that would allow mothers on public assistance to secure gainful employment was a high priority for Tillmon, and local welfare rights groups in Los Angeles privileged this objective in their work, even giving one such refuge Tillmon's name. The Tillmon Center opened in 1974 and instilled in the children it served "a positive ethnic identification and a potential to succeed at their own pace."[56]

Yet Tillmon put equal energy behind defending the right of AFDC recipients to privilege homemaking and child rearing if they decided such options were most feasible or important to them.[57] There was no one solution for the millions of women in need of public assistance, Tillmon understood, just as there remains no one solution today. Reflecting back on her activist aims and approach in 1984, Tillmon described the logic undergirding her stamina to fight for welfare rights, even after the NWRO ceased operations in 1975. "I think the fight is the same. . . . I don't like to change until I've got something complete. And so, I'm still with ANC Mothers and the [California] Welfare Rights Organization 'cause I don't think it's complete. I don't think my fight is complete, even after 20 years. It probably won't be completed until I'm dead and gone."[58]

Tillmon *did* complete the work of raising a family. Her children became both financially independent and socially responsible. After spending her childhood and teenage years picking cotton and working in other seasonal and temporary industries, and after twenty-three years of employment as a laundress and nine years as a welfare recipient, Johnnie Tillmon was proud to acknowledge that all of her six children had grown up to be productive citizens with "nondomestic careers," and she attributed her parental success to the father who raised her.[59] However, as a very young woman, Tillmon pledged never to accept another domestic position after a White family she looked after "asked her to eat lunch with the dog."[60] This humiliating experience undoubtedly played a role in the nondomestic careers her daughters selected for themselves.

Tillmon's resolve to place her dignity before the denigrating domestic work most Southern Whites had reserved for Black girls and women was a dress rehearsal not only for successful motherhood but also for the years she would spend as a welfare-rights activist and organizer. There was much to organize around when it came to Black women's welfare and forbidden Black love. Tillmon and many others who worked to abolish man-in-the-house and other similar AFDC policies disproportionately targeting Black women did not couch their intentions in terms that identified the systemic nature of what this book has named forbidden Black love. Yet in effect, this is exactly what they were describing when they contested AFDC federal-state impositions upon their marriages, relationships, and natural human desire for companionship.

By 1968 welfare rights activism and wider civil rights campaigns had taken their toll on the welfare system. The landmark US Supreme Court case *King v. Smith* officially outlawed AFDC's man-in-the-house, suitable-home, and substitute-father regulations, allowing in some estimations more than one hundred thousand families across the nation to receive welfare benefits.[61] The appellee, Mrs. Sylvester Smith, and her four children lived in Dallas County, Alabama, and had been welfare recipients for "several years" before being rendered ineligible for benefits on October 11, 1966. According to the Supreme Court opinion delivered by Chief Justice Earl Warren, "This action was taken by the Dallas County welfare authorities pursuant to the substitute father regulation, on the ground that a Mr. Williams came to her home on weekends and had sexual relations with her."[62] Williams, it turns out, was a married father of nine children, none of whom he shared with Smith. Her deceased husband had fathered her first three children, while the father of her fourth child had abandoned their home in 1963 and neglected his offspring for more than half of the child's life. Court records state that while he clearly was carrying on a romantic and perhaps complicated love affair with Smith, Williams actually lived with his wife and children and was not supporting Smith's children, as he was under no legal obligation to do. With a weekly salary of around eighteen dollars, working as a cook and waitress from 3:00 in the morning until 2:00 in the afternoon, Smith was eligible and in dire need of public assistance for her family.[63]

Smith's legal counsel left no stone unturned bringing the court's attention to a shameful legacy of controversial and downright cruel legislation that unfairly punished children for their parents' decisions. "Between June, 1964, when Alabama's substitute father regulation became effective, and January, 1967," Justice Warren's opinion acknowledged, "the total number of AFDC recipients in the State [of Alabama] declined by about 20,000 persons, and the number of children recipients by about 16,000, or 22%."[64] Smith's counsel further convinced the Court to see that "the Alabama regulation is aimed at punishing mothers who have nonmarital sexual relations," and that "the economic need of the children, their age, their other means of support, are all irrelevant. The standard is the so-called immorality of the mother."[65]

So-called is an appropriate modifier here, because whether an AFDC-enrolled Black mother's romantic life revolved around a stable marriage, a cohabiting relationship, a serious courtship, intermittent dating, or serial sexual partners, she was branded, at best, a thief who'd swindled the state into financing her children's welfare in lieu of her husband or partner and, at worst, the promiscuous and dysfunctional head of an "unsuitable" household environment for her minor children, at risk of having them removed from her care. In both cases, she was judged "unfit" not only for AFDC support but for mothering children at all. "What's 'welfare'?" Johnnie Tillmon asked in 1972 before promptly answering with textbook precision: "Welfare's when the government passes a law to give aid to the poor and then tries to keep the poor from getting it."[66]

Well into the 1970s, many states across the country would indeed "keep the poor [Black women] from getting it." In defiance of the Supreme Court's 1968 ruling, for example, fifteen states had gone on with business as usual, continuing to uphold outlawed man-in-the-house and substitute-father regulations and purging women and children from their welfare rolls in 1970. It's no wonder

Third World Cinema Corporation saw it relevant to produce *Claudine*, a movie that would dramatize such welfare violations on the big screen for all to witness in April 1974. The fact that Tillmon, a NWRO chairperson and later executive director, was still denouncing these AFDC abuses in her speeches and interviews years after the *King v. Smith* decision made it obvious that some states remained out of compliance with the Supreme Court ruling. Her famous and highly cited 1972 *Ms. Magazine* article, "Welfare Is a Women's Issue," addressed the "man-in-the-house" policy as if the *King v. Smith* ruling never occurred: "In half the states," she pointed out, "there really can't be men around because A.F.D.C. says if there is an 'able-bodied' man around, then you can't be on welfare."[67]

Tillmon's life story maps the terrain of America's welfare-rights grassroots organizing that aimed to disrupt the government's giving with one hand and taking away with the other. At fifty-nine years old, the experienced activist shared her view that only a radical reconstruction of welfare would ever meet the criterion of humane treatment for the poor:

> You have to blow it up, and you have to tear it down, and then you have to build it like it should be built, from its own foundation. . . . And our . . . social security program goes back to 1935, so that means we'd have to dig up—do a whole lot of blowing up dynamite and then laying up some foundation. Now, I'd like to see that done. I don't . . . believe that in the 80s and the 90s that that's going to be done by anyone. I think they're still tacking . . . boards on top of boards. . . . Each one comes in, he tacks a little bit. . . . Instead, let's stop, and let's just tear this whole thing down. . . . The sad thing about it is everybody that comes thinks his thing is better than everybody else's, and it's the same thing! You're dealing with the same congressional people. . . . If I had my way, I'd just tear the whole thing down.[68]

When Tillmon died of complications from diabetes in 1995, she had not succeeded in tearing down the whole system. Yet no one could deny that through organized activism and coalition politics, she had chipped away at many of its imperfections, including policies that targeted and strangled Black love. The public service road Tillmon walked as a welfare reformer, however, began with personal acts of insubordination and self-assertion when confronted with racist assaults and exploitation at different points in her life. This path was not unfamiliar to other Black mothers on public assistance who took daily measures and moment-by-moment decisions to protect their dignity and right to love. Their acts of resistance flew in the faces of the caseworkers and public welfare departments that supplied them with lists of the grocery items they were allowed to buy and official permission letters indicating when they could purchase a television.

In *Claudine* we see such buoyancy in our protagonist's determination to thrive and her eventual act of marrying her beloved "Roop" (Rupert Marshall), despite the consequences. More than a decade before American audiences were party to Claudine and Rupert's big-screen wedding, the same level of defiant pride was at work to save Black love. When a twenty-five-year-old mother of four children experienced firsthand that the welfare she signed up for was indeed "a law the government had passed to give aid to the poor while endeavoring to keep the poor from getting it," she swiftly revoked her enrollment. Upon receiving her first visit from an ADC "investigator," the young mother "admitted that she was employable, stated that she did not want investigators coming to her home and voluntarily signed a statement requesting withdrawal from the ADC assistance program." Perhaps sarcastically and with the kind of impudence Tillmon would have appreciated, she sealed the fracture with unabashed declaration of her freedom to associate with and love whomever she desired: "Now I can have all the men I want in my home," she declared, "and you men can't do a thing about it."[69]

BLAMING AND SHAMING BLACK MOTHERS FOR
LOVING AND SUPPORTING THEIR FAMILIES

It is true that severing ties with intrusive state agencies allowed Black women to reclaim their right to love, marry, and pursue upward mobility as they wished. However, Black women on welfare (and indeed all Black women in America) have never been able to free themselves from enduring stigmas of pathological mothering and hypersexuality. One of the most vivid expressions of these indelible tropes was Assistant Secretary of Labor Daniel Patrick Moynihan's 1965 study "The Negro Family: The Case for National Action."

Through his research, Moynihan had intended to win support for policies and programs that would address the nation's staggering rates of Black poverty. However, his analysis identified a long tradition of Black matriarchy and Black culture—shaped by slavery, segregation, urbanization, and unemployment—as the cause of persistent Black poverty. Moynihan's study assessed Black family structures and gender roles through the lens of heteronormative patriarchal conceptions of masculinity, femininity, parenting, labor, and family life. Black families, he warned, were headed, too often, by domineering single women, and the outcomes of such arrangements emasculated Black men, who often struggled to find gainful employment to care for their wives and children. The solution was multipronged, including elevating Black male authority and employability at the expense of Black women.[70]

Although Moynihan hoped to inspire policies that would close the poverty gap between Blacks and Whites in America, his report misinterpreted and misrepresented the actions of poor Black women, especially those on welfare. For generations, black women have been blamed for their victimization and even despised when overwhelmed by the oppressive forces structuring their lives in part because Moynihan and the elite social scientists who endorsed his study failed to acknowledge how poor Black women, such as those discussed in this chapter, subverted and protested an unjust system.

In failing to capture poor Black women's narrative of undaunted self-determination, social scientists and policy makers failed to see love as a fundamental civil right.

A century after Black women's emancipation from slavery, it would only make sense that their impoverished descendants, struggling to make ends meet with inadequate public assistance, would not be embraced with sympathy and genuine concern for disrupting systemically induced cycles of poverty engulfing them and their families. The nation's general antipathy toward Black women has infected how individuals view and treat them. But the women and the stories introduced in this chapter unveil the systemic sources of their economic impoverishment and alienation from the stable love and coupling they often desired and deserved.

Despite the merciless reach of structural power in their lives, we encounter nobility in their stealth and self-respect in the strategies they devised to navigate the AFDC and its partnering government apparatuses. As Elaine Riddick's sterilization case discloses, the AFDC's most nefarious means of amplifying America's long tradition of forbidden Black love was to enlist other state entities in its operations. Just as public welfare departments and eugenics boards collaborated to ruin Black girls' and women's pursuit of love and marriage, public housing authorities, the penal system, and public welfare departments also have worked hand in hand to destroy Black women's relationships with incarcerated Black men. Beginning in 1997, the US Department of Housing and Urban Development (HUD) issued regulations that empowered public housing agencies across the nation to prohibit convicted felons from participating in their programs.[71] These regulations shut the door on cohabitational reunification for the Black women residing in those projects and their postincarcerated husbands and partners with felony records.

CHAPTER 4

Black Love in Captivity

Mass Incarceration and the Depletion of the
African American Marriage Market

No other institution has perfected America's project of forbidding Black love better than the contemporary prison industrial complex (PIC). Racial enslavement, racial terrorism, and welfare each possessed a particular capitalist mood, and each applied its own bitter coating to the pill of forbidden Black love. The prison industrial complex, however, is a mechanism of subjugation that impedes Black love and marriage with unmatched methodical precision. Extending and exaggerating the capitalist moods of previous eras, since the 1980s, the PIC has produced a conquered army of Black male "criminals" to generate billions of dollars in revenue.

Black men are incarcerated at much higher rates than any other group in the United States, even when convicted for the same crimes. Today this contingent of more than 500,000 outnumbers incarcerated Black women by nearly 490,000.[1] Although the percentage of Black women coming under the surveillance of correctional facilities is increasing daily—the Bureau of Justice predicts that 1 in 16 Black women will experience imprisonment in their lifetime compared to 1 in 111 White women[2]—1 in 3 Black men can expect to be imprisoned at some point in their lives.[3] And while the erroneous statistic that more Black men are incarcerated than in college has been thoroughly debunked,[4] the chilling report that more Black men were under correctional control in 2013 (1.88 million) than were enslaved in 1850 (872,924) is enough to deflate any sense of hope that the nation is turning a progressive corner.[5]

Through statistics like these, researchers have sought to calculate the devastating cost of the nation's mass incarceration crisis to Black communities and the American society in general. With attention focused on a range of public safety and public health concerns, both real and manufactured, articles have appeared in rapid succession attempting to distill the causes and effects of the staggering rates of Black male incarceration in America. Even after Michelle Alexander's bestseller, *The New Jim Crow: Mass Incarceration in the Age of Colorblindness*, enough can never be said about the impact of mass incarceration upon Black individuals', families', and communities' mental and physical health, gainful employment, housing opportunities, and educational trajectories.

Embedded within this constellation of social concerns is the relationship between mass incarceration and Black love and marriage. Demographers have attempted to put this relationship into perspective for our current moment. However, estimates vary based on the different approaches they take to Census population data. Some determine, "For every 100 black women not in jail, there are only 83 black men."[6] Others maintain that, after adjusting for the fact that unincarcerated Black men have been repeatedly undercounted in decennial censuses, there are approximately 100 unimprisoned Black women to 91 unimprisoned Black men.[7]

Among the "missing" Black men, those in prison have had no choice but to make new homes out of the small cages holding them captive. If we trace the paths connecting inmates with their domestic neighborhoods across America, some of the most traveled roads would be between the cells of Black male inmates and the residences of Black women and children. As the phenomenon of mass incarceration unfolded during the 1980s and 1990s, Marc Mauer aptly called it a "race to incarcerate."[8] During this period, Black people, particularly Black men and adolescents, were also, for all intents and purposes, *the* "race to incarcerate." This is why author Michelle Alexander actually defines mass incarceration as a racial caste system "designed to warehouse a population deemed disposable—unnecessary to the functioning of the new global economy."[9]

When we add the numbers of Black males locked away in jail cells to those serving prison sentences, our nation's carceral facilities actually house nearly 1 million Black men today.[10] One African American male inmate personalized his experience of this mass incarceration, calling his prison cage "home for a while, whether we like it or not. This is home for a while. This is home for a while."[11] America's prison cells have actually become home for a *long* while to hundreds of thousands of Black men since the Reagan administration's War on Drugs put into effect criminal justice policies that sent disproportionate numbers of Black men to prison with felony records, beginning in the 1980s. In some cities across this nation, up to 80 percent of Black men were being incarcerated on drug crimes by the late 1990s.[12] In fact, America's penal response to public health problems and transgenerational structural oppression—mental illness, drug addiction, joblessness, poverty—would elevate the overall national rate of incarceration in record time. By the late 1990s, 1 out of every 34 adults was either imprisoned, on parole, or on probation,[13] and Black men were grossly overrepresented among these figures relative to their population size.

In 1980 143,000 Black men were incarcerated. By 2008 that number climbed to 846,000.[14] How did mass incarceration close in so quickly? Under a Republican administration, the political and economic climate of the mid-1980s allowed a vast web of institutions to consolidate its powers and engineer the mass incarceration of Black men in America. And this network extends beyond the cooperating units of the criminal justice system. The corporatization of incarceration, the rolling back of citizens' rights regarding police searches and seizure of property in circuit courts and the Supreme Court, the culture of corruption contributing to the overpolicing of Black communities, the criminalization of poor Black people and police preying upon poor Black residents as a source of revenue and to attract federal grants, the prosecutorial process of plea deals and coerced confessions that often leads to the ethically—if even legal—wrongful conviction of poor Blacks for crimes they did not commit, and the private industry lobbyists and campaign contributors representing companies that profit into the millions from the expansion of prisons have been among some of the most predatory means of placing Black men under correctional control in America over the past thirty-five years.[15]

Complementing, funding, and rewarding these strategies was the 1994 Violent Crime Control and Law Enforcement Act, especially known for its "Three Strikes" statute that has made prison *home forever* for thousands of Black men. A US Department of Justice Fact Sheet summarizes the parameters of the Three Strikes provision as "mandatory life imprisonment without possibility of parole for Federal offenders with three or more convictions for serious violent felonies or drug trafficking crimes."[16] The federal government's Three Strikes statute, however, appeared in the wake of Washington State's 1993 enactment of the first Three Strikes law. By 1995 nearly half of the nation's state legislatures had followed suit, although with some variation in how each conceived and enforced the statute.[17]

But if some Black men will die in prison as a result of Three Strikes legislation, what are the odds of the thousands who must make America's prisons their "home for a while" returning to productive lives upon release from their iron cages? For those navigating the world with felony records, their chances for successful reunification with spouses and family members, obtaining adequate housing and gainful employment, and participating in civic duties such as voting and serving on juries are grim. Long after exiting the criminal justice system, ex-felons struggle to recover from the shattering effects of perpetual social and economic exclusion.[18] Michelle Alexander, in fact, calls the felony record a "badge of inferiority . . . that relegates people for their entire lives to second-class status."[19]

After a decade and a half of federal, state, and private entities' efforts to "get tough on crime" and deter recidivism, the Obama administration took some measures to ameliorate punitive federal housing policies and tamper the predatory environment that fed the prison industrial complex. Besides the president signing into law the 2010 Fair Sentencing Act, reducing the sentencing disparity between convictions related to crack and powder cocaine,[20] the Justice Department also launched a "Smart on Crime" initiative in 2013. This legislation sought to bring about equal sentencing for use of cocaine, no matter how it was distributed to the body. Among the initiative's aims was the promotion of "fairer enforcement of the laws," the alleviation of "disparate impacts of the criminal justice system," and the strengthening of "protections for vulnerable populations."[21]

Publicly acknowledging the criminal justice system as "skewed by race and by wealth, a source of inequity that has ripple effects on families and on communities and ultimately on our nation," Obama became the first sitting president to actually tour a federal prison in 2015.[22] Under his Clemency Initiative, Obama also began commuting prisoners' sentences. While prison reform activists legitimately grumble over the number of petitions Obama denied or left unaddressed by the end of his term, America's forty-fourth president actually commuted the sentences of more inmates than his twelve predecessors combined. In addition to the 1,715 sentences he commuted, Obama pardoned more than 200 nonviolent inmates, most of whom were serving sentences for drug-related crimes.[23] His 2016 "ban the box" rule also prohibited federal government employers from asking applicants to disclose whether they have criminal records. Within a year, nearly thirty states had begun to implement ban-the-box policies.[24] These kinds of policies can potentially diminish racial disparities in employment, since criminal records reduce the likelihood of employment by half for Whites and two-thirds for Blacks.[25]

Surprisingly, the shift toward prison reform did not entirely halt with the end of the Obama administration. Despite the vitriolic tough-on-criminals rhetoric Donald Trump and his surrogates spewed during the 2016 election season and after, two years into his presidential experiment, Trump signed a bipartisan criminal justice reform bill. The First Step Act affords federal prisoners additional pathways to clemency, including the 2010 Fair Sentencing Act, which now can be applied retroactively for the first time since it was put into effect.[26] Many agree that the First Step Act is the most powerful and sweeping criminal justice reform legislation in the era of mass incarceration.[27] The recent wave of progressive district attorneys elected on platforms of ending mass incarceration adds to this slowly unfolding culture of criminal justice reform. Since 2016 new DAs across the nation have been pledging to implement equitable and compassionate prosecutorial practices premised on justice rather than a blind obsession with conviction at any cost. Many of these DAs provide support for one another through networks and forums where they gather to share resources and discuss operable reform strategies.[28]

Federal and state criminal justice reforms in recent times could lead to positive appreciable outcomes for Black communities. Yet even with reports that Black adult imprisonment rates have dropped in recent years, current trends still bear the footprint of previous administrations that set mass incarceration in motion.[29] And with such astronomical numbers of Black men still entering the prison system at rates far above Black women over the past three and a half decades, Black love and marriage, especially among the most poor and vulnerable classes,[30] have faced daunting challenges and remain on the receiving end of our nation's protracted war on drugs and crime.

By the mid-1990s, a general population survey of low-income urban Black women revealed that 22 percent were romantically involved with (most likely low-skilled Black) men who had experienced incarceration.[31] What else should we expect when one in four Black men born since the late 1970s was incarcerated by his midthirties?[32]

THE DELETERIOUS IMPACT OF MASS incarceration on Black love and marriage surfaces not only in tabulating the large number of men who are missing from the Black marriage market, but also in comprehending how mass incarceration ruins love relationships and affects the daily experiences of those challenged by the constraints of living behind bars. The ensuing stories bring us into the homes and hearts of Black women who love, marry, and struggle to stay connected to their incarcerated husbands and partners. They witness years of humiliation and abuse at the corrupt hands of the predatory capitalists behind the prison industrial complex and the public servants connected to it.

Navigating the correctional system demands patience, unrelenting inner strength, and flexibility. Resilient couples have found creative ways to survive the impunity with which officers of the law and the wider criminal justice system violate their rights and human dignity. But many marriages have crumbled under the exigencies of this ubiquitous enterprise. Beyond the emotional price incarcerated men, their wives, and their children pay as they accommodate new constraints, for poor Black families the financial cost of imprisonment is unsustainable. In many cases, criminal justice legislation of the 1980s and 1990s punished ex-convicts even after release from prison, impacting their chances to rebuild their lives and preserve their marriages. Most troubling of all, mass incarceration feeds and feasts on policies regulating public housing, welfare, and other social services. When Black couples are trapped within the web of these intersecting systems, there seems to be no way out. Their relationships often deteriorate, their marriages disintegrate or never materialize at all, and their children are repeatedly victimized. Since mass incarceration affects a significant number of Black women and Black marriages, it is important to survey its damaging legacy through their eyes.

BLACK WOMEN PRISONERS OF INCARCERATED LOVE

In the twenty-first century, the predicament of loving an incarcerated Black man has become a fact of life for increasing numbers of Black women across the nation. Thus, if 44 percent of Black women today have a family member in prison, what do their lives look like when that family member is a husband?[33] Over the past forty years, Black women have come to know all too well the truth of the refrain "no one . . . no one to love" from Luther Vandross's 1986 hit song, "Give Me the Reason." Among them are the tens of thousands whose fiancés and spouses are not quite "missing" but simply *absent*. These "prisoners of [incarcerated] love," women such as Khadijah Abdullah-Fardan, Jackie McPhail, and Asha Bandele, know what it's like to be engaged or married to men behind bars.[34] Their stories of loving incarcerated Black men are the palimpsests upon which Tayari Jones inscribed her narrative *An American Marriage*. Roy and Celestial, the two central characters of Jones's novel, reveal the truth that Black marriages are increasingly entangled with the carceral state and its imprisoning institutions in America. Jones is not wrong to name this arrangement "an American marriage" because America's public officers and servants—from the highest officer of the nation to the officers policing the streets—have indeed turned millions of Black women into "'prisoners of love' . . . married to men serving sentences." Sadly, our democratic republic's wider heritage of slavery, White racial terror, and White privilege has made the phenomenon of "incarcerated Black marriages" as American as apple pie.[35]

A powerful indictment of America's increasingly common marital arrangement channels Jones's protagonists' reflections and exchanges after Roy is arrested for allegedly raping a woman "six years older than his mother" while lodging at a hotel during a trip to his hometown of Eloe, Louisiana. Celestial recounts the events of that early morning, emphasizing the discrepancy between what *she* knew to be true and false and what the police and Roy's accuser reported. "I was still awake when the door burst open. I know they kicked it in, but the written report says that a front-desk clerk handed over the key and the door was opened in a civilized manner." Comparing her version of what occurred on the evening in question with the accuser's surfaces a tension that resides between beliefs and knowledge.

The accuser was confident that the man who "twisted the knob" on her door just before midnight was Roy, the same man who had helped her carry her ice bucket back to her room after he noticed her arm in a sling during a chance encounter at the ice machine. Roy had even lifted a window in her chamber that she could not manage to lift on her own, stopped the water from running in her toilet, and alerted her on his way out that the doorknob was not secure. "It was dark, but she believed she recognized Roy, the man she met at the ice machine. . . . Roy, she said, may be smart, and he may have learned by watching TV how to cover his tracks, but he couldn't erase her memory. But she couldn't erase mine either," Celestial immediately thought. "Roy was with me all night. She doesn't know who hurt her, but I know who I married."[36]

Despite Celestial's testimony that after returning to the room with a filled bucket of ice, Roy laid next to her the entire night, his conviction changed their futures forever. Celestial soon underwent her initiation into the unenviable life she would lead as the wife of a convicted felon. There were new codes and taboos to follow if she ever hoped to see Roy while in prison: "Show no skin. Don't wear an underwire bra unless you want to fail the metal detector test and get sent home." Rehearsing the dress-code policy reminded Celestial of a time at Spelman, her undergraduate college, when she attended a required convocation lecture delivered by "a man . . . who had been wrongfully imprisoned for decades." Celestial poured her recollections into the words she saved for Roy, recalling too that the "white woman who pointed the finger at" the ex-con spoke along with him. "Even though they stood right there in front of me," Celestial confessed, "they felt like a lesson from the past, a phantom from Mississippi. . . . I knew that things like this happen to people, but by *people*, I didn't mean us," she wrote to her husband after her first trip to visit him behind bars.[37]

BEYOND FICTION

The visitation rules Celestial obeyed in order to see her husband behind bars are enforced not only in fiction. Accomplished author and activist Asha Bandele seems none other than a living and breathing Celestial. She too was chastised for wearing an underwire bra during her first prison visit to the man who would become her husband. When she initially encountered Rashid behind prison walls in 1990, Asha was just a twenty-three-year-old college student. She eventually married him in 1995 and gave birth to their daughter, Nisa, in 2000. Once their relationship turned romantic after two years of volunteer teaching at Rashid's prison, Asha faced a new set of obstacles every time she approached the entrance to the "castle" that housed the man she loved.

As a girlfriend rather than a teacher, Asha was handled differently by prison guards. Though tempered slightly by the fact that she had been a regular volunteer there, the degree of animosity was still daunting. Asha was now lumped in with all the wives, siblings, and parents of inmates who were "treated with hostility and suspicion." After she married Rashid and the couple was allowed conjugal visits, the scrutiny was unbearable. "Getting processed into visiting rooms across New York State means police have the right to scan even my tampons and hold them up to the light," Asha explains in her memoir, *The Prisoner's Wife*. But as she describes the typical scene leading up to her private moments with Rashid, the surveillance goes even deeper:

Before I enter the trailer site where Rashid and I will spend our time, it will be my panties, diaphragm, and K-Y Jelly that male officers hold out in public often as a company of inmates is walking past five, maybe eight feet, from us. They have fingered my black silk panties, the ones I bought for only Rashid to see. They've shaken down my bra, my nightgown, even though it is sheer.[38]

Asha soon realized that the scrutiny and exposure she faced undergoing clearance at the prison paled in comparison to the strip searches her husband and his fellow inmates endured daily. After years of experiencing, observing, and listening to others undergo "inspections, interrogations, suspicions, and searches," Asha arguably reached the most unexpected conclusion for those whose lives remain untouched by incarceration. "There's a kind of freedom in being forced to place yourself in the hands of people who hate you, have them hold you up to the light, scan you, scrutinize you. This is what I've come to believe, finally, that there is a purity in sharing when there's nothing left to hide, no spaces for modesty or retreat."[39]

Asha's awareness of how prison policies seem to leave no place for human dignity to reside is what ultimately disclosed a deeper truth about the human condition and about Black love in captivity. In the prison environment of perpetual isolation and exposure, Asha realized that she and Rashid "have no camouflage, are as naked and displayed as the Venus Hottentot. . . . All we have, all we are, and all we hope to be," she declares, "is out on the table, dissected and documented. We can either wither apart and give in to the madness, or else struggle, keep honoring that, despite everything, we can still love and make the love feel good." Making the love feel good between them—the "holy communion" they shared—allowed them to claim their dignity and recognize their freedom while under surveillance.[40] This was worth the four-hour bus rides she regularly took to visit her husband. But it was an arrangement they would have to endure longer than they hoped.

After losing an appeal to overturn her husband's second-degree murder conviction, something fell off Asha's shelf inside and broke.[41] For fourteen years, the couple had suffered the humiliating intrusions from prison guards who desecrated their sacred intimate moments—their only moments as a couple to be free, human, and authentic. Perhaps most brutalizing of all were the times Rashid had to leave the trailer during their conjugal visits to verify his whereabouts.[42] Such security checks occurred at least seven times per visit, yet Asha held on to the hope that her husband would be released into her arms one foreseeable day. When Rashid told her that they experienced time *differently*—that with each passing day, "you see a little bit of your life slip away," while "every day that goes by for me is one day closer to having what I've always wanted"—Asha "was silent, saddened, and scared by the truth."[43] Her struggle to come to terms with their irreconcilable temporal locations left her suspended between that newly unveiled raw truth and the thick blanket of hope she was so accustomed to wrapping around her heart. Somehow, among the riotous thoughts raging through her mind, she always chose hope.

At the impossible crossroads of Rashid's denied appeal, the thing that fell off the shelf and broke was not her love for Rashid. "After all these years," Asha determined,

> I owed myself and I owed Rashid and I owed our relationship more than disappearing. In the very least, even if from that day forward, I never went up into a prison again, if I never saw Rashid again, I owed us the truth. The whole, entire, out-loud, in-public truth, which meant I had to admit that despite all of the losses and all of the hurt, there were these moments in Rashid's arms that were a luxury of bliss. There were these times when we shared an absolute embarrassment of love. There were days that had set a standard for days.[44]

Asha's memoir testifies to the enduring power of love in the midst of tragedy. As the years passed, Asha found sanctuary in the "embarrassment of love" she and Rashid established to nurture one another through an impossible situation. Despite all the trespasses upon the sanctuary their love provided, Asha and Rashid's love nurtured their imagination and, in fact, transported them to another *shared* temporal location, one that transcended the captivity they could not escape. Captivity—the carceral state—inevitably conquered their marriage, but not their love. After spending seven years in prison; meeting, marrying, and conceiving a child with Asha over another ten years; and dreaming across yet another nine of a victorious appeal that never came, Rashid was released from prison but not into Asha's loving arms. He was immediately and permanently deported to his native Guyana in 2009.

For twenty-six years behind bars, Rashid had fantasized about his release day. Twelve years into captivity, Asha took center stage in the scenarios he imagined—days, years, decades when he would be free to love his wife without limits. And seventeen years into his sentence, the birth of their daughter, Nisa, only intensified Rashid's reveries. He had five love languages for his wife and daughter and no chances left to demonstrate his fluency in each.

With her Black love story bruised and dismembered, Asha would end up raising Nisa alone in New York, away from the only man who "knew [her] body, its fears and its every nerve and yearning."[45] The inner turmoil, loneliness, and irreversible punishment of Rashid's deportation depleted Asha's resources and compelled her to follow through on a decision she knew she would regret for the rest of her life but still had to make:

> I couldn't play at house or marriage anymore. I think that's what I said to Rashid finally. I needed the real thing, or I needed to woman up and do this on my own. That breakup, though it left me with a grief so profound it has no name I can call, is something that feels akin to losing my husband, best friend, father, and brother on the very same day. Not losing them so much as sending them away, banishing them.[46]

Asha and Rashid eventually divorced not because their love had expired but because the accumulated wounds of a life spent married to an incarcerated man imposes a prison sentence of its own on innocent wives, especially those who are poor and exploitable.

Poor Black Wives: Financing and Surviving Mass Incarceration

Asha's experience, as difficult as it was, could have been much worse had she not had the resources to sustain herself and her daughter. Although she underwent rough financial patches, including the time when she aborted her and Rashid's first pregnancy shortly after they had married, Asha was college educated and a self-supporting poet and author. Thousands of Black women with incarcerated husbands find financial resources hard to come by. Therapists concur that financial constraints are among the principal causes of marital conflict, alienation, and dissolution, and Black marriages, arguably the least wealthy in the nation, are overrepresented among financially troubled and broken marriages in America.[47]

For Black women contending with an incarcerated spouse or partner, the capitalist enterprises of America's prison industrial complex saddle them with exorbitant fees reminiscent of the days of peonage and sharecropping. Among America's imprisoned population, the strain of paying for one's crime in time spent behind bars, underpaid *and* unpaid labor, and the almighty dollar can be unbearable for the vast majority of prisoners and their families.

Since numerous studies have shown a strong correlation between poverty and crime,[48] it's not surprising that most Black women with husbands and partners in prison are poor. With the proliferation of the prison industrial complex and the bevy of crime legislation intended to deter illegal drug activity and other criminal behavior, Black men were locked up at astonishing rates to pay for their violations. However, they paid financially as well. If they were married and attempting to sustain a relationship with their wives, their spouses too were forced to foot the bills of private and state entities. These entities, including private telephone companies, security companies, vending machine companies, and commissaries, charge exorbitant fees for their products, forcing inmates' wives and partners to choose between sustaining their relationships with the men they love behind bars and supplying their own basic necessities and, in many cases, those of their children.

The phone call is one of the most immediate and consistent means of spousal reunification after incarceration has occurred. While some incarcerated men deliberately distance themselves from their wives and families, others lose motivation or adopt new identities within the prison culture when they are not able to connect with their wives or partners through regular phone calls. In one study of incarcerated African American fathers and family relations, a forty-two-year-old participant, with the pseudonym Lamar, maintained contact with his children through weekly telephone calls, but he had not spoken with his wife since his incarceration. Lamar's "drug problem" had scarred their marriage, and his incarceration for a burglary committed to support his habit made matters only worse. Another twenty-nine-year-old participant called Ed spoke about the loneliness and abandonment his wife experienced. "Me and my wife just had a serious confrontation because I forgot about my wife and focused all of my attention on the kids," he explained.[49]

Ed's neglect of his wife might be just what wives who have legitimate concerns about maintaining intimate connections with their incarcerated husbands prefer. Even when conjugal visitation programs allow couples to enjoy the intimacy of sexual intercourse, some wives have important reasons to hesitate or disengage. This was Jerome and Lawonda Williams's predicament. Jerome had sampled drugs while serving in Vietnam during his ten years of service in the Marine Corps. After returning home with "marketable skills," job insecurity led him down the path of substance abuse. Jerome's wife, Lawonda, a licensed practical nurse, harbored serious concerns about her sexual and personal heath and actually refused intercourse because she feared she might become infected with HIV. Her husband was not only "a former intravenous drug user," but also confined to an all-male facility where opportunities for coerced and desired same-sex relationships abounded. Lawonda was "afraid that [Jerome] may have had homosexual activity while in prison, which would also put him at risk of AIDS."[50]

Others who have the means, time, and desire to visit their incarcerated husbands combat emotional alienation through regular face-to-face contact. Murielle tried to stick it out with her incarcerated husband and remained married to him for a decade after he went to prison. Eventually, she found that her resources could no longer sustain her in the marriage, as she tried to make the best choices for her daughter and carry the load of parenting alone:

> To be honest, I did not take and expose my daughter to that a lot because I didn't want her to see the environment and I didn't want her to see her father incarcerated. . . . And the couple of times that I did take her down, she couldn't understand. . . . [W]hen you get to that door and you have to say good-bye, they want to know why you can't get on the van or the bus. And they [the children] turn around with this look on their face. Isn't he coming, Mom?" "No, he's not coming, he has to stay here."

In fact, the fathers of Murielle's two daughters were incarcerated, and although she ultimately severed romantic and marital ties with both of them, she was determined to keep the lines of communication open between her daughters and their daddies. The weight of financing the phone calls from two inmates, however, demanded that she compromise. When her ex-husband called, she had to pay ten dollars if her daughter spoke with him for ten minutes, basically a dollar per minute. That was money she just didn't have lying around, and so Murielle insisted that her ex-husband use cost-effective means of communication with his daughter:

With Christelle's father I had to put my foot down, and I told him that he couldn't call for awhile, because it became too expensive for me. And I told him. . . . "I understand that you want to talk to her, but you know, you're gonna have to find another way of doing it. Call Christelle just to say hello and how-you-doing and then pick up the pen and write her. You know, she can write. She has very good penmanship. She's gonna have to start writing you, because it becomes so expensive, and the cost become [sic] so enormous that it takes away other things that you could be doing with your money." . . . I said, "I'm not trying to be mean. I'm not trying to be the B-I-T-C-H in this, but I have to look out for my well-being and my children's well-being because I'm the only source of income they have.[51]

Murielle's predicament illustrates how Black women's incomes drive the flow of capital required to sustain relationships with incarcerated Black men. During the 1990s, collect phone calls—the only calls prisoners could make—entailed both collect-call fees at long-distance rates and a surcharge for each call placed, yielding revenue of up to $15,000 per year for each installed phone in a prison facility.[52] While Murielle placed a serious limit on the amount she would give to filling the coffers of private predatory phone companies, Asha regularly paid monthly phone bills of $500 and $600. In some months, her bill even reached the $800 range. Knowing that Rashid was not at liberty to call her when he wished, Asha was forced to take expensive cab rides and cancel appointments to make sure that she was home on time to receive her husband's planned collect call.[53]

Current prison reform activism at the state and national levels has advanced steps to outlaw predatory policies requiring prisoners and their families to pay exorbitant fees for collect calls. Among recent failed and ongoing efforts was the bipartisan 2018 Inmate Calling Technical Corrections Act, introduced by Senator Tammy Duckworth (D-IL) at the 115th Congress on March 8, 2018. The bill would have prohibited decades-old telecommunications policies in all carceral facilities nationwide, if only it had not stalled in Congress.[54] Despite the setback of the federal bill, a small ray of hope is on the horizon within the Connecticut General Assembly, which is on the precipice of passing an act that will "provide cost-free telecommunications services for incarcerated persons."[55] Connecticut inmates pay some of the most expensive rates for collect calls in the nation, and the state's $7.7 million profits from collect calls alone during 2018 paint a clear picture of how ruthless the corporate entities behind such avaricious schemes actually are.[56] Undoubtedly, many will follow the outcomes of these critical efforts in ensuing years. However, extensive reforms are needed elsewhere to topple the PIC's stranglehold on Black families, not to mention Black love and marriage—after all, prisoners and their wives need more nourishment than words alone to maintain healthy and balanced lives. They need and deserve the sensual pleasures of life, eating together, shared vulnerabilities, romantic intimacy, and a therapeutic environment that rehabilitates and celebrates small victories, whatever they may be.

Most couples separated by incarceration know not to expect these comforts, not even the comfort of sharing a home-cooked meal together during visits. Since visitors are typically barred from bringing food into visiting rooms and are thus compelled to purchase meals from vending machines, often after costly long-distance journeys, the expense of purchasing food can be prohibitive. Family members also face restrictions when sending packages to their incarcerated loved ones. In some cases, they can purchase products only from approved mail-order companies and do not have the option of comparison shopping for the lowest price.[57]

The culture of surveillance family members encounter when visiting loved ones in prison is also costly. It reduces visitors to the status of criminal suspects and gives license to those in charge to treat them with indignity. And treatment can vary depending upon one's racial and class status. At the Londonderry prison in Burlington, Vermont, wives perceived to be "fast-living" were often strip-searched, while "good wives" seldom underwent the ordeal. One wife perceived to be "fast-living" described how strip searches were "especially degrading when I had my period because you have to remove your Tampax in front of them."[58]

Wives, partners, and family members of prison inmates describe visits as stressful and demeaning. They can find themselves standing on two-, three-, even four-hour lines before receiving clearance to visit with their loved ones. When lines extend beyond the prison doors, even in the deadening winter cold, no pity is taken on mothers with infants and young children. They have to wait their turn like everyone else. And while standing in line, visitors must learn the rules of when to ask questions and how to ask questions between pulsating shouts from overzealous prison guards to "shut up!" Visitors can also be turned away if their attire is deemed improper or unacceptable. One inmate's sixty-three-year-old grandmother was denied visitation "because she had on a sweatshirt that was the wrong color."[59]

The rules, especially when applied haphazardly and unfairly, produce an endless series of impediments. They wear down wives, partners, and family members and erode life-giving connections with loved ones that research shows are essential to achieving the best outcomes for incarcerated men during and after their sentences. Shanita Hubbard says that "visiting an inmate you love is its own kind of prison" and, in many respects, aptly identifies the family member or friend intending to see a loved one behind bars as a "visiting inmate." At least, this is how visitors are typically treated at carceral facilities. In a 2017 article, Hubbard provides a gripping account of what it means for visiting inmates to *wait* at New York City's infamous Rikers Island, where the experience is "particularly vile":

The line consists of mostly black and brown women and children, with a few men. You all have an unspoken agreement to keep the small talk to a minimum. Even without words, the looks on everyone's faces as the dogs stalk around tell a deeper story. . . . You see shame on the face of an older black man that's told to shut up by the guards when he says he can't stand for very long. . . . You wait in line for two hours without any clarity or information. The dogs disappear. Did they detect drugs? Was there an issue inside the building? Lockdown perhaps? What's taking so long? You all wonder, but only one amateur visiting inmate makes the mistake of asking a correction officer. No one has told him the rules to this joint, but when the CO screams "Shut the fuck up or lose your visit!" he quickly learns. . . . It's now been three hours of just standing, waiting and stewing in rage. You finally enter the building, only to be met with . . . more lines. You wait in line to be searched. . . . Someone is screaming "Open your fucking mouth!" in your face. You freeze. The CO screams louder. "Open your fucking mouth or go the fuck home!"[60]

Hubbard's exposé invites us into a universe of endless violations of the body, soul, and psyche, committed by the very civil servants empowered to *prevent* violations of the law and of persons. It's no wonder many wives not only experience stigma when their husbands go to prison, but also feel "their husbands' punishment . . . [has] been imposed directly on the family."[61]

In the arena of romantic intimacy, this feeling is particularly true, because both wives and husbands are denied the normal comforts and rewards of uninterrupted cohabitation. For wives such as Asha, fortunate enough to have access to conjugal visits, they can at least look forward to the bittersweet experience of confronting the mood-wrecking security-clearance procedures and enjoying some hours of romantic privacy with their husbands in a reserved trailer.

Others without conjugal visitation privileges sometimes find other means to experience the sexual intimacy they deserve. It's not uncommon for couples to protest intimacy deprivation by actually copulating in the public space of the visiting room. They usually try to hide behind vending machines or in restrooms to conceal their lovemaking. In one case, a couple "consummated their marriage in an Oklahoma visiting room with other couples as their lookouts" and remember that day as "a moment of daring that gave them hope for the future."[62] But others feel no shame in assuming cuddling positions in the main visiting area that allow them to engage in sexual intercourse. One inmate's wife not only confessed that she and her husband "had sex in the visiting room," but also admitted, "I knew that the people who were visiting saw us having sex . . . way in the corner."[63] While some prison guards deliberately turn the other way during such moments, others respond tyrannically. Sociologist Megan Comfort reports that while conducting fieldwork at San Quentin, "six lifers were placed in solitary confinement due to allegations by other prisoners that the men and their partners repeatedly engaged in illicit sex in the Mainline visiting room."[64]

Not all wives are ready and willing to indulge in intimate acts in public visiting rooms. Many refuse to trade privacy for a compromised moment of pleasure, no matter how much they miss the warmth of their husbands' bodies. They complain that such desperate attempts at sexual gratification are inappropriate and even "pretty gross." Some intentionally leave their children at home when visiting their husbands to avoid exposing them to such obscenities.[65]

Incarceration and the cultures of surveillance and survival it produces punish everyone in an inmate's family who cares to remain connected.[66] Marriages too are severely punished because correctional control extends to wives' sexual, physical, and emotional bodies.[67] The ten-year ordeal of managing a marriage under impossible conditions intensified when Tina's husband, Dante, was transferred to a private prison in the state of Ohio, far away from the Washington, DC, metro area, where Tina and her children were living. The decision from on high to transfer Dante, a common practice in the industry, robbed her of the one ritual she had to cushion the blow of her husband's absence: regular visits to see him behind bars. "Our life is on hold," Tina confessed. "That's what I feel like. And being as though our life is on hold I really can't spread my horizons without my husband. I accepted his wrongdoing, because I just wanted our family to rejoin and reunite." Tina, an ambitious and willful student and working mother, did not have the liberty to travel to visit Dante at his new facility, and this fact devastated her to the core. "All I ever do . . . is hope that it's over. All I can do is hope and dream." But her enduring question remains: "When is it going to manifest? When is it going to materialize? What if they keep him for the duration of his time? What does that leave me as his wife?"[68]

Thinking back on it, Tina admitted, "I went through it so bad when he went to Ohio, but I kept saying the whole time that I wasn't stressed, because I was still functioning. . . . I struggled through school, because every week I was sick. . . . Mentally, I was making myself sick." But Tina was not just mentally sick. She developed migraines and lost a tremendous amount of weight. Her doctor diagnosed her with anxiety induced by the separation Dante's incarceration imposed on their marriage, especially because "in our five years of being together, we had never been separated," Tina explained. Family members actually saw how sick she was, and word got back to Dante in prison. When Tina finally had a chance to visit him, he noticed right away, with his own eyes, that something was terribly wrong. Facing him through a glass divide, Tina recalled that Dante "told me to pick up the phone."

> I picked up the phone. He said, "Look at you." He said, "I'm gonna tell you just like this. . . . As much as I love you and as much [as] I want you in my life, this thing has taken a toll like the way I see you looking." He said, "I want you to walk out that door and don't come back in here. Get yourself another man 'cause you're killing yourself." He said, "Look at you. You've lost weight, your eyes all

sunk, you look terrible." . . . So I was, like, "I'm okay." He say, "You're not okay."[69]

The dance of denial and protection performed by couples coping with incarceration only intensifies the stress consuming wives and husbands. When they meet for such limited windows of time per visit, many Black wives admit to concealing their woes from their incarcerated husbands. They prefer to discuss lighter matters that sustain a happy and hopeful mood. Incarcerated Black husbands too have hidden their troubles behind bars from their wives when asked, "How are you doing?" or "What's wrong?" Despite knowing that they had to navigate a humiliating screening process just to make it past security to the visiting room, some even refuse to see their wives if conflict with another inmate or a prison guard left them physically or emotionally wounded.

Inmates often undergo reassignment to different prison facilities during their sentences. As was the case for Tina's husband, Dante, for no apparent reason at all they are constantly moved, far from their families, making visitations unduly difficult and even impossible for some. In one case, across twenty years of custody, "T" Lawson had been relocated eleven times. His prison odyssey took him from Washington, DC, to Kansas, Oklahoma, Indiana, Wisconsin, Georgia, Pennsylvania, Washington State, North Dakota, Tennessee, Ohio, and Virginia.[70]

With the heightened stress and loss of agency wives of incarcerated husbands experience, it's astounding that some report an improved quality of interactions with their husbands during imprisonment, which they testify enhances the overall health of their marriages. Women do find that they are able to love and remain married to men behind bars against the odds, and many credit the frequent exchange of extensive letters as the source of their satisfying relationships. As one woman explained:

I think the strain that's been put on us has made us closer. . . . [W]e don't have a choice but to communicate in ways and learn how to read each other. And I think we've done that. And I think that's what's really different is we're more friends. Because we don't have sex. We don't you know cuddle all day or anything like that. So we're friends. And I think that you really have to be friends in order for your relationship to work . . . and I think we've got that down. It's a good thing in a way that he is there [in prison] because it's brought us closer.

Another woman described the emotional fulfillment her partner's romantic imagination and "letters upon letters upon letters" brought her. Within one month the couple shared a total of one hundred letters, forty-five scribed by her partner: "We weren't able to touch or see each other. . . . But being romantic with each other he knows how to draw. He draws me roses. Instead of going out and buying me a dozen roses and sending them to the house he draws me a dozen roses and sends them to the house. . . . He draws me pictures with hearts with a rose through it and clouds in the ocean and everything. He draws me how he feels and what he wishes he could give me."[71]

These moving testimonies are not necessarily representative of isolated experiences. Yet far more women describe a life fraught with disappointment, loneliness, stigma, depleted resources, and perpetual adversity. They know the emptiness of deferred desires year in and year out. Wives of incarcerated men harbor what Asha expressed as a singular wish for a normal marriage, a different American marriage than the one this nation has arranged for far too many Black couples. "At the end of the twentieth century," she wrote,

when there were some people who, more than anything else, wanted the stock market to keep booming, and some who wanted to lose another fifteen pounds, and some who wanted to become

big stars in small films, and some who wanted brand-new sports
utility vehicles, and some who wanted [Bill] Clinton impeached,
and some who wanted to rock Hilfiger gear daily, and some who
wanted to write rhymes and make phat beats, and some who
wanted their next ten-dollar bag of whatever they could sniff or
shoot or smoke away, and in the time when most of us wanted
cures for AIDS and cancer and a realistic way to keep our blood
pressure down, the greatest of my own personal needs was for my
husband to come home to me.[72]

For Asha, there was nothing more pressing, nothing more
needed in a world of troubles and disasters, than Rashid's freedom
and presence at home. But added hidden obstacles await to tie up
Black love even after incarceration comes to an end.

BARRIERS TO RETURNING HOME

One of the greatest obstacles to reunification after Black men are
released from prison is the restriction that state and federal policies
place upon assisted housing opportunities for ex-offenders. Just as
public welfare departments and eugenics boards collaborated to ruin
Black girls' and women's pursuit of love and marriage in the past,
public housing authorities, the penal system, and public welfare departments have also worked hand in hand to destroy Black women's
relationships with incarcerated Black men.

During the 1990s, the US Department of Housing and Urban
Development issued regulations that empowered public housing
agencies across the nation to prohibit convicted felons from participating in their programs.[73] And although the Obama administration worked to reverse such regulations, ex-offenders are still refused
housing based on their criminal backgrounds. When they are allowed to join family members already living in subsidized housing,
many low-income Black women find themselves in the precarious
position of having to provide shelter without adequate financial

sustenance for their unemployed husbands, sons, fathers, or partners. For the thousands charged with minor violations, they often are forced to pay exorbitant fees for ankle bracelets and other monitoring devices they must wear while awaiting trial or as a condition of their release from prison. A 2014 NPR survey discovered that forty-nine states "allow or require the cost [of monitoring devices] to be passed along to the person ordered to wear" a monitoring device, which can easily amount to $400 per month.[74]

The laws that encourage such housing restrictions serve to criminalize drug addicts and other ex-convicts long after they complete their sentences behind bars. Hence, they pay twice for their offenses. And while the mid-1990s saw the most venomous legislation passed to deny government subsidized housing to ex-offenders, after the ratification of the Anti–Drug Abuse Act of 1988, public housing authorities were compelled even then to update their leases with clauses prohibiting leaseholders, their family members, and guests from "engaging in criminal activity on or near public housing premises" and "declaring such criminal activity to be a cause for terminating the tenancy."[75]

Circumstances worsened in 1996 and 1998 when President Bill Clinton signed into law the Housing Opportunity Program Extension Act and the Quality Housing and Work Responsibility Act. Federal and state housing authorities swiftly weaponized the law to exclude millions of previous drug offenders, and "criminals" in general, from establishing residency in federally assisted housing. Borrowing phrasing from famous War on Drugs legislation, the US Department of Housing and Urban Development instituted what it labeled "the toughest admission and eviction policy that HUD has implemented." HUD's "One Strike and You're Out" policy was unforgiving. As Bill Clinton announced in his January 23, 1996, State of the Union address, "From now on, the rule for residents who commit crime and peddle drugs should be one strike and you're out."[76] Ostensibly, this meant that "one strike" of just one person could displace an entire family—all members sharing a household with the offending party.

The 1996 and 1998 acts specifically allowed for standardized screening and application processes that authorized the government to investigate the criminal backgrounds and drug-offending and -treatment histories of all applicants. In some cases, applicants with criminal backgrounds have been required to wait years to become eligible for public housing. While states and local housing authorities exercised discretion over how they would align their local policies and practices with federal laws and regulations, just twelve months after the 1996 law was passed, a whopping "75 percent of the 1,818 housing authorities responding to a HUD survey indicated they had adopted the 'One Strike and You're Out' Initiative's policies." Incentivized to reject applicants with drug offenses or other criminal activity on their record, public housing agencies went from denying 9,835 applicants housing to denying 19,405 applicants opportunities to access low-income housing within the first six months of the new dispensation.[77]

Having an address, a stable place to lay one's head, is an essential pathway to productive citizenship and wealth building. However, since the late 1980s, elected officials invested in austere antidrug and anticrime policies, assuring the American electorate that they prioritized public safety. Through calculated efforts, they were determined to cleanse the nation of dangerous criminals who preyed upon law-abiding citizens.[78] The impact of anticrime public housing policies has been devastating for poor Black ex-convicts, many of whom are left to fend for themselves in an unforgiving world, alienated from most social service institutions.

In a 2012 interview, Gavin, a convicted felon, explained the call-and-response nature of crime and punishment for Black men with no place to live. Handicapped by their criminal records, they quite understandably cannot withstand the deluge of compounded criminal justice, public assistance, and social service policies toppling over them like endless walls of dominoes. "I am homeless, a grown man, and I ain't got a place to sleep," Gavin lamented.

> I'm fifty years old, but have to go more backwards because all I can do is go and live in the shelters, where drugs and stuff makes it rough. The housing situation for people like me [with a felony] is not there to help nobody. The charge just brings you down, and makes you want to go back to doing what you were doing [illegal activity], because really, to tell you the truth, I can't do nothing legal with that [felony] charge [on my record.]. All I want is to stay clean [off drugs], and get a safe place to stay so I can live. I need that to have a chance [to re-enter], and I don't. I got nothing with my name on it. I'm nothing, a nobody.[79]

Gavin and many other ex-offenders are direct casualties not only of decades of political rhetoric that "permanently cast drugs, crime, poverty, racial minorities, and public housing as synonymous terms," but also of the laws "politicians designed . . . to socially disable those who fell into each of these categories."[80] Whether deliberately or apathetically deployed, the laws and policies that feed the prison industrial complex exacerbate existing and create new social disabilities. However, in addition to recidivism, homelessness, joblessness, physical and mental illness, addictions, and other public health problems, the missed and ruined opportunities for healthy Black love, coupling, and marriage to thrive and anchor Black families and communities must be counted among the social disabilities impacting African descendants in America today.

Studies from the late 1980s to the present reveal that many incarcerated Black men's worst fears of spousal alienation after release actually do materialize even if their marriages don't terminate in divorce.[81] They know better than any that the prison industrial complex is a foe to Black love and marriage because it separates and taxes the finances of Black couples. But beyond these piecemeal assaults, it destroys hope, smothers the fires of love, and forecloses opportunities for actual rehabilitation when Black men are released from prison.

Since the 1980s, the "New Jim Crow" has engineered an inferior and impotent caste of Black men barred from fully obtaining and exercising citizenship rights and responsibilities. Similar to the Old Jim Crow, it has provided structural niches for American ways of life that exploit and discard Black people and, in the process, deny them the comforts of love and marriage on their own terms. Leaving, in particular, millions of Black women (who desire romantic coupling and marriage with Black men) hopelessly single or saddled with undesirable and toxic relationships, the New Jim Crow is the fulfillment of America's centuries-long investment in forbidden Black love.

Accenting the fragility of Black relationships under the governing authority of the prison industrial complex, the stories explored in this chapter disclose the crippling reach of mass incarceration into the homes and hearts of Black women whose partners and husbands remain behind bars. As scholars and activists constantly explain, mass incarceration and its "collateral consequences"[82] turn innocent and rehabilitatable Black men into repeat offenders, overwhelmingly rendering them unemployable,[83] unmarriageable, and undesirable in the eyes of many Black women. Researchers have found too that a stable and supportive marriage actually discourages crime, even among men with "histories of delinquency." The obligations and expectations that attend marriage and family relations incentivize men to embrace prosocial family roles and curtail their fraternizing with other men "whose recreations veer into antisocial behavior."[84]

OTHER COLLATERAL COSTS OF MASS INCARCERATION

Mass incarceration's depletion of the Black marriage market has led to other troubling outcomes for Black women. Social scientists point out that the shortage of Black men in some communities has encouraged some men to develop simultaneous relationships with multiple women. Beyond this, Black women, seeing options disappear before them, lower their standards and lose leverage in the relationships they do forge. Black heterosexual men know their value in the age of mass incarceration, and they have the luxury to take as much time as they want to settle down. Why rush when there is an unlimited supply of Black heterosexual women around to choose from, not to mention women of other racial-ethnic backgrounds? Black heterosexual men marry outside the race twice as much as Black heterosexual women, further depleting the pool of available Black men for most Black single heterosexual women who, as the data show, overwhelmingly choose to marry Black men.[85]

Undeniably, some Black women have transgressed prison gates to find acceptable men for love and marriage.[86] This was not exactly Shanita Hubbard's situation, but, with no preparation, she did end up sharing her love with a Black man through prison bars. One day, Hubbard's fiancé did not come home as expected. He had been arrested for a crime committed long before their first encounter. His subsequent indictment, prosecution, and five-year prison sentence incarcerated Hubbard every bit as surely in what she calls a "prison of shame." Hiding her fiancé's fate from her middle-class circles of family, friends, and colleagues, Hubbard dodged questions about his absence and their prolonged engagement. "How exactly was I supposed to tell them . . . ?" writes Hubbard. "Was I supposed to squeeze it in between talks about intersectionality and feminism? Would it have made great small talk in the car on the way to pick up one of their husbands from yet another business trip? Or maybe when we had our yearly college homecoming, I could have spilled the beans in between party-walking and pretending I could still step like an undergrad." A professional with advanced degrees, Hubbard "didn't think [she] was the 'typical' face of the woman who secretly spends weekends taking long-distance trips to see her fianc[é] through a glass." Eventually, Hubbard revealed some details about his arrest to close relatives and friends. In disbelief, they queried why a beautiful, young, educated woman would place her life on hold for a man behind bars. "Before I could provide a real answer, and not just a response designed to silence them," Hubbard confesses, "I had to own my truth. My truth was that I stayed because I loved him."[87] But whether Shanita Hubbard's love will be enough to survive the impositions of the carceral state on her relationship is still unknown.

The testimonies of Black women throughout this chapter confirm something my mother said that cut right into the center of the blissful love I had been enjoying with the man who would become my current husband. When he met my parents for the first time and conveyed his plan to move from a foreign country to marry and start a new life with me in America, my mother responded that "sometimes love is not enough."[88] My mother's admonition was not a callous attempt to throw cold water on my intended's noble plans and genuine excitement. She wanted to be sure that he had thought carefully about the perils of transitioning to an unknown territory where he would have to learn a new language and launch a new career as a middle-aged man.

For proof that love is indeed not always enough, we need only look to the experiences of Black women who have struggled but, by no fault of their own, failed to transcend incarceration in pursuit of love. The vicissitudes of life under normal circumstances *are enough* to derail what a woman believes to be her unadulterated love for her husband and vice versa. Add in the leviathan of the carceral state, and it's no wonder Black love and marriage are facing perhaps their darkest days since the first Africans landed on the American shores.

While mass incarceration afflicts the poorest and most under-resourced Black persons and communities, middle-class Blacks are not immune to the effects of the carceral state. Not only are many of their relatives poor and vulnerable to being locked up, if they're not already, but middle-class Blacks are also more likely to find

themselves facing probation or incarceration than their White counterparts.[89] Increasingly, middle-class Black women, such as Shanita
Hubbard and Asha Bandele, are marrying or making plans to marry
Black men before, during, and after incarceration. If Black male
imprisonment continues at disproportionate rates, more and more
Black women will fall in love with and marry some of these men.
Thus, when Michelle Alexander writes that "mass incarceration
is, metaphorically, the New Jim Crow and that all those who care
about social justice should fully commit themselves to dismantling
this new racial caste system," I would add that mass incarceration
is the newest battleground in America's war on African American
marriage.[90] Moreover, all who care about social justice must commit
themselves to ending this war for the sake of Black women, Black
men, Black children, and the health of this nation.

Even at a time when the state is sponsoring official initiatives in
support of "healthy marriage" among poor and dependent populations,[91] mass incarceration is far more powerful and effective in preventing and dismantling Black marriage than government programs
launched to promote marriage. This is because the state is more pre-
occupied with controlling Black men than it is with rendering them
marriageable. And make no mistake about it, the state is no hopeless-
romantic actor behind the scenes. No different from its position in
the immediate decades after slavery, where the state today seems
willing to invest in Black marriage, its first priority is to alleviate its
responsibility to subsidize poor Black women and children in need of
public assistance. Once married, in the eyes of the state, it is Black
men's patriarchal obligation to support their wives and children.

Welfare's Patriarchal Logic in the Age of Mass Incarceration: Still a Barrier to Black Marriage

Examples of how state-enforced patriarchy absolves the state of cul-
pability for systemic poverty and other social constraints oppressing Black people today can be found in the management of welfare

programs across the nation. The welfare state tracks and holds poor Black men accountable for the subsistence doled out to their wives or ex-wives and children even decades after issuing final payments. I personally know a Black man in New York in his sixties whose Social Security check continues to be garnished to repay the government for the decade of subsidies his ex-wife and children received between the 1980s and the 1990s. Although he began receiving his Social Security benefits only a few years ago, the state has a long memory. Until his debt is paid in full, he will collect reduced monetary payments. It doesn't matter that this particular Black man was not able to find steady employment while his children were growing up. It doesn't matter that when he tried to relocate to another state for greater opportunities, he was denied motor vehicle privileges, which quickly dashed his hopes of independence and gainful employment. Nor does it matter that his life was beset by one trauma after another. America, with its patriarchal heritage and conception of marriage, has no sympathy for the millions of Black men it has actually excluded from patriarchal privilege and trapped in cycles of imprisonment, labor exploitation, or unemployment and poverty since the earliest days of debt slavery to the rise of the prison industrial complex.

Although American presidents have given welfare new names across the decades—ADC, AFDC, Temporary Assistance for Needy Families (TANF), and others—its patriarchal logic remains constant. Federal and state welfare policies typically require women seeking government aid for their children to sue the absent fathers (husbands, partners, boyfriends) for child support that the government will subsequently collect to replenish its own coffers. Fathers earning less than $10,000 per year were responsible for two-thirds of the nation's child-support debt in 2006, and these poor men easily could have seen the majority of their salaries garnished and their driver's licenses suspended or revoked.[92]

Though these findings were published more than a decade ago, the policies remain in effect across many states, often sowing seeds of bitterness and distrust between young unmarried couples who might otherwise develop healthy and cooperative means of coparenting—couples who might even preserve their romantic bonds and eventually seal them with marriage vows. When mothers are "forced to name absent fathers, and then sue them—and sue them again and again," poor fathers find themselves trapped in a closed system of utter privation. "Because the fathers are often also poor, the vast amount of assigned child support goes unpaid and insurmountable arrearages quickly result. The fathers who try almost always fail as the automated enforcement mechanisms throttle endlessly: a trucker's license is suspended, so he cannot work; a laborer's wages are garnished at sixty-five percent, so he cannot afford to pay his own rent; a father obtains a new job and then loses it after being incarcerated for contempt because of his child support arrearages."[93]

Welfare-cost recovery often works against the stated goals of the TANF program, especially those of encouraging and sustaining two-parent families. In 2017 twenty-seven states were enforcing the harshest TANF policies. Although the federal government mandates TANF recipients to "assign their rights to child support payments to the state," it does allow states to determine if a portion of noncustodial parents' child support will be "passed through" to custodial parents of children receiving aid. States have the authority also to disregard child-support payments when determining TANF applicant eligibility. Even when states do adhere to pass-through policies, the amounts are minimal, most ranging from a flat $50 to up to $200 for two or more children.[94]

My friend's twenty-eight-year-old son finds himself at war with the government and with his ex-girlfriend every month as he struggles to support their child and his own expenses. The source of contention: the state of New York garnishes his wages to replenish the TANF benefits his ex-girlfriend receives for their six-year-old son. "Every month we go to battle about this," Teddy complains, "because she tells me what the government gives her is not enough, and she needs additional support from me. But my hands are tied. I'm working as much as I can making nineteen dollars an hour, and even doing overtime. I don't have any money stashed away that I can draw from, and I have to be able to cover my rent and monthly expenses to even be in a position to remain in my son's life."[95] Although Teddy's work history has been somewhat sketchy, he has held a few stable jobs over the past ten years, including his current position in the construction business. Yet scholars have shown that "child support enforcement disproportionately impacts young African-American men and has a contributing negative impact on their participation in the workforce."[96]

Similarly to Teddy, Zion, a Black male high school graduate in his early thirties with two children, has struggled to sustain himself and his children due to the wage reduction he faces every month.[97] The state of New York garnishes his wages, collecting $800 per month to pay current and overdue child support. Zion has reached his limit when it comes to navigating the family court system—a place he says "is not made to be there for the male." He respects his younger daughter's mother and calls her an "excellent mom," but he feels tremendously burdened by a situation that traps him in a vicious cycle he is at pains to escape. "I don't want to tarnish the mother of my child," Zion explains,

> because she's very respectable and works very hard to take care of my child. So, I don't want to discredit her in any way; but because she was susceptible to getting on welfare, when I had my daughter, she didn't want me to put my name on my daughter's birth certificate. She felt like, if she ever did move to a place of needing assistance, she would have a better chance of receiving help from the government. I insisted though. I told her, "No, I want my name on my daughter's birth certificate, because my older daughter's mother did the same thing and my name was omitted from her birth certificate!" I wasn't gonna go through that again.

Once I put my name there though, when they're [TANF/wel-fare personnel] checking the record for the father, the name on the certificate, whoever's name is there, they're gonna pay. They're gonna ask, "Is the father in your life and how much money does he provide?" They want to know how much he provides so that they can cut you even shorter on the money that you're getting. That's why it feels like it's such a big scam because they want to know everything I'm doing to help out so that they can shorten how much they help out.

Zion had always been an engaged father when it came to pro-viding emotional and financial support for both of his daughters, so he actually experienced a rude awakening when he "started getting letters in the mail."

They were telling me my passport is not nothing. . . . I can't get a passport and my passport is not valid because I owe over a certain amount of money. If you owe over a certain amount of money, you can't drive—your driver's license is suspended. If you get pulled over in your car on a suspended license, and you have unpaid child support, you're going to the jail. Absolutely demoralizing! You're a hardworking person, and so psychologically what it does to you is it makes you feel like you have to be more selfish so that you can have enough for yourself. The money is going and being spent everywhere. It's like, where's the money for yourself.

Talking to Zion left me with the impression that the welfare state functions like a temporary lender that will stop at nothing to recu-perate from partners, husbands, and fathers as much of the money it dispenses to the mothers of their children as possible. "I know some-body that's on supplemental income," Zion added, "and, you know, the state is taking back their money from that inadequate source of support. Whatever money you get, they will be right there to take their little cut." Another of Zion's acquaintances received a large settlement after being on welfare for several decades, and the state "took like fifty to sixty thousand of it. It's definitely not free aid," Zion concludes, "because they got the system down to a science, and any reported income—any money coming in to you—if you put it in your name, in your account, it raises flags, and they will collect from you what they think you owe them."

Today's TANF programs create for many young parents explosive entanglements of finances and the heart—cocktails of love, responsibility, ambition, desperation, and despair that lead them down paths of resentment and hostility. Zion confessed that "sometimes it was to the point where I started to hate the mothers of my children. I'm not in that place anymore because I have to understand that money is not everything." Undoubtedly, "money is *not* everything," but it is critical for personal and family stability. And Zion grapples daily with the instability in his life that the disparity between his aspirations and his inability to actualize them causes.

The money the state wrests from him weekly, which he knows is not going entirely or directly to his daughter or her mother, chips away at his sense of manhood. He describes how many men among his circles of friends and neighbors share his situation of struggling to work a steady job and provide for dependents. "When you're striving to assert yourself as male in this world," Zion contends,

you need to have certain things and you need to be saving money and need to do certain things to be an assertive man. Males want to assert themselves. It's very hard when you can't save money. When you only making something like [he pauses in frustration]. Sometimes my checks be like, 330 dollars. And if I don't do overtime, my weekly salary—it drops from 700 and something all the way to 330 dollars. Now I am forced to work extra which forces me away from my kids, sometimes on Saturdays when I could be spending time with my kids instead of working. Holidays come up and I'm not paid for days off, so the money is extra short. If I do get to work on Saturday to replace the day off, I need to be in the overtime surplus category to really make money. And it's like the more I make the more they'll take, so you don't really wanna work. Some males, they don't even work, because they're just like, "Naw! they not gon take *all* my money!" And then to know that the mother not even getting all the money. It's one thing if the mother is getting all the money, but it's another thing if this guy is doing everything, and he still dealing with this. So I spend money, my mother spends money, my aunt spends money, everybody spends money to support my daughters, and it's like, I get hit twice, double, and it's not a good feeling . . . at all!

Thirty-five years ago, Johnnie Tillmon concluded that our nation's welfare programs needed a complete overhaul and an entirely new foundation. She observed then that, over the decades of her activism, each American president devised and implemented supposedly "new" welfare programs, promoting them as "better than everybody else's," but from Tillmon's purview, they were only advancing "the same thing!"[98] In many respects, our current federal and state welfare policies continue to impact poor Black aid recipients no differently than they did during the height of Johnnie Tillmon's welfare rights activism. Their power to divide Black couples—to give financial support to the family unit with one hand and still take away financial support with the other hand—is eerily familiar.

Tillmon's insight and wisdom are needed now more than ever because an effective and supportive welfare program demands loftier ideas, ethical commitments, and goals to address disparities and inequality centuries into the making, especially when it comes to Black men's alienation from stable employment opportunities. If the government genuinely wants to reduce the number of Black children living in poverty, it will have to devise welfare, training, and employment programs that financially assist poor Black men, acknowledging that most have been denied patriarchal opportunities to provide adequately for their families under the laws and customs of both the Old Jim Crow and the New Jim Crow.

Given the poor employment outcomes for Black men with criminal records,[99] we can only imagine how TANF policies might be impacting their wallets and their already limited opportunities to secure a livable wage in today's society. A 2019 study now confirms that the decline in Black men attending college over the past few decades is directly related to the passage of the Anti–Drug Abuse Act of 1986. Clinton-era criminal justice legislation designed to wage a war on drugs also placed specific barriers between men incarcerated for drug offenses and a college degree, including laws that denied them access to Pell Grants and in some cases even federal aid.[100] "The fact that more than half of the young black men in many large American cities are currently under the control of the criminal justice system (or saddled with criminal records) is not—as many argue—just a symptom of poverty or poor choices, but rather evidence of a new racial caste system at work."[101] No matter how much the government wants to pretend that poor Black men are at liberty to assume "patriarchal" responsibility for their wives, partners, and children (as if patriarchy is a benign or unassailable system of kinship and social organization in the first place), the history of mass incarceration in America unveils the hypocrisy and delusion behind this unwarranted posture.

Too Late to Turn Back Now

Predictions for Black male mass incarceration in the twenty-first century are proving accurate. To make things worse, Black women are being imprisoned at concerning rates, and their overrepresentation in women's prisons has extended roots reaching back to the nineteenth century.[102]

While still a drop in the bucket when compared to Black men, Black women are incarcerated nearly twice as much as White women.[103] Today the United States criminal justice system houses 2.3 million persons—adults and juveniles—behind bars, and close to 1 million of them are Black. Despite their racial minority status in this country, Americans of African descent make up 40 percent of the nation's incarcerated population.[104] They also make up 30 percent of the additional 840,000 persons who are on parole and the 3.6 million persons on probation.[105] The untenable numbers of Black men under correctional control are neither an accident nor an indication of any natural propensity for criminal behavior on the part of Black men. Rather, they reveal something more sinister about America's ever-evolving institutional determinants of Black life and, yes, Black love.

America's ongoing project of forbidden Black love has finally found its most hospitable home in its sprawling prison industrial complex. If the institutions of racial enslavement, lynching, race massacres, and welfare each proved painfully effective at discouraging or even disrupting Black love, the prison industrial complex has succeeded in this on another level altogether. The prison reform advocacy organization Worth Rises phrases it best with its summation that America has "built an industry and economy dependent on human caging and control that capitalizes on crime and prevents justice."[106]

Stymied by its thirty-five-year legacy of unprecedented human caging and the gross violations associated with mass incarceration, the nation now finds itself at a crossroads. In a political moment fueled by heated debates about the value of Black lives and increasingly visible activism on the part of those aiming to dismantle the PIC and eliminate its effects on poor and vulnerable communities, politicians of all stripes at the state and federal levels are taking notice and responding.[107] However, it is not easy to determine whether the darkest days of mass incarceration are actually behind us.[108]

Prison reform activists are making strides in convincing legislators of the dangers of the PIC and the mass incarceration it orchestrates. Even many Republicans are supporting suggested re-forms meant to overturn counterproductive laws so as to ameliorate or in some cases terminate policies and practices that encourage re-cidivism. Yet America has always preferred punishing Black males for their antisocial (and at times even prosocial) responses to their structural victimization. As a result, we have reached the point where progressive policies at this late hour may not matter in the end. Mass incarceration has already done its job so perfectly that the Black community—Black love and Black marriage—may not recover from its effects before the end of the twenty-first century.

In this age of mass incarceration, forbidden Black love and its historical antecedents in America have left millions of heterosexual Black women wandering through unstable landscapes of love-lessness, unsatisfying marriages, divorce, and most prevalently singlehood. But there are models of resilience that Black women can champion interpersonally for inspiration and support. In spite of America's racist-sexist heritage, there are nevertheless Black cou-ples whose shared love and successful marriages provide hope to Black women still in search of Black love. Their examples reveal the quality of love heterosexual Black women can and do experience in lifelong commitments with Black men. Together, their stories make an incontrovertible case for why our democratic nation should care about Black women and Black love.

CHAPTER 5

Will Black Women Ever Have It All?

Michelle Obama, Kheris Rogers, and African Americans' Shifting Landscapes of Love

Every once in a while, one of my besties, Courtney Brown, sends me articles featuring elderly African American couples whose fifty-plus-year marriages have withstood America's legacy of forbidden Black love. As the cultural and linguistic anthropologist who taught the session "Observing Black Love" in the inaugural 2004 iteration of my Black Love course at Emory University, Dr. Brown is well poised to notice the resilience and longevity of Black love in a nation designed to destroy it. Set against the painful history examined throughout this book, the stories framing each couple's deeply rooted relationship are simple and inspiring.

Studying their lives affirms the conviction that love conquers all because for all of the stories we have seen thus far of black love denied or destroyed, these centenarian stories demonstrate that enchanted Black couples can defy the odds, sometimes for many years. Most illustrative of blissful Black love are the only two stories in my files thus far featuring couples celebrating more than eighty years of marriage. Ninety-eight-year-old Varrie and her 104-year-old husband, Lawrence Player, of Benton, Louisiana, had celebrated eighty-three years of marriage by Valentine's Day 2018. During a 2015 interview, the happy couple claimed they had "never had a fight in 80 years." The Players' lineage extends across nine children, thirty-seven grandchildren, fifty-eight great-grandchildren, and five great-great-grandchildren.[1]

Another happy centenarian couple doesn't lay claim to a prodigious family tree, but Willie Williams and her husband, Daniel (100 and 103, respectively), are proud parents of one daughter and one granddaughter. Explaining the secret behind her marriage's longevity, Willie said she and Daniel have "never been the type that will fuss and fight. . . . We just find funny things to talk about."[2] Lawrence Player said something similar about his marriage to Varrie: "I treat her nice and she treats me nice. We've had a good life together."[3] The Players' and the Williams's unions are sources of unadulterated love, a fortress in the face of America's war on African American marriage.

Both couples have lived through virtually all of the racist horrors and abuses described in every chapter of this book except those of slavery. While they did not witness Reconstruction, they were born in the middle of the reign of terror. Their successful marriages offer flesh-and-bone examples of the rewards of Black love. They are the canvas upon which many Black Americans have painted their admiration and aspiration for the quality of everlasting love. Acknowledging Black couples whose love has triumphed over decades of marriage is important in a discussion such as this because it is easy to forget the sterling examples of resilient Black love in our midst.

Another, higher-profile, example of black love actually unfolded before the eyes of the nation during Barack Obama's two presidential campaigns and terms of service as the forty-fourth president of the United States. The incessant media coverage of the Obamas' powerful romantic bond caught the attention of many Americans.[4] However, the most interested and involved observers of the Obamas' love and marriage were millions of Black women in America. They are the population most vulnerable to living, working, and dying in this country without love and marriage, forced to make do with a menu of poor options for courtship and coupling. Becoming acquainted with the nation's new Black first family was *personal* for Black women. Whether young or old, coupled or single, Black women followed the discussions on the Obamas' glamorous and appealing marriage, celebrating and idolizing the couple's love and intimacy.

But Michelle in her own right was particularly irresistible to African American women. Many took her for a real, live Clair Huxtable on steroids. Michelle's public career, even as the wife of a Black presidential candidate turned president, seemed impossible in the United States of America. If ever there was a time in this nation's history when a majority of Black women likely pondered the modern woman's question—whether they could actually "have it all"—it happened during Michelle Obama's tenure as a Black presidential candidate's wife and the nation's subsequent first lady. As one professionally successful single Black woman who "sometimes thinks of the Obamas in assessing her own failed romantic history" put it, "What's so different about Michelle compared to a lot of these other women who are not married, including myself? . . . Did she just happen to be at the right law firm at the right time? Is it just the luck of the draw?"[5]

Michelle's elite legal career and celebrated marriage to Barack Obama gave some Black women at least a glimmer of hope that they might one day have it all. However, her admittedly rare public and personal success conveys something else as well: the idea that highly accomplished Black women in the public eye need no longer pass the implicit "brown paper bag test." Gone perhaps are the days when Black women with skin shades darker than a brown paper bag found themselves barred at the doors of American opportunity. America's project of forbidden Black love, it would seem, has finally met an equal match in the marital assets of the nation's first Black first lady. Vanessa Williams said it well in her article "Dark and Lovely,

Michelle." After giving President Obama props for marrying a woman of dark complexion, she told no lies in declaring, "A lot of black women fell for Barack Obama the moment they saw his wife," because "sisters who look like Michelle Obama seldom become cultural icons, aesthetic trendsetters—a proxy for the all-American woman."[6]

Still, rather than an anchor of promise, Michelle's good fortune is at best an inspirational sign for Black women in search of intraracial romance and marriage. Sadly, as inspiring as her public profile and healthy marriage may be, Black love is still far from flourishing in America. Black women not only confront a shortage of Black men, but also wrestle with internalized and interpersonal color consciousness, legacies of poverty, "wealthlessness,"[7] patriarchal marriage, and stereotypic tropes that render them undesirable, hypersexual, difficult, and intimidating. Attentive to both Black women's and men's perspectives on love and marriage, including interracial relationships, the final sections of this book explore these obstacles to the flourishing of Black women and Black families, identify areas of focus requiring immediate consideration in any program aimed at curtailing forbidden Black love, and outline policy recommendations and strategies that build on resilient features of Black kinship and family formation as well as resourceful insights from Black scholars, public figures, and influencers.

Color Matters

With Michelle Obama ranking among the most influential Black women across the globe, her barrier breakthroughs have been celebrated on a world stage. Yet for all the love she exudes and attracts, Michelle has her share of detractors. Many are White citizens from her natal land who have bemoaned her accomplishments and first-lady status. Michelle has spoken candidly about such insults, reminding America that, after Donald Trump's presidential victory, Pamela Ramsey Taylor, a White West Virginia county worker at the time, welcomed the change of power with her assessment that Melania Trump embodied the beauty, class, and dignity that Michelle Obama, an "ape" fronting as first lady, could never display.[8] From where I stand, it's no accident that this remark targeted a dark-skinned Black woman. The White imagination has been conditioned to make effortless associations between dark-skinned Blacks and apes.[9]

Even though Michelle broke through the color barrier that sometimes poisons Black men's minds, she still had a steep hill to climb to win widespread support for her presence in the White House. And Black women, especially those with dark skin shades, have a steep hill to climb yet before reaching the marriage altar that Michelle at least was able to reach. Colorism and phenotypic stratification remains a persistent discriminating factor among African Americans, not to mention other Americans, and has a great deal of power over the Black marriage market. The research of Darrick Hamilton, Arthur Goldsmith, and William Darity reveals how treacherous the incline from singlehood to marriage actually is, especially for dark-skinned Black women.

In their study of 1,579 Black females between the ages of sixteen and twenty-nine, "55 percent of light skinned black females had been married, but only 30 percent of those with medium skin shade and 23 percent of the dark skinned females had ever been married." In addition, within the same sample, "Twenty percent of light skinned black women have a child under the age of 18 but have never been married, whereas 38 and 35 percent of medium and dark skinned black women have such a child and have never been married." Even after controlling for key demographic and socioeconomic variables among Black women, there was a roughly 15 percent higher chance of "ever being married" associated with having lighter as opposed to medium or darker skin.[10] Unsurprisingly, "the penalty attached to dark-skinned women becomes more pronounced with high status."[11] Related studies show corroborating results, and sociologist Margaret

Hunter underscores the price that women with dark skin tones pay for their phenotypic inheritance. "Black women in general marry less than other races but darker-skinned black women," she explains, "marry men of lower social status than the lightest-skinned black women."[12]

Social and digital media have provided numerous venues for Black women to fill out these statistics and observable trends with harrowing accounts of rejection and exclusion. One writer, Dream McClinton, wraps her own dark flesh around these statistics in a candid article describing her dating experiences and those of her friends who share dark brown skin tones. McClinton confesses to establishing a dating profile online because, as a woman with "deep mahogany skin," "men don't talk to me any other way." Confirming results of the often-cited 2014 OkCupid study,[13] Jasmine Turner of the Chicago-based dating enterprise BlackMatchMade has noticed that "Black men will say, 'complexion doesn't matter,' but they might give that lighter complexion woman who is very comparable to a darker-complexion woman a chance, when they wouldn't give that darker-skinned woman a chance."[14] McClinton thickens Turner's composite Black male profile with one anecdote after another—Black men keeping her and all demonstrations of affection for her out of public view, a Black man telling his dark-skinned girlfriend that he "wants a white family," and even an unattractive one with the same dark brown hue as hers who wrote on his dating profile, "I only date light-skinned women."

As a dark-complexioned Black woman with a dark-complexioned father who always celebrated my natural beauty, I moved through life not noticing how ugly and undesirable I probably was to so many Black men I encountered on a daily basis. Yet I was not entirely shielded from colorism and phenotypic stratification. I have felt the weight of CPS when navigating our nation's anti-Black social world premised upon aesthetic perceptions of what is phenotypically valuable and invaluable, safe and dangerous, beneficent and malevolent, and so forth.[15] Though I knew about the psychology of beauty and desire in Black communities, which situates light-complexioned Black women as ideally beautiful and desirable relative to darker women, I couldn't help but be shocked after reading study after study and personal story after personal story, and online post after online post, that reinforce the Black community's (not to mention the wider society's) standard stratification of beauty by hues ranging from the lowest, darkest stratum to the highest, lightest stratum.[16]

Perhaps this is why a dark-complexioned National Football League (NFL) athlete Jahleel Addae and his White fiancée, Lindsey Nelson, shared an intimate digitally recorded toast with a group of friends shouting one after another, "Cheers to more light-skinned kids!" The February 2019 recording lasts only about ten seconds, but the person holding the camera (purportedly Nelson) does scan the guests around the table. Of the four Black men within view, three of them are darker than or as dark as Addae. Although it's unclear whether Addae first proposed the toast or if he joined the echo chamber of voices that repeated it, Addae certainly raised his glass with his left hand while holding his "light-skinned kid" with his right arm.[17]

The video went viral. Black women and even Black men have rebuked the NFL player and his posse with anger and sadness for what the scene suggests about Black self-hatred and the disdain for Black women that far too many Black men harbor. The Black men seated around the celebration table are exactly the type Dream Mc-Clinton's dark-complexioned friend Larissa had in mind when she described how determined some Black men are to acquire a seat at precisely those kinds of tables. "Sometimes, I can kinda feel their eyes sliding off of me to go to the pretty white girl next to me, or even the fairer-skinned Yara Shahidi type," she revealed.

It was the sheer accumulation of these kinds of insults, devaluations, and dismissals of Black women, especially dark-skinned Black women, that propelled some Black women activists to withdraw support from a high-profile campaign protesting the fatal police shooting of Stephon Clark. On March 18, 2018, the twenty-two-year-old father of two was executed by Sacramento, California, police who fired twenty shots in his direction, seven of which penetrated his body, mostly from behind and several after he had fallen to his knees or flat on the ground behind his grandmother's house. As protesters swelled the streets demanding justice for Stephon Clark in the weeks after his tragic death, news circulated that the same Black male casualty of overpolicing and racial profiling Black women had pounded the pavement to honor had posted disparaging remarks online about them as early as 2015. To make matters worse, Clark shared his views with his non-Black girlfriend (of Vietnamese and Indian heritage), who also posted insulting comments about Black women.[18]

Clark's unsavory tweets provoked a much-needed conversation in the Black public square concerning the price Black women activists pay for "Black" solidarity with men who don't respect or value them. Among Clark's most egregious comments was his response to the assertion "Black is beautiful." Clark seemingly disagreed, writing, "Black bitches <<< I don't want nothin black but a Xbox, dark bitches bring dark days." He also posted, "I don't want no black baby. I'm already black. I don't need no black baby." And he seemed boastful when he wrote, "Got an Exotic bitch, you would think I'm racist. If you're wondering why I wanted my son to be mixed with Asian, they two steps ahead."

The response to Clark's misogynoir has been mixed, but one person wrote with arguably righteous discontent, "Black Women here is what #StephonClark thought about you. Stop marching/protesting for this fool that did not care about you. He would NOT have done the same for you."[19] Another tweet carried the message, "Shout out to #StephonClark for hating the same black women that are carrying the torch for his dead body." One tweeter even went as far as describing Clark's views as "normal for black men" and vowed to "never fight for someone who hates me." She also predicted that "black women will back out of his individual case of police brutality/ discrimination," and while some did, others such as Danielle Young displayed empathy for Clark. Young urges her viewers to remember that he was only nineteen years old when he posted a number of his misogynoir comments and that the struggle for racial justice and human dignity is larger and more important than Stephon Clark's missteps and ignorance.[20]

The Clark and Addae incidents illustrate the deep contempt for Blackness, and Black women—especially dark-skinned Black women—in Black culture and Black consciousness more than 150 years after racial slavery was abolished in this country. The brutality and violated bloodlines at the root of America's inveterate fascination with White people and disdain for Blackness and Black people set the stage for the bold displays of colorism and phenotypic stratification and misogynoir we see not only in the Clark and Addae incidents but also in daily occurrences across Black America and the wider nation today.

I take no delight in citing such hurtful and harmful episodes and have no interest in further lambasting the Black men responsible for them. I would simply argue that, as these examples illustrate, colorism and phenotypic stratification is not a thing of the past. It remains operative in twenty-first-century Black communities, affecting some of our most important decisions in life. Our diverse Black cultures— Southern, Northern, national, transnational, international—harbor and bequeath across the generations Euro-colonial ideologies that reinforce CPS and misogynoir. Encouraging Black women to inhabit an empathetic rather than dismissive stance toward Stephon Clark, author, activist, and blogger Hannah Drake reminds audiences that Clark is no anomaly in the Black community. Rather, he "is a product of a nation that has told him everything Black is wrong and everything not Black is right. And perhaps at 22," Drake surmises, "he had not gotten past the self-hate that so many of us must

learn to overcome as we mature and step into the fullness and great-
ness of being Black."[21]

Clark did not formulate the derogatory ideas he espoused
about Black women—nor Addae his preference for lighter skin—
independent of a wider subculture in the Black community and the
overarching racist ideologies of American culture. Across class differences, the Black community's quotidian conversations and cultural conventions demonstrate that Black people have not escaped
the ghosts of Thomas Jefferson, Archibald Gaines, Robert Newsom,
James Henry Hammond, and other countless White slaveholders
who were also architects of CPS and misogynoir.[22] As painful as it
is to accept, these "isms" infuse Black cultural and aesthetic perceptions of Black women, and dark-skinned Black women are the most
haunted and punished, especially in the arena of love and marriage.

This claim is borne out not just by anecdotal evidence. Perhaps
the largest study conducted on dating preferences in recent years indicates that Black women are the least likely to be selected for dates
by men of any racial-ethnic background at online dating sites. Ok-
Cupid collected the study's data in 2014,[23] and for the data showing ratings of women by men on dating sites, based on their profile
matches, we should be able to predict whom the men would select
for dates. Messaging and response rates show, however, that racial
biases can weigh heavily on people's attraction. With all the buzz
in the air about Black men's insatiable appetite for White women,
it might be shocking to some that the study's results indicate that
Black men actually place a discount on White women and a premium on women of color when seeking online dates. However, the
premiums placed on Latina and Asian women are twice as high as
the premium placed on Black women. When looking at other men's
ratings, Black women are more deeply discounted by Latino, White,
and Asian men.

The data look quite different when examining women's ratings of
men, as something very striking appears in the racial configurations

of the women's dating preferences. Black women, as a group, prefer their own race *only*, while Latina, White, and Asian women prefer their own race *and* White men. Despite the difficulty Black women face in finding Black male partners and spouses, over the past few years Black women who did marry were selecting Black male partners at a rate of at least 88 percent (meaning that Black women who marry, for the most part, want to marry Black men).[24]

SOME RESIST THIS GLOOMY PORTRAIT of Black women's dating and marriage options, citing a lesser known statistic that most Black women over the age of fifty-four will experience marriage with at least one partner.[25] But not all Black women will take comfort in this revelation. Many of those desiring a long life of coupledom with children will miss out on bearing offspring with their husbands as well as the economic benefit of nearly doubling the wealth potential of a two-income family if they are forced to delay marriage until their early fifties.[26] In fact, the wealth inequities between White and Black families caused by slavery and other compounded forms of systemic racism bear heavily upon the dearth of Black men who are available for marriage, in terms of their own sense of readiness and their potential partners' perception of their marriageability.

WEALTHLESSNESS AND MARRIAGEABILITY

While social scientists correctly point out that "marriageability" is often loosely defined or not defined at all in many discussions of low marriage rates among African Americans, the concern about a potential mate's financial stability emerges as a high priority, according to data collected from both Black men and women. In a 2009 study that analyzed survey results from 344 Black women and men, researchers found that, overwhelmingly, both Black women and men desired spouses whose salaries significantly "surpassed their own." Most respondents indicated a strong desire to acquire and sustain middle-class status through spousal income.[27] And this smaller study mirrors results from a national 2010 Pew Foundation study of social and demographic trends, which showed that African Americans prioritize financial stability over other racial-ethnic groups.[28]

Income and wealth potential appear to be strong indicators of whether Black men feel prepared to marry. But even Black men who earn lucrative salaries marry less often and later than their White counterparts, and more research is needed to understand why. According to family law professor Ralph Banks,

> Black men who are employed and economically stable are less likely to have ever married than white men with comparable incomes. Moreover, the marriage gap between black men and white men actually widens at the top of the income distribution. For white men, as income increases so does the likelihood of marriage. But a black man who earns more than a hundred thousand dollars per year is *less* likely to have ever married than a black man who earns seventy-five thousand dollars per year. The highest-earning black men are more than twice as likely as their white counterparts never to have married.[29]

Despite their impressive salaries, far too many middle-class Blacks are just a few paychecks away from economic instability, have little to no inheritable wealth, and often provide financial support to extended family members. Any way one slices the cake of Black financial mobility and stability, someone comes up short—Black women, Black men, or both, whether single or married.

The negligible wealth of Black women and men appears to be a strong factor impacting the Black marriage market and specifically Black women's options for marrying Black men. Understandably, scholars, commentators, and everyday people point many fingers at the carceral state as the principal source of the Black male shortage and the continued low rates of marriage among Black women in recent decades. However, Black men and women's inherited wealth-lessness is another factor in the equation that warrants examination. If a majority of Black men are either waiting to marry or never marry because they are seeking mates with significantly higher salaries than their own—mates who are not necessarily forthcoming[30]—then Black men's low wealth-building potential must be considered when attempting to understand the range of issues placing a tight squeeze on the Black marriage market.[31]

Black men and women's inherited poverty and wealthlessness as well as low earning potential are reflected in annual calculations of median incomes for both groups across the decades. For example, in 2017 the median income was $29,962 for Black males and $23,499 for Black females,[32] and in 2018 nearly 50 percent of Black children came from households within the bottom fifth of the nation's income distribution. By comparison, slightly higher than one in ten White children fell within the same income bracket.[33] But Black men and women don't need US Census Bureau reports and social scientific studies to alert them about their bleak economic circumstances and slim chances for measurable social mobility; their desire to marry mates who can help them tackle poverty and financial instability is the best indication of the sobriety with which they confront their common condition.[34]

BUT THE BLACK MARRIAGE DECLINE TRANSCENDS SOCIAL CLASS

Although scholars debate the underlying factors that have led to low Black marriage rates, especially since the 1960s, increasingly there is consensus that the factors cannot be limited to financial instability, the depletion of low-skilled employment opportunities across urban landscapes, and mass incarceration. Shifts in cultural attitudes and norms regarding marriage, sex, and divorce, some argue, also contribute to the marriage decline among African Americans. Despite the debates and different conclusions drawn, one thing seems clear: the marriage decline affects African Americans across social class.

While some highlight how poor Black women are most affected by the marriage decline, research on a large sample from the 1990s shows that the disparity is negligible, leading sociologist Averil Clarke to argue that "marriage opportunities and choices are highly related to African Americans' racial status rather than their class status."[35] Clarke's data sets, taken from the National Center for Health Statistics' 1995 National Survey of Family Growth, indicate that, during their childbearing years (ages fourteen to forty-five), Black women across three class divisions have virtually the same chances of being currently married, formerly married, or never married.

Black women with college degrees (21.57 percent), some college (20.94 percent), or only a high school or general equivalency diploma (GED) (21.59 percent) who were married at the time of the survey were basically in the same boat. This holds true for Black women of the three class levels who were formerly married (college, 8.74; some college, 9.73; high school/GED, 10.90) and never married (college, 66.17; some college, 66.36; high school/GED, 64.57).[36]

The only notable difference that showed a class disadvantage for Black women in the marriage market appeared when two figures were calculated for Black women with less than a high school diploma. Only 15.29 percent of women in this category were married, and 73.07 percent were never married at the time of the survey. However, 10.83 percent of women without high school degrees were formerly married and thus actually fared better than women with college degrees (8.74 percent) and some college education (9.73 percent) while virtually rivaling the percentage of women with a high school diploma/GED (10.90 percent) who were formerly married. Yet even the variances between the lowest class of Black women surveyed and the three higher classes are not significant. What *is* significant are Black women's shared history of racial oppression, and quite often, their shared patriarchal expectations of marriage.[37]

Round Two: Reconsidering the Sources of America's Patriarchal Marriage Ideal

Millions of Black women and men believe patriarchal marriage is socially and morally compulsory because it was designed by God and revealed in the Bible. However, patriarchal marriage in the United States, its attending nuclear family structure and gender roles and its perceived biblical foundations are Euro-American traditions and ideations. Some would push back on this point with claims that African patriarchy was resurrected in Black American communities during and after slavery. If this is true, I have yet to see any compelling evidence to support such claims. African historians, archaeologists, and anthropologists, especially those studying precolonial Africa, have documented diverse marital arrangements and family systems that accorded power and privilege to men *and* women based on seniority, kinship, and social belonging. African women were not confined to the domestic sphere; they held political office, worked and provided for their families, and occupied roles generally assigned to men in Western societies. The concepts of "head of household" and the "nuclear family" are also notoriously Western. African family structures privileged consanguineal over affinal ties. They also encompassed matrifocal units, complex conceptions of siblings that included relations Euro-Americans would deem as cousins and members that Euro-Americans would call "extended" kin. It was also commonplace to privilege maternal heritage within monogamous and polygamous marriage and family systems.[38]

The patriarchy that remains nonnegotiable for so many Black women and men today is not African patriarchy;[39] neither is it God's patriarchy. Rather, it is White America's patriarchy—the Black community's entrance fee to the dark margins of national belonging. Today there are countless Black purveyors of White American patriarchy, and the most influential voices can be heard on Sunday mornings. The patriarchal marriage ideal is so embedded in Black culture that we can easily forget the historical moment when most African

Americans began to accept and practice it—the postemancipation period during which Freedmen's Bureau agents and White Southern proprietors required Black women and men to adopt patriarchal marriage as a precondition for obtaining labor contracts and the livelihood to sustain their families.[40]

The most ardent pushers of patriarchy in the Black community are revered Black male pastors, but Black church cultures in general reinforce inherited White American patriarchal values that prescribe roles for husbands and wives. A good wife is subordinate and takes a back seat, while her husband governs their marriage and family. She handles domestic duties, cooking, cleaning, child care, and so on. By the same token, a respectable husband is an excellent provider and leader—the authoritative household head and final arbiter of all family decisions. Some even believe that a good husband should earn enough money to handle his family's financial needs so that his wife's salary is supplemental, if she works at all. All of these husbandly roles and responsibilities are tied as well to notions of ideal manhood. Trouble arises not so much regarding who does what in a marriage—who is the caregiver and who is the breadwinner—but whether those actions and accomplishments are valued unequally or tied to norms that affix manhood and husbands to stereotypic masculine tropes and womanhood and wives to stereotypic feminine tropes. Naturalized conceptions of what it means to be a husband and a wife don't leave room for adjustments, personal style, talents, preferences, flexibility, and growth.

Led by their pastors and spiritual mentors, many African Americans appeal to Christian biblical texts to justify their patriarchal conceptions of marriage as consistent with God's revelation. They cite passages from the Genesis creation stories in chapters one and two, noting that God created Eve to be Adam's helper. They also cite many Pauline and Deutero-Pauline epistles that they believe provide instructions for gender-based spousal duties and roles. Contextualizing and interrogating the authorial intent of the persons who wrote these and other related scriptural passages are beyond the aims of this volume, and there are many prominent African American (and other) biblical experts who have combined a range of tools and methods to situate scriptural passages and texts in their historical, cultural, linguistic, and literary contexts. Instead, it is perhaps more interesting to interrogate why Black Christians are unwilling to apply the same critical skills they use to decode and interpret the texts they read and hear in other cultural contexts—graphic novels, poems, comic books, hip hop lyrics, and the like—when reading and discerning the meanings of the scriptures.[41]

The diverse historical contexts in which the books of the Protestant and Roman Catholic Bibles were written and disseminated and the processes through which the actual Bibles were compiled were ideologically driven, politically fraught, and even polemically contested. If certain factions within the early church had been more influential, the West and the peoples it conquered would have different Catholic and Protestant Bibles today. Christian Bibles are compilations of multigenre texts, written across epochs for specific purposes, and translated from their original languages into Western languages, often in service of ruling classes who could deploy the scriptures to pacify their oppressed subjects. The books of the Bible reflect both divine revelation and Hebrew and Christian people's attempts to access, interpret, and apply divine revelation within the boundaries of their flawed cultures, traditions, and worldviews. Many leading biblical experts and theological scholars argue that the Bible contains both the Word of God and the words of humans. This means it also contains the cultures, power struggles, and ideologies of humans that are often mistaken for the Word of God. My seven years of theological studies training lead me to agree and encourage Black Christians to embrace informed and intelligent interpretive approaches to the Bible.

In every domain of life that demands expertise, we don't hesitate to consult an expert to handle problems. We wouldn't seek advice from a layperson about a serious legal matter or health concern; we would solicit expert advice from a lawyer or a doctor. However, when it comes to studying the scriptures and understanding biblical texts, many Christians dismiss too quickly scholarly *experts* who are also persons of deep Christian faith with the credentials and training to teach laypersons about the far and distant worlds of the Bible and the eras that produced its contents. In addition, God's revelation is not limited to the Bible. We live in a complex world, a digital and globalized age far removed from the epochs that produced the texts of the Bible. Yet Christians testify constantly about the effects of God's messages and continued revelation over their lives.

A concrete example that many Christians might appreciate can be found in a compelling contemporary argument for canonizing Martin Luther King's "Letter from Birmingham City Jail" and including it as a book of the Bible. According to Jerome Stueart, a White American Christian blogger, "If churches across America had *The Book of Birmingham* in their Bibles, pastors would be obligated to look at it as relevant, preach on it, talk about it." In his wider post, Stueart discusses how the first-century world of biblical Christianity is so far removed from our twenty-first century context that "the Bible is overdue for a Modern addition" and "*The Book of Birmingham* is that addition." Explaining in greater detail the urgent social conditions underlying his appeal, Stueart writes:

> Today, we face a lot of racial tension in America, and outright racism within individual Christians and churches. Because there is no text in the Bible that brings this to our attention on a Sunday by Sunday basis, we are free to avoid that topic on a regular basis. Free to believe that all the work is done, and that everyone is equal. Or that race doesn't matter. . . . The work of Justice is not done. With so many 1st Century AD problems clouding the cultural context of scripture, it's easy to dismiss it as "their" problems and NOT see our problems. King shows us our problems. We

cannot escape that gaze. Events in Dayton, Ohio, and Ferguson, Missouri and Charleston, South Carolina, shootings of unarmed black citizens, protests, civil unrest—means we have a LOT of work to do to overcome race issues in America.[42]

Stueart is convinced that canonization will "give MLK's letter the weight, the importance, the authority, the urgency it deserves in Christian lives. Put it in that book, people will read it," he declares. "Put it beside Paul, people will read it. And we need Christians everywhere to read it."[43]

Stueart's 2014 argument was not without precedents. At the Black Theology Project's 1979 national conference, Black theologians and biblical scholars queried, "Why not add a Black book to the existing 66 books of the Holy [Protestant] Bible?"

According to the BTP director at the time, Reverend Muhammad Isaiah Kenyatta, many theologians thought King's "Letter from Birmingham City Jail" epitomized Black sacred literature and was "a prime candidate for canonization." The Baptist minister and lecturer explained, "The sacred letter or epistle is a common Biblical form. Martin Luther King, the Black Christian, writing to the White churches of Birmingham parallels the Apostle Paul, a Jewish Christian, writing to the Roman churches."[44] The reflective and critical interpretive work Stueart is undertaking today at the layperson's level is exactly what Black biblical scholars and Christian theologians were doing decades earlier, at the academic level, and are doing still today. Their professional training and faithful commitment to the Christian tradition equip them to wrestle in expert fashion with the question of how to recognize and apprehend God's revelation in the Bible and in the world.

By now, many Black Christian scholars have also taken up the subjects of patriarchal marriage and gender roles for husbands and wives, yielding tremendous resources to help Christians discern God's revelation and distinguish it from cultural structures that facilitate subjugating hierarchical relations in the marital union and the human family. Reputable scholars, commentaries, and biblical and theological scholarship are increasingly accessible in our digital culture, and Black Christians should be placing them in conversation with their favorite preachers and mentors. Unfortunately, the academic world of biblical scholarship and the ecclesial world of biblical preaching do not intersect as often as they should, leaving many parishioners at a loss for where to begin if they want to access the research and knowledge of biblical experts.[45] Contrary to what some have been taught to believe, faith and scholarly inquiry are not incompatible, and through archaeological, historical, textual, literary, philological, and other methods of critical study, biblical scholars have uncovered extensive information about the complex cultural universes in which the peoples of the Bible lived out their dynamic faiths.

I should say that I privilege Christianity in this discussion because 79 percent of African Americans identified as Christian in 2014 and roughly seven out of ten Black Christians identified as Protestant. Moreover, 54 percent of Blacks read the Bible at least once per week outside of church settings, while only 24 percent reported seldom or never reading the Bible.[46] However, Black Americans do practice other faiths, including Islam, Buddhism, African heritage, and neo-African religions such as Yoruba-Ifa and Ausar Auset, Hebraic traditions, and a host of other religious expressions. The number of religiously unaffiliated African Americans also grew from 12 percent in 2007 to 18 percent in 2014.[47] Learning from other religious traditions that have edified Black populations can also enhance a national conversation about patriarchal marriage and religious values across the entire Black community.

When scholars surveyed nearly 350 Black adults in northeastern Ohio and western Pennsylvania to inquire about their criteria for marriage, they discovered that "both African American men and women seek well-educated, financially stable, monogamous, and affluent partners who are spiritual, religious, self-confident, and reliable."[48] If this admittedly small sample is any indication of the national importance of religion and spirituality to Black couples, there is a high probability that religiously inspired patriarchal values are actually diminishing the quality of married and family life that Black wives, husbands, and children actually seek. The financial strain that most Black families experience across poor, working, and middle classes makes the patriarchal marriage ideal untenable and a likely culprit in the removal of decent and respectable men from the Black marriage market. In 2016 the median net wealth of Black families (approximately $17,000) paled in comparison to White families ($171,000). Thus, for every dollar a white family possesses in wealth a black family has only a dime.[49]

A 2013 study that surveyed 33 Black men revealed that 32 viewed marriage as a stabilizing force and affirmed "increasing marriage rates among African Americans as a worthwhile goal." Of this number, 26 lamented the fact that "too many African American families are missing strong fathers serving as the heads of their households."[50] The state of Black marriage today and the studies discussed earlier invite us to query whether "too many African American families are missing strong fathers" *because* Black men are expected to "[serve] as the heads of their households," often with inadequate resources for this burdensome role.

I recommend abandoning this futile and divisive Euro-Western "head of household" title altogether, if not legally then at least culturally. Instead of normalizing the patriarchal "head of household" role that most Americans tend to take for granted, Black families should consider privileging opportunities to nurture the health and wellness of the entire kinship structure through the sharing of adult responsibilities and prerogatives. Furthermore, in a nation that has impoverished Black men systemically and trampled on their sense of masculinity and preparedness for responsible fatherhood, the best way to address the dilemma of absent "strong fathers" is through aggressive structural programs designed to move Black men out of poverty and build inheritable wealth for their posterity.

SINGLE BLACK MOTHERS: SCAPEGOATS FOR THE FAILURES OF PATRIARCHAL MARRIAGE

In recent decades, demographic data have indicated high national rates of Black single-parent homes. In 2017, 69 percent of Black babies were born to unmarried women, and 65 percent of Black children were being raised by one parent.[51] Since most Black children residing in single-parent homes are being raised by their mothers, fervent discussions about responsible Black fathers have unfolded, from President Obama's speeches to Sunday-morning sermons. Quite often these discussions are premised upon patriarchal assumptions about masculinity and fatherhood. As a result, the urgency with which some Black men (and women) advocate for patriarchal fatherly presence in the home has served to reinforce stereotypes that pathologize Black mothers. A common criticism is that Black mothers cannot raise Black sons to be men, often a veiled jab at minoritized masculine sexual identities and Black women's "poor" parenting skills.[52]

In her *New York Times* opinion piece "A 'Daddy-Daughter Date,' Queer Single Mom-Style," Asha French criticizes the social pressure single mothers bear of having to secure daddies for their children and carrying excessive guilt if they don't. Using her own life choices as an example, French explains that some single Black mothers purposefully enter motherhood alone and admits, "I sometimes find myself hypermotivated to give [my daughter] everything children with 'normal' two-parent families have, including braces and a mortgaged home and a dinner date to a place where the staff treats kids like royalty." But French goes to the heart of the issue, naming the special pain that single Black mothers feel when they compare their unenviable lives with the romanticized images of daddy-daughter dates in our national culture and consciousness. Thinking about her own immediate matrifocal family, French writes, "What hurts us . . . is the social and emotional toll of scholars and pundits suggesting, as they have for generations, that our very family unit—a black mother, a black daughter and no one to ring the doorbell with a suit jacket on—is a liability and the cause of any difficulties we may experience."[53]

French's intervention provides an opportunity to reiterate a larger point of this book—that not only should Black love and Black marriage *not* be patriarchal, but they don't even need to be heteronormative.[54]

By now, I hope readers are convinced that single Black mothers who want to be married are *not* the problem, nor will husbands solve all their problems. Rather, single Black mothers who want to be partnered or married are victim-survivors of systemic forces far more powerful than their deepest desires for enduring romantic relationships. For heterosexual Black women, including single mothers who *want* and *deserve* romantic partner love and marriage with Black men, they should not have to accommodate the systemic and structural barriers that prevent them from even finding Black male significant others, let alone spouses.[55]

Human beings, including Black women, were not designed to endure loneliness and isolation. The common assertion that we are social animals is trite but *true*. Social exclusion and the lack of meaningful connections with others, including partner love and companionship, can cause "a serious problem that has deep roots in [our] biology as well as [our] social environment." Human displeasure with loneliness is founded in a "genetic predisposition" to sociality and a "high sensitivity to feeling the absence of connection." When deprived of meaningful connections with others, our perceptions and behaviors can become distorted, leading to negative, even dire, consequences for our holistic health.[56]

The answer for single Black women in search of love and partnership with Black men does not lie in normalizing singlehood and life without intimacy and meaningful connection to a partner. And it certainly doesn't lie in scapegoating Black women for the sins of a patriarchal, misogynoir society. Those who care about Black women and Black love should refuse this arrangement with the same force with which many have refused slavery, lynching, disenfranchisement, segregation, redlining, underresourced schools for Black children, disparities in health care, racial profiling, mass incarceration, and all other civil and human rights violations Black people have suffered in this nation. Creating the conditions for quality Black marriages is a social good that benefits the nation overall.

Interracial Relationships

With unprecedented numbers of Black women missing out on not just Black love but love period, some recommend that Black heterosexual women date outside the race. Citing the well-known fact that Black women outnumber Black men nationally and also in terms of educational attainment,[57] they advise Black women in search of love and marriage to cast their dating nets widely and to include men of other racial and ethnic heritages. Doing so gives Black women a broader range of options and lessens the chances of them lowering their standards when they can't find Black men who are financially stable or who have comparable levels of educational and professional attainment. For example, Ralph Banks proposes that "if more black women married nonblack men, more black men and women might marry each other." Banks explains further this closing recommendation in his book *Is Marriage for White People?* "If black women don't marry because they have too few options, and some black men because they have too many, then black women, by opening themselves to interracial marriage, could address both problems at once. For black women, interracial marriage doesn't abandon the race," Banks contends, "it serves the race."[58]

Others explore the world of interracial dating and marriage through in-depth interviews with Black women who have pursued love across racial borders. In her 2018 text, *Interracial Relationships Between Black Women and White Men*, sociology professor Cheryl Judice presents vignettes of Black women who are dating, married to, or divorced from White men. Judice conducted sixty interviews to offer firsthand, "thought-provoking insights on the lives of those willing to cross the racial divide in pursuit of personal happiness."[59] Advancing the personal fulfillment of Black women motivated her to write the book after hearing so many young Black women complain about their nonexistent dating lives and after witnessing so many of her friends' and acquaintances' Black sons get married and Black daughters remain single. "It is my hope," Judice conveyed in a 2019 interview with PBS Chicago,

> that presenting their stories will cause more black women to intentionally seek to broaden their idea of suitable dating and marriage partners. This book is not intended to diminish black males—only to present another dating and marriage option for black women who wish to get married and who recognize that the continuing numerical imbalance between black men and black women in this country reduces the likelihood of marrying within their racial/ethnic group.[60]

In another interview, Judice reported that since the publication of her book, several of her Black women readers actually changed their online-dating profile preferences, one who spent her entire twenties waiting for a Black man who "never materialized" had begun to date a White man, and another had begun to date a "Hispanic man."[61]

This scholarly conversation about Black women and interracial dating and marriage is attended by the recurring buzz of gossip that echoes across Black social media whenever high-profile celebrities such as Serena Williams or politicians such as Kamala Harris marry White men. Do such pledges of love to White men signal a turn in Black women's marital partnering aspirations? Should Black women remain "loyal" to the idea of marrying Black men and Black family formation even if it means they may never marry or will marry closer to or during their postmenopausal years? When Issa Rae suggested in jest that Black women should start dating Asian men since they were both the least likely to be selected for dates via online-dating sites, Black women and men lambasted her for her remarks. Black men were especially vile and rude in scorning her body and face even several years after she published her comments in *The Misadventures of Awkward Black Girl.*[62]

As raucous and emotional as the debates surrounding interracial dating can be on social media, I seek to contribute to the conversation from a different vantage point. While personal happiness and emotional health can be deeply impacted by extensive periods with no emotional or sexual intimacy with a romantic partner, I approach the crisis of Black women and Black love with a view toward attacking the causes rather than the outcomes of the crisis. When I listened to Judice explaining why she wrote her book, I felt that she had taken the words concerning my own journey with this book out of my mouth. For my entire adult life, I have heard similar stories and witnessed my own share of Black women with no one to love. When I was completing my doctoral degree, one of my Black female friends, then pursuing a PhD in clinical psychology, told me she was emotionally exhausted from living a life without any Black male company. Forget the fact that she was not partnered. She just wanted Black male energy and presence in her life in some way. She told me that she could go an entire week, even several weeks, without having a substantive conversation with a Black man who was not her brother.

Each time I discuss this topic with friends, they respond with dozens of parallel stories. The situation is serious, and I respect the position of those who want to stop the bleeding right now for Black women who desire and deserve to fall in love and get married. However, what should we do about the structural forces that have created a population disparity between Black women and Black men as early as their teenage years?[63] Should we not attempt to curtail the intersecting injustices—inherited poverty and wealthlessness, domestic White terrorism, misogynoir and misandrynoir laws and policies, calculated and strategic disappearance, colorism and phenotypic stratification, mass incarceration—that have directly and indirectly punished Black love and marriage for centuries in this nation? It is a daunting prospect to take on the machinery behind America's history of forbidden Black love, but do we really have a choice? And isn't it our moral and social responsibility to change the landscape of love for Black women and Black men in a democratic nation whose citizens profess "to establish Justice, insure domestic Tranquility, provide for the common defence [sic], promote the general Welfare, and secure the Blessings of Liberty to ourselves and our Posterity?"[64]

Black women do not suffer alone through this crisis. Black men and Black children suffer directly with them from the loss of familial support and parental presence and guidance, wealth and financial stability, affirming and healthy conceptions of Black beauty and value, and much more. But in addition to African American individuals, families, and communities, our nation suffers too from its destruction of human talent and resources, fiscally and socially absorbing cycles of inherited poverty and wealthlessness, antisocial attempts to survive systemic oppression, overpolicing, incarceration, and the physical and mental health consequences of the burden of literally four hundred years (1619–2019) of what some scholars actually brand as "racial capitalism."[65] The weight of this kind of use and abuse of people of African descent and the wasting away of their right to healthy love and marriage take a toll on our entire American society.

Admittedly, encouraging Black women to date White men and men of other racial-ethnic heritages does expand their pool of available men. But this advice will go only so far if we don't address colorism and phenotypic stratification as well as misogynoir in American culture and consciousness, ideologies that have painted Black women in the most undesirable light in the minds of many non-Black men. If too many Black men don't value and desire Black women with dark complexions, there are likely to be many more White, Asian, and non-Black Latino men who feel similarly.

The collective conscious and unconscious memory of Black women's sexual trauma at the hands of White men during and after slavery, and White men's exoticization of, disrespect for, and cultural distance from Black women—to say nothing of the fact that Black women are the least likely to be selected by men of *any* race at online dating websites—expose some powerful internal and external deterrents to interracial dating and marriage between Black women and White men.[66] A 2009 study involving 134 White male respondents to in-depth questionnaires exposed the trenchant emotions and perceptions influencing "white men's consistent exclusion of black women as relationship partners." Respondents resided in thirty-eight states from all regions of the country, and while 34 percent reported short-term dating relationships, 30 percent reported sexual relationships, and 14 percent reported long-term relationships with Black women, none reported long-term dating leading to marriage with a Black woman.[67]

Ranging in age from eighteen to over fifty, respondents, nearly half of whom were middle class, disclosed disturbing perceptions, emotions, and desires. "Many . . . perceived black women as unattractive unless capable of a white normative standard, as possessing a negative 'black' culture, and as possessing negative and 'unfeminine' attributes that make them complicit in their own rejection."[68] White men with little to no meaningful contact with Black women revealed deeply embedded negative, even vulgar, views of Black women involving "elements of animalism, disease," and sensorial displeasure. They often described Black women as loud, violent, abusive, and obnoxious. In addition, respondents' views of Black women's bodies could seesaw from the exotica end to the pathologizing end of the scale of attraction versus repulsion. For example, Drake confessed, "I am sexually attracted to most all women, but black women have a certain 'exotic' look to them, and I like that. Specifically, I really love black women with bubble butts and nice legs, and who are fit." Reginald, a White man with no Black female friends and no connections to Black people "aside from having sex with a black prostitute," characterized most black women as "unattractive" and displayed no delicacy in sharing graphic details of the sexual fantasies he wanted to fulfill with a Black woman: "I like the thought of having a black woman with bigger lips for oral sex," Reginald confessed. "I like the thought of having anal sex with a black woman with a big round butt but she should not be too heavy. I would like [to] give oral sex to a black woman with clear not too blotchy skin." Another respondent, Tyler, expressed his unadulterated superiority over Black women and even assessed the Black woman as "not even good enough for a Black man." Despite his low opinion of Black women, Tyler disclosed his sexual involvement with two Black women for their "darker skin and sexual appetites."[69]

I presume many White men will not recognize themselves in some of these remarks. However, the study's author attributes the disparaging narratives and views White men disclosed about Black women to "deep frames" that typify their identities; engage the senses, emotions, and cognition; and operate unconsciously and automatically. Coined by cognitive and linguistic scholar George Lakoff, "deep frames" is a term that refers to people's fundamental worldviews. Many well-meaning persons, including some White men, might be unaware of how those frames are culturally constructed over time, internalized, and unknowingly triggered.[70]

Undoubtedly, Black women have found love and satisfaction with White men and men of other racial-ethnic heritages.[71] Some, like Christelyn Karazin, have even devoted their lives to helping other Black women "swirl" through the terrain of interracial and interethnic dating. Karazin's experience with love, motherhood, and marriage reflects a journey that straddles several themes discussed in this chapter. In 2010 she launched the "No Wedding No Womb" movement to urge women to make marriage a condition for having children. Some have misunderstood Karazin's campaign as focused on proscribing premarital sex, but she clarified that hers is a proactive movement "advocating the use of what's available in terms of birth control." Karazin was raised by both of her parents, who were married for forty-five years when her father passed away. While she valued and desired marriage, she quickly learned when she became pregnant at twenty-four while in college that her Black boyfriend did not share her views. Although he was a churchgoing, college-educated man with no children and no history of imprisonment, Karazin's assumption that they would simply tie the knot given their discussions about marriage prior to her pregnancy was quickly put to rest. Her boyfriend reportedly told her, "Just because you're having my baby doesn't mean I have to marry you." Karazin explains that he came from a family background where his parents never married and his half-brother is nine months his junior.

Karazin describes the daughter her college relationship produced as having "a nice life," but explains that "there is a part of her that suffers because she is not living in the same household as her father."[72] Karazin went on to marry a White man and have three additional children with him. As an active blogger, author, and YouTuber, she utilizes multiple venues to address the topic of interethnic and interracial relationships and share her experience of deep marital satisfaction and family fulfillment with unlimited audiences.[73]

With more visible publications and personalities exploring the subject of interracial dating with Black female audiences, more Black women will likely transgress cultural prohibitions and date a wider pool of racially and ethnically diverse men. But what about the millions of Black women who will never be selected for dates or marriage by non-Black men? And what about the Black women profoundly inspired by Michelle Obama's Black love story—those who find it important to provide healthy models of Black romantic love, marriage, and family in an anti-Black country? What word of encouragement do we have for Black women who anticipated in every fiber of their bodies the moment in that *Being Mary Jane* episode—you know the one—when Gabrielle Union in the character of Mary Jane Paul finally breaks down and tells her White male romantic experiment, Eddie, "I like Black men. I want Black love"?[74]

BLACK MEN WANT AND DESERVE BLACK LOVE TOO

Assumptions about the shortage of "marriageable" Black men prevail today given the paucity of research on Black men's actual perceptions of and attitudes toward marriage. Preliminary studies, however, have yielded useful clarifications as well as complicated and multifaceted explanations for the low rates of marriage among African Americans. One obvious fact that discussions such as this sometimes lose sight of is that there *are* Black men to love and there *are* Black men who want Black love too. After conducting in-depth interviews with thirty-three African American men residing in the Louisville, Kentucky, metropolitan area, researchers found that most of the participants "desire to be married and can articulate the benefits they derive from it."[75] Despite class and age differences, most men in the study associated marriage with "partnership and commitment." When asked to elaborate more on his conception of marriage as a partnership, thirty-five-year-old Peter, who is married with two children, responded:

> You know when you get married . . . you're taking on someone else's beliefs, you're taking on their family, you're taking on their habits, whether they're good or bad, and you have to mingle that with your situation because you become one. The old me died when I got married and that doesn't mean that the old me was a bad person, but I couldn't continue with the same lifestyle, mentality, everything when I got married. The same thing [goes]

for my wife. You know we entered into a new partnership, a new thing; it's a whole new ball game.[76]

Nick, a forty-three-year-old single father of two, also offered the following response:

More so from a personal perspective, [marriage is] about having a partner, someone that I can depend on and help me make it through life and other social things. . . . [Marriage is also about] support for one another. I'll say in all ways whether it's mentally, spiritually, physically, emotionally.[77]

The authors of the study report that participants repeatedly mentioned the importance of strong and healthy Black family formation and its necessity for building and empowering Black communities. For example, forty-seven-year-old Thomas discussed how marriage is "foundational to building strong families, and when children are growing up in our communities and they see strong marriages, they can gain confidence and experience first-hand that marriage is worthwhile and that it can be an achievable goal or reality."[78] A much younger participant, twenty-one-year-old Rex, concurred, declaring:

Wow! I definitely feel like it is a worthwhile goal, just seeing the state of the Black family right now. Stability is a big thing and if we can't have stable households, now I'm not saying that we're having all unstable households now, I'm just saying that it would be good if we could get more families married for the kids in our communities, so I definitely say it's a worthwhile goal.[79]

Seven of the thirty-three men felt so strongly about creating conditions for quality marriages in Black communities that they answered affirmatively when asked if the government should play an active role in supporting African American marriages. Their rationale echoes some of the themes pursued in earlier chapters of this book: the government had played a divisive role in pushing Black men out of their homes through disruptive public assistance policies and other structural injustices. Christian identity and biblical teachings were powerful sources of several participants' beliefs and attitudes, as they connected their views of marriage with religion and specifically Christian biblical texts that inspire their values pertaining to marriage and family life. Chad, a married fifty-year-old father with three children, spoke to those values even when answering a question about what characteristics distinguished his wife from other women:

> Well, I think just how she was able to articulate to me who she was and how she shared some of my values when it comes to children and relationships and a walk with Christ. And also, when I think about my wife, she does so much . . . she does so much in helping me with my walk. She demands . . . and when I say she demands, I'm talking about how she does it by the way she walks, her lifestyle, demands that I give her respect. I think if I can give an example from my first marriage, I didn't have that. . . . you know, I grew up without a father and what I lacked was the guidance to know how to treat a woman so I made a lot of mistakes. And growing up in a large family, I was always one who enjoyed relationships and what they were about and having someone around, so there was no doubt that once I was divorced, I knew I would get remarried. And so when I met my wife, she was that person who helped me be who I wanted to be just by her lifestyle and just her walk with Christ.[80]

Round Three: Partnership, Not Patriarchy

While some participants in the study associated marriage with religious values, none attributed fulfilling and enduring marriages to patriarchal values and gender roles, perhaps a hopeful indication that there is space to seriously rethink the patriarchal marriage ideal in the African American community today.[81] In so doing, even our Black centenarian couples, whose marriages were sealed during periods when patriarchal marriage and traditional gender roles were taken for granted, will have much to contribute. In a 2015 interview, reporter Courtney Spradlin captured more details about the inner workings of Lawrence and Varrie Player's shared married life, the same couple whose story features in this chapter's preliminary pages. Responding to his interlocutor's query, Lawrence Player made it clear that the secret to a long and satisfying marriage is loyalty, communication, and cooperation. "All you have to do," he remarked, "is be loyal toward each other. Make sure you agree on the things you are doing. Be loyal, and when you plan to do or build something, both need to come along in agreement." Varrie concurred, describing a peaceful existence with her husband across nearly a century of marriage.[82]

I find these reflections telling for a couple that married in 1935 and apparently maintained a traditional marriage in which Varrie assumed domestic responsibilities. According to Spradlin, "Lawrence said he told Varrie before they were married that if she cooked his lunch and kept his clothes clean, 'that's all she has to do. And that's what she done.'" The couple's daughter, Barbara Player, indicated that her mother didn't just prepare lunches. She cooked three meals per day for her husband. "And I mean cook," Barbara emphasized. "She doesn't open a can of something. She cooks—even makes homemade biscuits." But biscuits and ironed clothes for a Black patriarch who brings home a paycheck and handles the finances are not what surfaced when Spradlin asked the perennial question of the enduring lovers. The Players discussed qualities and experiences that are cherished in romantic love but also in other kinds of relationships. And these qualities—communication, cooperation, loyalty, peacefulness, and kindness—also surface in scholarly studies of healthy and enduring marriages.[83] Simply put, in the words of daughter Barbara

Player, "I learned from them how to love. They taught us we need to treat people like we want them to treat us."

Patriarchy is not the secret sauce of long, healthy marriages no matter how much Black couples may strive to achieve this Euro-American familial model of the breadwinner husband and the caregiver wife. In a 2017 Pew Research Center survey of 4,971 adults, 84 percent of Blacks (compared to 67 percent of Whites) said it was "very important for a man" to be "able to financially support a family when it comes to being a good spouse or partner."[84] If black husbands can't perform their patriarchal role because of inherited poverty and wealthlessness, how does it affect their sense of manhood, their wives' and children's perceptions of them, and their overall marriages and family lives?[85] And how many wives have submitted themselves to abuse and toxicity at the hands of their patriarchal spouses because they have accepted subtle and overt cultural messages to mind their place and preserve their marriages at any cost?

Too many, according to Tamara Harris. "American society," she contends, "has conditioned us for 'traditional' heterosexual matrimony sustained by domination and female pain." Harris quotes actual scripts that women have been fed to shrink themselves, curtail their ambitions, or mold their bodies for the superficial life of the trophy wife: *"No man will love you unless you lose weight. It's almost impossible for smart women to get married because men are too intimidated by them. Having an opinion on everything isn't ladylike."* She confesses to being most disturbed, however, by the piece of advice a successful Black female writer received from her grandmother when she was just a teenager: *"Your husband will beat you because you talk too much."* Harris maintains that "Black women are particularly vulnerable to this emotional terrorism and our communities are aggressively devoted to dispensing it." Her solution is to abandon traditional marriage and instruct Black girls and women to redefine marriage altogether. Instead of the word "traditional" affixed to marriage, Harris introduces modifiers that affirm and nurture. She welcomes nothing less than "liberating," "supportive," "fun," and "sustaining" marriages for Black women.[86]

When discussing the quality of Black marriages, Black women *and* Black men must own the conversation about patriarchy. Therefore, it is important to acknowledge that Black men also need nothing less than liberating, supportive, fun, and sustaining marital unions. To achieve these ends, they have to escape the plantations of patriarchy that hold them captive. As more Black men enjoy the rewards of marital partnership and discover modes of healthy Black masculinity in the process, it is imperative that they share their experiences with Black boys, adolescents, and peers. Black men have a unique role to play in emancipating Black communities from the stranglehold of patriarchal marriage and family formation. Establishing Black marriage and kinship as institutional spaces of partnership and shared responsibilities/privileges for Black mothers, fathers, spouses, and children involves empowering Black men who defy patriarchy to speak candidly and courageously about their experiences.

Black communities must open the floor for Black men to reflect on their experiences as both perpetrators and victims of patriarchal abuse and their journeys toward a new inhabitance of manhood, of humanhood, that supports healthy love, marriage, and kinship structures.[87] Toward this end, wider institutional investment in the promotion of partnership over patriarchy in Black marriages and families can enhance the resources available for sustained transformation. And with purposeful preparation and commitment, Black churches can position themselves to play a vital role. According to the National Healthy Marriage Resource Center, "79% [of] African American married mothers and 68% [of] African American unmarried mothers reported being interested in a religious relationship program," yet only 3 percent of Black churches in America offer marriage and parenting programs.[88] As the Black community continues to grapple with the state of Black love and marriage, assembling well-vetted teams of clergy, theological and biblical scholars,

gender and sexuality scholars, social scientists, clinicians, and therapists to devise criteria and templates for religious relationship programs that Black churches can implement nationwide is a critical
next step in addressing this country's most camouflaged civil rights
issue since the slave period.

THE PROSOCIAL IMPACT OF AFRICANA KINSHIP STRUCTURES

Patriarchy situates a man as the head of his household and distrib-
utes his power in nuclear fashion over his wife and children, who
are submissive to him. This antivillage family arrangement has been
seared into many Black people's perceptions as the ideal marital aspiration. However, truth be told, aspects of extended African family
systems are still features of African American family life today. The
protracted debate about whether the so-called pathological patterns
shaping African American family life derived from the destructive
practice of racial slavery or from Black people's African cultural
background (also categorically and incorrectly perceived as destructive) has long missed the point.[89] In reality, an African heritage with
imperfect yet richly resourced and flexible marriage and family systems has left some imprint upon African American life that, ironically, the injurious institution of slavery perpetuated as well.[90]

Slavery actually did make necessary the matrifocal unit, a stabilizing and healthy African institution. Slavery also created the
conditions for what many scholars have called "fictive" extended
families. I prefer to simply call them African heritage or Africana
kinship arrangements and family structures that allowed African
captives and their descendants in the Americas to retain their sense
of purpose, family, and community and to express sociality in anti-
Black, anti-African, and antisocial environments. Within Africana
kinship networks there is no concept of the "single mother" because
the mother-child (matrifocal) unit is embedded within a social web
of the most intimate human bonds that make up a large family system of support, the kind of support that Chicago migrant Ruby

Daniels profited from in her Black cultural world of the Mississippi Delta. Even when marriage failed, family seemed eternally faithful in Ruby's estimation. Reflecting on her life, an elder Ruby had witnessed only one happy and stable marriage—that of her aunt Addie Green, who herself had to divorce twice before stumbling into a good relationship worthy at last of the ceremonial vows she knew so well.

When Ruby found herself at the front door of her local Chicago welfare office, she had given birth to three children by two different men, and when she received her last welfare check, she had brought four more children into the world with a new man, Luther Haynes, the second man she would marry and also divorce. The South she knew was not home to strong Black marriages, but it had provided a nurturing, reliable kinship network beyond the nuclear family. In *The Promised Land*, Nicholas Lemann describes well Ruby's "kinship wealth," which can easily escape notice when juxtaposed against approved Eurocentric conceptions of family formation. According to Lemann:

> Ruby's feelings about her blood relatives . . . were entirely positive. She loved both her parents, understood their failings, and harbored no resentments against them. Her circle of acquaintances outside her immediate family, especially her aunts, had been a crucial source of support when she was growing up. People with minimal resources of their own had taken her in, as if she were their own daughter, whenever she needed help. Underneath the disorganization that outsiders saw was an extended-family system that had real strength. The network of friends and relatives got one another through the constant round of crises that made up the sharecropper life.[91]

Instead of bemoaning and devaluing the fact that Africana kinship networks continue to organize (rather than disorganize) Black life in

America, especially among the poor and working classes,[92] the time is ripe to explore and exploit the stabilizing features of these kinship arrangements.

Several studies from the 1990s and early 2000s have found that White children of divorced parents have poorer educational outcomes than Black children, and scholars propose that extended family embeddedness and socioeconomic stress are pivotal factors accounting for why Black children are less negatively affected by the consequences of divorce.[93] Adding her 2020 longitudinal study to this body of research, Harvard sociologist Christina Cross drew from data collected between 1985 and 2015 and found that family embeddedness and socioeconomic stress both help explain racial differences in the effects of family structure on children's educational outcomes. To her surprise, socioeconomic stress was more impactful, accounting for nearly 50 percent of the gap in on-time high school completion rates between Black and White children. However, extended family embeddedness still explained 15–20 percent of the gap. As a result, Cross cautions, "If minority children are less vulnerable to the adverse effects of parental separation than white children, then valorizing the two-biological-parent family over other family forms is unwarranted and may prove to be unfruitful in reducing racial/ethnic disparities in child outcomes."[94]

With additional research, we can gain further insight into the prosocial salience of Africana family structures in the educational outcomes of Black children and the sense of support and well-being such extended kinship networks provide their members. However, to shift the landscape of Black love and marriage in America, kinship wealth must be paired with financial wealth. The only effective way to do this is through deliberate structural interventions aimed at dismantling inherited poverty and wealthlessness among African Americans. Black wealthlessness is so widespread that it can be more tempting to throw our hands up in despair rather than seek viable solutions. But policy recommendations are within our reach. Those invested in supporting healthy Black love and marriage should not leave it to politicians and cultural leaders alone to scrutinize and implement structural change and new cultural messaging. We can and should ignite critical conversations by examining proposals that aim at systemic reform.[95]

BUILDING BLACK WEALTH THROUGH BABY BONDS

Inherited poverty and wealthlessness are staples of African American life so much so that "the financial advantages that come with marriage, like having two earners, qualifying for tax breaks for dependents, and the ability to share expenses, are insufficient to close the racial wealth gap."[96] Even though married couples' dual-income households are expected to generate close to four times the wealth of a single-income household over the course of a lifetime, the combined wealth that Black marriages produce is nothing to speak of when compared with the wealth White single-income households generate. To add to this, Dorothy Brown's pioneering research has shown how "federal tax laws that hurt dual-income married couples disproportionately hurt African-American households."[97]

Bold solutions are needed to address this structural bleeding of Black finances and the systemic racism that reproduces Black poverty and wealthlessness in this nation with special consideration of the peculiar misogynoir *and* misandrynoir circumstances that render Black women and men financially vulnerable and immobile for different reasons. We need to cultivate a new national affect regarding Black love and marriage—one that never forgets Zora Neale Hurston's vernacular theorization, that the Black woman is "de mule uh de world," and one that simultaneously creates what Alisha Gaines calls "empathy plus" for Black males and their structural alienation from gainful employment as well as wealth-building resources and opportunities.[98] The lives visited throughout this book illustrate how the trap of patriarchal manhood has been weaponized against Black men, from the lynching of Reverend Simmons in 1944 Mississippi to the garnished wages of single-father Zion in 2019 New York City. I feel compelled to reinforce this point because our nation reserves a special callousness for Black men that remains dangerously unacknowledged.[99]

The systemic sources of Black men's alienation from their own wealth-building potential can hardly be denied. Yet this nation continues to place emphasis on the antisocial measures Black men take to surmount their alienation. In "The Inheritance of Black Poverty: It's All About the Men," Scott Winship, Richard Reeves, and Katherine Guyot make a monumental claim that identifies a starting point for structural change strategies aimed at promoting Black love and marriage. "Breaking the cycle of intergenerational poverty for black Americans," they contend, "requires a transformation in the economic outcomes for black men, particularly in terms of earnings." Their accessible report elucidates a larger 2018 study, "Race and Economic Opportunity in the United Sates: An Intergenerational Perspective," and presents complementary statistical analyses that "confirm the stark differences in upward earnings mobility for black men compared to both black women and whites."[100]

In the end, however, *it's all about what America has done to the men . . . and the women.* Black women, in fact, are most economically fragile relative to Black men and Whites when considering their mobility in the context of adult family income.[101] Black men and women's inherited wealthlessness and economic immobility warrant deeper theorization and structural innovation to understand and overcome it. But I want to linger on Black males' economic fragility for a moment because, as I noted earlier, it apparently encourages Black men who *are* marriageable to remove themselves from the marriage market.

The explanatory work that theorists of "racial capitalism" have been doing provides one of the most comprehensive frameworks for understanding the roots and development of Black men's enduring financial imprisonment. In America predatory capital accumulation has required "loss, disposability, and the unequal differentiation of human value," and "racism enshrines the inequalities that capitalism requires. . . . by displacing the uneven life chances that are inescapably part of capitalist social relations onto fictions of differing human capacities, historically race."[102]

In the US context, the intersectionality of race, class, and gender and the unique threat that Black masculinity has always posed to White imperial (and patriarchal) power make Black men specially targeted victims of racial capitalism today (for example, mass incarceration) and lower the national rate and quality of Black marriage. At the same time, a report by the conservative think tank Institute for Family Studies reveals that marriage is among "the three major factors that are linked to the financial success of black men in midlife today." The other two factors are "a college degree and a full-time job."[103] For millions of Black men, none of these three achievements is an easy feat. However, a proposal that has been receiving increasing attention in public outlets could spark an economic sea change for Black men, women, and children in the presumable near future.

Economist Darrick Hamilton is the architect of "Baby Bonds," or, more accurately, "Baby Trust," a wealth-generating policy-based initiative grounded in the values of economic rights. First advanced in America during the 1940s under Franklin Delano Roosevelt's administration, the concept of economic rights lost ground beginning with the Nixon administration and the emergence of neoliberalism. Hamilton envisions "Baby Bonds" as a structured federal government program that would provide seed capital for every newborn infant in America on a wealth-based rather than income-based sliding scale. If implemented, Baby Bonds would ensure a more equitable distribution of the nation's wealth over time since children born to the wealthiest families would receive nominal accounts as low as $500 and poor children (many of whom are Black) would receive much larger trust fund investments into the tens of thousands. In fact, the plan is based upon precise calculations that commit the federal government to providing the poorest American children between $25,000 and $60,000 that they can access and use to develop more wealth as adults.

Baby Bonds would be organized as federally managed trust accounts with an expected annual growth of roughly 2.5 percent interest. To finance a federal Baby Bonds program in America, Hamilton proposes innovations and modifications in our current tax policies, which "privilege existing wealth" over "establishing new wealth." Recognizing that "when it comes to economic security, wealth is both the beginning and the end," he conveys better than any the necessary value of wealth building in an American and global society deeply impacted by the growing divide between the rich and the poor: "Wealthier families are better positioned to finance an elite independent school and college education; access capital to start a business; finance expensive medical procedures; reside in neighborhoods with higher amenities; exert political influence through campaign finance; purchase better legal counsel if confronted with an expensive criminal justice system; leave a bequest; and or withstand financial hardships resulting from any number of emergencies."

Wealth is the stabilizing force for achieving and sustaining personal, familial, and social wellness and sufficiency. Therefore, when Baby Bonds recipients become adults, they can draw from their investments "for some asset enhancing activity like financing a debt free university education, a downpayment to purchase a home, or some seed capital to start a business."[104] With Baby Bonds capital awaiting Black men, marriage might soon be one of the assets increasing numbers of them will be able to secure at earlier stages of life and sustain both financially and emotionally into their twilight years. Certainly, adult Black female Baby Bond recipients who want to marry Black men would find themselves in more advantageous financial positions to marry, for the long term, men of comparable socioeconomic status before the onset of menopause.

During the 2020 primary election season, Democratic presidential hopeful and New Jersey senator Cory Booker adopted Hamilton's Baby Bonds program as his "Big Idea." When asked by NBC correspondent Harry Smith how he would respond if some Americans say "Baby Bonds" is "just a different word for reparations," Booker had a politically expedient yet true answer: "Well, it goes to every single child." He also affirmed the economic rights platform upon which Baby Bonds was conceived: "We know there['re] differentials in wealth that are inherited from bigoted policies of our past that excluded families from doing the things that created wealth."[105] Booker is correct. Baby Bonds is not a reparations plan. But like never before, the demand for "reparations" now stems from a wide range of constituents across America.

Today's new movement of those calling for economic and wider material and immaterial restitution for the descendants of enslaved Africans in America seems determined to stay in the public eye. Of course, social media is a major ally in spreading the aims of reparations activists and advocates. The reparations question comes up regularly during presidential debates, and most politicians find themselves cornered when queried about their positions on the issue. They usually dodge and deflect rather than address the topic directly. Still, while most presidential hopefuls were dancing around the issue, on June 19, 2019, concurring with Juneteenth,[106] the US Congress held a hearing on the subject of reparations. It had been ten years since the last reparations hearing, and much was made about author and journalist Ta-Nehisi Coates's testimony before Congress, given his widely read 2014 article, "The Case for Reparations."[107] Although chances are slim that the HR 40—"Commission to Study and Develop Reparations Proposals for African-Americans Act," sponsored by Representative Sheila Jackson Lee (D-TX), will pass the Republican-controlled Senate, the issue will likely not go away anytime soon.

As reparations scholars and activists sharpen their arguments for the debates that lie ahead, the opportunity should not pass to consider our nation's history of forbidden Black love and its costs to Black women, men, and children. In recent decades, reparations proposals have addressed a range of material and immaterial resources, but none that I have seen has addressed directly the delayed and denied windows for childbearing and family building that millions of Black women face every day due to their heavily restricted dating and marriage options. Even with a slight increase in Black women opting to marry men of other racial and ethnic backgrounds (12 percent in 2013), most Black heterosexual women want to marry and have children with *Black* men. They should not have to settle, look outside the race, or lose the opportunity to bear children because of the accumulated effects of structural injustice—including slavery, White racial terror, Jim Crow, substandard education and racist-sexist educational infrastructures, divisive welfare policies, redlining, and mass incarceration.

Reparations proposals and other policies that reflect our nation's preparedness to tackle its history of forbidden Black love with empathy for Black women's particular sufferings must include programs that support Black women's reproductive health and family planning. Reparations reproductive health initiatives might address delayed childbearing and the fertility concerns older Black women face when attempting to become pregnant. They should also account for the historic disproportionate sterilization of Black women in this country and their high rates of premature births, perinatal deaths, and maternal deaths related to childbirth.[108] These steps are necessary to tackle and dismantle forbidden Black love and its consequences for Black women. However, because the Black community lacks a sustained focus on the roots and long-term manifestations of forbidden Black love across four centuries, and because we have neglected to frame Black women's low marriage rates as the civil rights issue that it is, our ability to change the love, marriage, and child-bearing outcomes for Black women is severely hampered.

DISMANTLING COLORISM AND PHENOTYPIC STRATIFICATION

In addition to the obstacles of inherited wealthlessness and poverty and patriarchal marriage, colorism and phenotypic stratification poses a third threat to healthy Black love, marriage, and family formation. While CPS is a global phenomenon impacting populations of color beyond Africa and its diasporas—Asians, Middle Easterners, and others[109]—the darker one's skin and the more stereotypically "African" one's overall phenotype, the lower one is on the CPS stratification scale. Addressing this Goliath of immaterial and material proportions—self-loathing, depression, skin bleaching, and other harmful body modifications—is beyond the scope of this book. Only multipronged initiatives can marshal the resources to adequately confront perhaps the most elusive of all three obstacles tackled in this chapter. But some reflections on a way forward are nevertheless warranted and critically important.

It is abominable and untenable that the world hates dark skin and stereotypic African features, but it's even more egregious that people of African descent have internalized this hatred so deeply. As we have seen, the consequences of CPS for Black love, especially lower rates of marriage for women with medium and dark complexions, are psychologically and physically wounding. However, research has linked CPS to higher rates of punishment for Black children of darker hues, harsher prison sentences for Black people of darker hues, and stratified employment outcomes for light- versus dark-skinned Blacks.[110] All of these patterns directly or indirectly impact the state of Black love and marriage.

What we need in Black America to tackle CPS is an all-out, unapologetic war against this deleterious and degrading ideology. We need a social and cultural movement of proportions analogous to the #MeToo movement, one that will override our current programming of bias and discrimination against those targeted by CPS. This movement might be called #AbolishColorism, or perhaps something else, but whatever we name it, it must be potent enough to shatter the ideological, aesthetic, and cultural standards that feed CPS in every corner of human existence and interaction, in every institutional space—from the family to the church, from the advertising and television industries to schools and universities, from the sports industry to the tourism industry.

All Black persons who promote CPS, especially those determined to welcome a different day for the state of Black love and marriage, must do their part to liberate their spirits, thoughts, tongues, and actions from this psychic poison, so long a lethal concoction bathed over the collective soul life of African descendants in this nation and beyond. While all Black skin tones and phenotypic features have to be valued, if we are to overcome CPS and enhance marriage outcomes for all women, a strategy for doing so has to include what social media influencer Chrissie calls "corrective promotion" of "dark skinned women."[111] There are signs that an anti-CPS movement is on the horizon—its strength and reach slowly building in some spaces across our nation.

I BEGAN THIS CHAPTER ASKING the question "Will Black women ever have it all?" One "Black Girl Magic" phenom who presents and acts as if she fully intends to have it all is Kheris Rogers. The thirteen-year-old entrepreneur launched her clothing line, "Flexin' in My Complexion," when she decided that she would no longer be the target of her classmates' CPS jokes and insults. Since the first grade, fellow students threw lines at a Kheris such as "You've been in the oven too long. You're a dead roach. You're a burned biscuit." Physically assaulted, and abandoned by playmates, Kheris's self-concept was so impacted by these traumatic experiences that, while still in the first grade, she told her older sister she wanted to spend extra time in the bathtub "in hopes that her skin would get lighter."[112]

With support from her maternal family, Kheris soon relieved her trauma with a T-shirt line meant to affirm her patrons with empowering messages about their value and uniqueness. "I was being bullied for my complexion," she explains, "so I wanted to empower others by making my T-shirt line saying 'Flexin' in My Complexion.'" With direct support from her sister turned manager, Taylor Pollard, Kheris sold more than ten thousand shirts during her first year of operation. Her endorsers include decorated actors, screenwriters, and entertainers such as Lupita Nyong'o, Lena Waithe, Alicia Keys, and Snoop Dogg. The young fashionista's inventiveness has also created new paths for her to spread her message and her brand, taking her from her native Los Angeles to New York City as the youngest designer to display her clothing line at the September 2017 New York Fashion Week.

The most important lesson from Kheris's story is the transformative intervention the women in Kheris's family engineered when they rallied behind their legacy to ease her suffering and rehabilitate her self-concept. The support from her maternal lineage was potent enough to disrupt the narratives Kheris was receiving at school. Her grandmother, mother, and sister wrapped what scholars from my academic neighborhood would call their loving "womanist" arms around her injured body and soul and affectionately affirmed her deep Black beauty.[113] In a 2018 interview, CBS correspondent Jamie Yuccas asked Kheris what she sees when she looks in the mirror. Kheris saw exactly what her matrifocal unit—her womanist nation—prepped her to see. "I see Black beauty," she replied. "I see melanin poppin'."[114]

The charm of this young advocate for Black love is already unmistakable. Kheris is as infectious as Michelle Obama, and I want so much to believe that she will one day have love, professional fulfillment, and compensation commensurate to her education and experience and comparable to her White and male counterparts'. I want to believe that if she desires heterosexual union with a Black man in her adult life, she will have dating access to a range of appealing Black men among whom she will find her life mate. And I want most of all to believe that these assets (of love and marriage) will accrue to her early enough to bear children with her husband if they choose to parent natural-born children of their own.

Although the odds are against us, it is not fanciful for Black girls and women to admire and aspire to the quality of love and marriage Michelle Obama experienced before, during, and after her term as first lady. Despite the plastic lives so many celebrities and public figures come to symbolize, Michelle's life is anything but plastic. Her love is not made for television, and her high-profile, enviable marriage discredited Fox News's pathetic attempt to reduce her to "Obama's baby mama."[115] In fact, Michelle transformed the White House into the Black House by establishing its first Africana familial tradition when Michelle's mother, Marian Robinson, moved in with her daughter to help care for her granddaughters. The Africana matrifocal unit made it from the slave quarters to the nation's headquarters, illustrating the African proverb that Hillary Clinton loved to quote but did not actually demonstrate with her own family—"It takes a village to raise a child."[116]

Asked by CNN correspondent Randi Kaye how she felt when she saw Michelle Obama "walk out on that stage in Grant Park, in Chicago" the night her husband declared his victory in the 2008 presidential election, Michaela Angela Davis replied, "She looked like she belonged there. And that's how I felt. I felt like . . . I belong here. And all my ancestors, they belonged here. Everyone that dreamed about her was validated in that moment."

The moment I watched Kheris Rogers walk out on that stage to model her clothing line at the 2017 New York Fashion Week, I too felt like she belongs here. Knowing in my own Black flesh that all her enslaved ancestors, especially her foremothers, had "proclaimed love as their salvation"[117]—had dreamed of her coming, and for some, even her belonging—as I watched her speak with magnetic flair before large audiences, selling her product and her influence, I imagined how generations of enslaved and nominally free Black women had to have yearned for this very hope-child.

Kheris is theirs to claim, their womanish baby girl with the audacity to name the dark, radiant skin she's in "melanin poppin'." No Margaret Garner–type scar creating a permanent runway on her face. No need to be told "Never marry again in slavery." But she knows, nonetheless, that her chances of marrying a Black man with assets suitable for enduring love are as slim as Margaret's were when she crossed the Ohio River more than 160 years ago with her husband, Robert, hoping to secure everlasting freedom.

The Garners' story and the narratives of other figures encountered throughout this volume unveil the terrible truth that, if we don't act now, America's war on African American marriage will likely deny Kheris the fundamental civil right to romantic love and marital coupling as it has so many Black women before her, from slavery to the present day. For Black women, in particular, discerning how to respond to what we often experience as an up-close and personal battle can invite immobilizing feelings of overwhelm and powerlessness. But we must respond knowing that with all the lovelessness and lawlessness that Black girls and women have endured for four centuries in this country, with all the abandonment and exclusion, we keep emerging as paragons of unconditional, tenacious love among our families, local communities, national population, and ourselves. Single and coupled Black women are even discovering new ways of loving and supporting one another and building sisterhood through international travel groups, exercise teams, book clubs, expos, conventions, and other activities that enhance the pleasures of life.[118] These womanist practices of solidarity and hospitality support sociality, heal brokenness, and mitigate the isolation and loneliness Black women can experience during long and even permanent periods of undesired singlehood.

Through practices of love, Black women have fashioned a womanist grammar of belonging, indeed a womanist "love language," that this nation must now learn to speak fluently. As we mobilize with allies who want to see new possibilities for Black women and Black love in America, this is the heritage we must remember and uphold.

Afterword

Being Mary Jane . . . or Not

B lack love seems to be on America's mind. Since the turn of the twenty-first century, a bevy of television series, online blogs, digital stories, and social media conversations have captured the interest of Black women (and others) with themes of Black love, both forbidden and found, that privilege Black women's dilemmas and dreams. From *Soul Food*, *Girlfriends*, and *Being Mary Jane* to *Insecure*, *Queen Sugar*, and *Sistas*, and from the reality TV show *#BlackLove* to the Oprah Winfrey Network's *Black Love* series, Black women across the nation explore nightly the uneven terrains of love, courtship, and marriage with their favorite television personalities who act out roles and emotions they know all too well.

Among these titles, the story line for the television series *Being Mary Jane* (2014–2019) echoed many of the themes explored in this book, and the producers of the finale appeared eager to answer Chapter 5's guiding question: in the end, Mary Jane Paul, a dark-skinned Black woman, does indeed get it all. When her last hope for Black love and marriage terminates their relationship, Mary Jane decides to finally go it alone. She accesses her previously frozen eggs and attempts pregnancy via artificial insemination using donor sperm. The pregnancy takes, and immediately after, her Black beau, Justin, returns to her with a change of heart. Following a few dramatic twists and turns involving a competing suitor, Mary Jane's concealment of her pregnancy from Justin, Justin's second exit after learning about his fiancée's concealed pregnancy, and Mary Jane's premature delivery of a baby boy, the financially secure couple finally settles into a firm commitment to marry and raise Mary Jane's baby boy in a loving two-parent household.

Mary Jane's trajectory parallels many of the realities Black women—even professionally successful upper-class Black women like her—confront today. Had she not frozen her eggs, she might not have been able to deliver a child of her own given her late-stage marriage to Justin. For the forty-year-old Mary Jane, just in the nick of time, everything falls into place. I mean everything—the baby, the suitor, the wedding. Ahhh, the wedding . . . the final scene before Mary Jane disappears from our lives, and Black women can no longer live vicariously through her accumulation of "it all." Closing scenes can make or break a show or film, and this is where *Being Mary Jane* actually does disappoint.

After spending several years illustrating the complexities of Black love and marriage—the shifting landscapes of the Black marriage market, for post–*Sex and the City* generations of Black women—the finale betrays the series's most substantive messages, with Mary Jane's final voice-over monologue, her ultimate awakening. "I realize," she declares, "the only affirmation you need is, 'Let go and let love!' Because the second you get out of your own way and stop orchestrating, it just happens. The moment you stop saying 'me' and—without thinking—[start] saying 'us,' that's the moment you're finally able to allow the love you want . . . in!"[1] At this instant, Mary Jane and her "at last" husband, Justin, are lip-locked and dancing at their wedding reception to Natalie Cole's "This Will Be." And the scene does convey that Black women *can* have it all. Even dark-skinned Black women can have the career, baby, life mate . . . *if* they know the right formula, the proven strategy to follow into the arms of a forever Black man. Thanks to Mary Jane Paul, the secret sauce has been divulged to all the single Black women in America who want what Mary Jane finally gets. Not quite.

In the scene, the family is dancing around the happy couple sur-rounded by wedding guests. As Mary Jane arrives at the point in her monologue of verbalizing the word "us," the camera zooms in on her and Justin escaping to a private sensual kiss. In the middle of the dance floor, crowded with people, the camera shot creates the ambi-ance that makes everyone else disappear for those last moments of her reflection. This is your world, Black women—your world of love, joy, companionship, and fulfillment (the scene suggests), and all you have to do is "allow the love you want in!" As soon as she utters that final preposition, "in," the camera slowly blurs out the scene, and Mary Jane and Justin loosen their lips and applaud the love and commit-ment they have vowed to preserve, ending the story line and the series.

THE LONG HISTORY OF FORBIDDEN Black love that this book has brought to the surface tells a different story of Black women's love outcomes. Only the rare Black woman has experienced love just "happening" the moment she "stopped orchestrating." Only the luckiest of the lucky have wrestled with the dilemma of *allowing* the love she actually *wants* in! There is something to be said about self-help approaches to the personal side of dating, self-improvement, and selecting a desirable partner for love and marriage. I will never deny the importance of the personal dynamics involved when seek-ing and securing good love, and this book is not meant to under-mine the works of others who seek out self-help or provide it. What I do hope to convey is that self-help approaches can unwittingly veil the actual systemic problems that create poor marriage outcomes for Black women. If anything, this book is an intervention meant to complement the best clinical and therapeutic advice on the mar-ket for self-improvement, and improving the quality of the love and marriage couples share.

Unfortunately, Mary Jane Paul, the dark-complexioned Black woman who gets to have the complete package, is a fiction. But all around her, real Black women of every complexion are holding up a mirror to the nation to see itself reflected in their undeserved love defeats. From where Black women stand, the current state of Black love and marital unions renders the problem of the twenty-first century the problem of forbidden Black love. It cannot be trivialized with assertions that Black marriage patterns reflect wider patterns in the American institution of marriage. That they do is true. But many social determinants of the alarming state of Black love and marriage are uniquely connected to Black people's involuntary presence in this nation, a nation that (across centuries of unchecked White terror and systemic racism) has refused to ensure the protection and liberties of its Black citizens, including the liberty of love and marriage. For this reason, the harmful consequences of America's overall diminishing rate of marriage and high rate of divorce for Black women and Black communities are more intense and deeply disproportionate compared to other American women and communities.

Forbidden Black love demands structural interventions and vigilant attention from our nation's most powerful stakeholders and most affected victims. If Americans believe in the founding documents of our republic, in the unalienable right of all Americans to life, liberty, and the pursuit of happiness, and in the civil right of marriage for all American adults, then Americans have a civic responsibility to address the structural causes of this crippling phenomenon.

Supporting Black love is not only an essential step in liberating Black women, men, and children from endless webs of related injustices, it is also a pathway to liberation from centuries of organized hate and apathy. America can learn to love Black people in part by institutionalizing the collective love and humanity Black people have shown this nation through patriotism, protest, prayer, and public vision. Beyond its effects in personal and private affairs,

Black love has performed political and public roles of demanding national repentance, justice, repair, and healing. And Black women know better than any that desired institutional changes are likely to occur once America accepts our long-standing invitation to claim Black love as its salvation.

Acknowledgments

MOTIVATION AND INSPIRATION ARE NOT mutually exclusive. So while the motivation for this book derived from personal and professional experience—my own, my friendships, and encounters with Black women from all walks of life, as well as from scholarly research and teaching on the subject of Black love—the inspiration for this project lies at the center of the love my maternal great-grandparents shared for the short duration of their marriage during the early twentieth century. Their marriage ended when my great-grandfather died in his late thirties. But their love survived his death. My great-grandmother carried their special bond with her to her grave, and its magic lives on in my lineage. The hope behind this book is a toast to Margaret "Mammy" Blissett and Nathaniel "Natty" Brown, and my deepest gratitude goes first to these two ancestors for demonstrating the infectious power of love. Without ever meeting me, they taught me that love satisfies, love saves, and love endures.

Many of the people discussed in this book also lived and died before I was born. I pay homage to them and to all whose stories grace the pages of this book. I pray that I have done justice to their experiences and historical legacies. The encouragement to investigate their lives, to inscribe my ideas about Black love, and to share them with a wider public came first from Carol Anderson, my colleague, friend, "twin sister," and mentor. She insisted I expand what I thought might be an article into a book proposal, and she connected me to critical resources that made this project realizable. I am eternally grateful to her for believing in this book and for the many tweets and articles she sent to me over the past four years, always with the subject heading "Black Love." Her support for this project went beyond initial encouragement, as she supplied a number of references for some of the arguments I undertake in this book. She also put me in phenomenal hands when she introduced me to her ingenious agent, Rob McQuilkin. Rob listened to my thoughts on Black women and Black love and found value in the patterns I identified. I cannot imagine working with a more committed and knowledgeable agent. Rob has been my cheerleader, advocate, and coach—collaborative but always prepared to insert his expertise at the right time.

My editorial and production team at Seal Press provided critical support every step of the way, patiently reviewing drafts and helping me to craft the language that could appeal to a wide audience while honoring the truth and power of the stories this book relays to unveil the long history of forbidden Black love in America. Brandon Proia worked extensively with my earliest drafts, helping me to polish and clarify my prose, and my production editor, Kelly Lenkevich, showed remarkable patience and attentiveness during the final editing phases. Her personable style, approachable demeanor, and excellent communication skills turned what is commonly a tedious process into a gratifying experience. My chief editor, Laura Mazer, not only acquired my project with great enthusiasm and belief in its message, but also shepherded me through the entire writing process. Laura was the dynamic force propelling me from the book proposal to the production stage, and her insightful vision for what this project could be strengthened it significantly. I am also grateful to my editor Brian Distelberg for stepping in during the final stages of the book's production and helping to carry me to the finish line.

A community of supporters, however, helped me to refine my ideas and arguments in a volume whose authority and persuasion rests upon historical contextualization and social scientific analysis. As a scholar of religious studies and African American studies, two multidisciplinary fields, I was aware that receiving feedback and suggestions from historians and social scientists was not negotiable. However, I never imagined how necessary the expertise of colleagues and friends would be for presenting a nuanced and complicated interpretation of historical events and statistical data. I offer my deepest appreciation to Walter Rucker, Alyasah Ali Sewell, Christina Cross, Tracy Rone, Meina Yates-Richard, Didier Gondola, Darrick Hamilton, and Regine Jackson. Terrence Johnson, Stephanie Sears, and Shively Smith, scholars in my own field of religious studies, also provided invaluable feedback and additional resources to support this book's most foundational arguments. I also extend a special thanks to my colleague Nathan McCall for reading drafts of my introduction while on leave and for encouraging me to move forward with this project. Other scholars, especially Daina Ramey Berry, Leslie Alexander, Nikki Taylor, and Trevon Logan, expressed great enthusiasm and provided rare resources for this project. I treasure their generosity, grace, and collegiality.

I owe a tremendous amount to my students, especially those who enrolled in my Black Love courses over the years, and to the graduate teaching assistants who provided instruction for those courses. BaSean Jackson (who inspired me to offer Emory's first Black Love seminar and served as my first teaching assistant), Nicole Morris-Johnson, Timothy Rainey II, Nicole Symmonds, Calvin Taylor, Shari Madkins, Marcelitte Failla, Lahronda Little, and Kimberly Akano have supported my scholarship and teaching and reinforced my commitment to this project.

Several people also contributed significantly to the compilation of source material and data for this project. I could not have written *Black Women, Black Love* without the meticulous research of Timothy Rainey II and Alphonso Saville, my graduate students at the time, and Clara Pérez and McKayla Williams, my undergraduate students at the time. Collectively, they assisted me with primary and secondary sources, permissions, digital resources, and other pertinent information.

I received generous support from Emory University to pursue and complete this project. My colleagues in both the Department of Religion and the Department of African American Studies have championed me throughout, especially my chairs, Gary Laderman, María Carrión, and Carol Anderson. Emory College deans Carla Freeman and Michael Elliott also supported this project through subvention funds and other resources. My senior fellowship at the Bill and Carol Fox Center for Humanistic Inquiry provided resources, space, and time to conduct the research for this book. Emory's Center for Faculty Development and Excellence provided technical support and funding for the book's promotion, and Emory's "Write to Change the World" workshop with the OpEd Project offered invaluable training to support the promotion of the book's message.

Other Emory colleagues also supported my journey to this project, especially Donna Troka, who first approached me with the idea to coteach the fall 2016 Power of Black Self-Love side-car course that received widespread attention across various media outlets. Richelle Reid, law librarian for research services at Emory's MacMillan Law Library, went to great lengths to help me access judicial decisions and other court documents. Toni Avery and La Shanda Perryman, senior staff in the Departments of Religion and African American Studies, respectively, were some of my greatest champions, and I thank them both for all they have done to simplify my professional life and help me access resources for the writing of this book. Angela Mamaril in the Department of African American Studies also deserves special acknowledgment for designing promotional materials and website-development support.

Words cannot express the love I feel for my dedicated group of friends Nneka Otim, Marqquita Copeland, Heather Searles, Sunni Tolbert, and Charlene Hucks, who read the book and posed critical questions that enhanced its message and accessibility.

Karen Marie Mason is one of a kind. Beyond her professional endeavors as an artistic consultant and promoter, she is a genuine seeker of knowledge and celebrator of Black love. I thank her for supporting my work and providing opportunities for me to disseminate my message.

Tracey Hucks heard and uttered "ashé!" to the incipient thoughts that found their way into this book, and she remained a powerful source of encouragement across the long journey toward its completion. My deepest appreciation endures for her cherished friendship and sisterhood love across more than three decades. My other three-decade friend and intellectual sister, Carla Beckford, anticipates the release of *Black Women, Black Love* with choreographed African dance steps. She sees courage in my efforts and told me that Black people need this book and can handle its claims upon our best and worst selves. I thank her for her confidence in this project, and I appreciate her intrepid spirit now more than ever.

As I worked through ideas for this book, conversations with my curious college-age nieces Tatyanna Stewart and Laetitia Babin helped me to appreciate its value for women in their twenties. I hope this book provokes them and other young Black women toward deeper reflection and uncompromising self-love as they mature into young women with hearts open for healthy love and companionship.

To other members of my Africana family, a family as wide as the oceans surrounding us, I thank you for showing me that a sacrificial, protective, and understanding love is the ligature that binds us eternally. At the heart of that love is my spouse and companion, Vital Fouemina—the love force through which I calibrate every day. He has taught me that loving another means respecting and supporting their freedom to be who they must be, a lesson I cherish and have grown to appreciate more profoundly with each passing moment we share.

My final note of gratitude goes to my parents, Ruby Burrowes Stewart and Roydel Stewart. They loved me before anyone else I knew on this earth. Their Black love set me free to be who I must be and to write what I must write.

Notes

Introduction

1. Marriage has been defined and designed differently across cultures and across time, and the diverse marriage rituals and institutions that communities worldwide uphold put into perspective the relative cultural expectations and social functions any given society might invest in marriage. Marital unions become official through religious rites and ceremonies, statutory procedures, or social sanction, and many societies honor multiple marital arrangements. Marriage can occur between two or more people or between people of the same or different sex. It can involve love and romance, or it can be founded upon political allegiances, the bridging of larger family networks, social obligations, or a combination of these and other incentives. Marriage is a long-standing institution in human culture that regulates kin relationships and resources. It has provided cohesion, orientation, and social recognition for parents and children across millennia. In this book, which explores the topic of Black women, Black love, and Black marriage, I am primarily concerned with monogamous marriage among heterosexual couples and the cultural expectation most Americans have that romantic love is seminal to sustaining a satisfying and rewarding married life. *Black Women, Black Love* is not intended to serve as commentary on the validity or moral integrity of nonromantic, nonmonogamous, nonheterosexual, or other marriage systems and marital unions that many human beings find personally meaningful and socially rewarding.

2. According to the American Psychological Association, "In Western cultures, more than 90 percent of people marry by age 50. Healthy marriages are good for couples' mental and physical health. They are also good for children; growing up in a happy home protects children from mental, physical, educational and social problems." www.apa.org/topics/divorce/.

3. By comparison, 43 percent of non-Hispanic White women between the ages of twenty-five and twenty-nine had never married in 2009. Rose M. Kreider and Renee Ellis, "Number, Timing, and Duration of Marriages and Divorces: 2009," US Census Bureau, issued May 2011, www.census.gov /prod/2011pubs/p70-125.pdf. Among the 71 percent of Black women who were unmarried in 2009, 5 percent were separated. For more information on

245

these estimates in comparison with other racial-ethnic groups in America, see the Centers for Disease Control's "Table 2. Marital Status of the Population 15 Years and Over by Sex, for Black Alone or in Combination and White Alone, Not Hispanic" (2009). In 2011, 26 percent of Black women compared to 51 percent of White women were married. See Julissa Cruz, "Marriage: More Than a Century of Change," National Center for Family and Marriage Research, https://www.bgsu.edu/content/dam/BGSU/college-of-arts-and -sciences/NCFMR/documents/FP/FP-13-13.pdf.

4. Pew Research Center, "Race in America: Tracking 50 Years of Demographic Trends," Social and Demographic Trends, August 22, 2013, www .pewsocialtrends.org/2013/08/22/race-demographics/.

5. R. Kelly Raley, Megan Sweeney, and Danielle Wondra, "The Growing Racial and Ethnic Divide in U.S. Marriage Patterns," *Future of Children* 25, no. 2 (2015): 89–109; R. Richard Banks and Su Jin Gatlin, "African American Intimacy: The Racial Gap in Marriage," *Michigan Journal of Race and Law* 11, no. 1 (2005): 115–132, esp. 120–123, https://repository.law.umich .edu/mjrl/vol11/iss1/7.

6. Several studies have shown that Black women's attitudes about the value of marriage and their desire to be married are not substantially different from those of other groups with much higher and more stable marriage rates. See, for example, Jerold Heiss, "Women's Values Regarding Marriage and the Family," in *Black Families*, ed. Harriette McAdoo (Beverly Hills, CA: Sage, 1981), 186–198; Robert Staples, *The World of Black Singles: Changing Patterns of Male/Female Relations* (Westport, CT: Greenwood Press, 1981); Belinda Tucker and Claudia Mitchell-Kernan, *The Decline in Marriage Among African Americans: Causes, Consequences, and Policy Implications* (New York: Russell Sage Foundation, 1995); Scott South, "Racial and Ethnic Differences in the Desire to Marry," *Journal of Marriage and the Family* 55, no. 2 (1993): 357–370; Kathryn Edin, "What Do Low-Income Single Mothers Say About Marriage?," *Social Problems* 47, no. 1 (2000): 112–133; and Daniel Lichter, Christie Batson, and J. Brian Brown, "Welfare Reform and Marriage Promotion: The Marital Expectations and Desires of Single and Cohabiting Mothers," *Social Service Review* 78, no. 1 (2004): 2–25.

7. Many scholars identify Daniel Patrick Moynihan's study, "The Negro Family: The Case for National Action," as the principal source that fed widespread assumptions about Black parents as either single mothers or absent fathers. For more on Moynihan's study, commonly referenced as the "Moynihan Report," see Chapter 3. Regarding single Black mothers, see also Lisa Rosenthal and Marci Lobel, "Stereotypes of Black American Women Related to Sexuality and Motherhood," *Psychology of Women Quarterly* 40, no. 3 (2016): 414–427. See also Dawn Marie Dow, "Negotiating 'the Welfare Queen' and 'the Strong Black Woman': African American Middle-Class Mothers' Work and Family Perspectives," *Sociological Perspectives* 58, no. 1 (2015): 36–55. Regarding absent Black fathers, the Centers for Disease Control and Prevention data now challenge myths that

associate father absenteeism with Black men. According to a 2013 study, Black men spend more quality time with their children than Latino and White men. See Jo Jones and William Mosher, "Fathers' Involvement with Their Children: United States, 2006–2010," December 20, 2013, www .cdc.gov/nchs/data/nhsr/nhsr071.pdf. See also Tara Culp-Ressler, "The Absent Black Father Myth," *ThinkProgress*, January 16, 2014, https://think progress.org/the-myth-of-the-absent-black-father-ecc4e961c2e8/; and Frank Walton, "The Absent Black Father Myth: Debunked by the CDC," May 13, 2015, www.dailykos.com/stories/2015/5/13/1383179/-The-absent-black -father-myth-debunked-by-CDC/. For more on Black single-parent families, see Daniel T. Lichter et al., "Race and the Retreat from Marriage: A Short-age of Marriageable Men?," *American Sociological Review* 57, no. 6 (1992): 781–799; and Michael Tonry and Matthew Melewski, "The Malign Effects of Drug and Crime Control Policies on Black Americans," *Crime and Justice* 37, no. 1 (2008): 1–44.

8. Sandra Lane et al., "Marriage Promotion and Missing Men: African American Women in a Demographic Double Bind," *Medical Anthropology Quarterly* 18, no. 4 (2005): 405–428. I often employ the qualifiers or nouns "male" and "female" to denote statistical references to bodies that are feminized and masculinized through cultural ascription and socialization. I also employ these terms when referencing girls *and* women (females) or boys *and* men (males). However, the reader should know that I do not perceive a strict demarcation between sex and gender as constructed in the Western imagination. I agree with Judith Butler that "sex itself is a gendered category" and with the analysis of Oyèrónké Oyěwùmí that sex and gender are "essentially synonymous" in the West, since Western ways of organizing social life "use . . . biology as an ideology for mapping the social world." Although it might be more current to use the nouns "men" and "women" as qualifiers in some instances throughout the text, because I understand male and female to be gendered concepts, I opt for the more conventional use of these adjectives—"male" and "female"—when qualifying a noun. I also am aware that not all humans are biologically male or female and acknowledge the limitations of this book, which does not account for the love and marital experiences of Blacks with intersex, nongender-conforming, or other sex identities. For more on biological sex as a gendered concept, see Judith Butler, *Gender Trouble: Feminism and the Subversion of Identity* (New York: Routledge, 1990), 7; and Oyèrónké Oyěwùmí, *The Invention of Women: Making an African Sense of Western Gender Discourses* (Minneapolis: University of Minnesota Press, 1997), 12.

9. Under President Bill Clinton's administration, the federal welfare reform legislation sought to "increase the number of two-parent families and to reduce out-of-wedlock childbearing." President George W. Bush's Healthy Marriage Initiative launched a concerted effort to address America's marriage decline and has been described as "the first positive step toward strengthening the institution of marriage since the Moynihan report four decades ago." See Robert Rector and Melissa Pardue, "Understanding the President's

Healthy Marriage Initiative," Heritage Foundation, *Marriage and Family Report*, March 26, 2004, www.heritage.org/marriage-and-family/report /understanding-the-presidents-healthy-marriage-initiative. Shortly after George W. Bush launched his HMI, M. Robin Dion questioned whether concrete healthy marriage programs actually responded to low-income couples with multiple stressors in "Healthy Marriage Programs: Learning What Works," in "Marriage and Child Wellbeing," special issue, *Future of Children* 15, no. 2 (2005): 139–156.

10. President Barack Obama's most noteworthy contribution to the Healthy Marriage Initiative was his "Responsible Fatherhood" programs, which addressed some welfare issues and provided inmate reentry programming. See www.acf.hhs.gov/ofa/programs/healthy-marriage. See also the following articles on Obama's criticisms of absent Black fathers: J. Weston Phippen, "What My Brother's Keeper Gets Wrong About Black Fathers," *Atlantic*, November 2, 2015, www.theatlantic.com/politics/archive/2015/11 /what-my-brothers-keeper-gets-wrong-about-black-fathers/433296/; Julie Bosman, "Obama Sharply Assails Absent Black Fathers," *New York Times*, June 16, 2008, www.nytimes.com/2008/06/16/us/politics/15cnd-obama.html; and Ta-Nehisi Coates, "How the Obama Administration Talks to Black America," *Atlantic*, May 20, 2013, www.theatlantic.com/politics/archive/2013/05 /how-the-obama-administration-talks-to-black-america/276015/.

11. "President Donald J. Trump's Economic Mobility Reforms Will Restore Independence and Dignity to Millions of Americans," April 10, 2018, www.whitehouse.gov/briefings-statements/president-donald-j-trumps -economic-mobility-reforms-will-restore-independence-dignity-millions -americans/.

12. For a discussion of studies indicating the high value that Blacks, especially poor Blacks, place on marriage, see Robin Lenhardt, "Marriage as Black Citizenship?," *Hastings Law Journal* 66 (2015): 1349–1350, http://ir.lawnet .fordham.edu/faculty_scholarship/655. For a comprehensive critical analysis of the Healthy Marriage Initiative and the African American Healthy Marriage Initiative, see Trina Armstrong, "Behind the Veil of the Village: A Womanist Practical Theological Analysis of Single African American Mothers, Cultural and Relational Trauma, and Relationship Education Programs" (PhD diss., Claremont School of Theology, 2014). Since HMI and AAHMI "curricula couch [relationship] skills in relation to marriage," Armstrong argues, "they disregard the well being of single African American mothers who head over half of the families in the African American community" (abstract, para. 3).

13. Economists Darrick Hamilton, Arthur Goldsmith, and William Darity argue, "An alternative means of expanding the level of marriage for black women, which is also capable of reducing the inter-racial marriage gap, is to enlarge the supply of marriageable men." See "Shedding 'Light' on Marriage: The Influence of Skin Shade on Marriage for Black Females," *Journal of Economic Behavior and Organization* (October 2009): 29.

14. I attended college between 1986 and 1990, a time when this ratio became a mantra for Black women of my generation. See, for example, how it shows up even in a contemporary article that brought visibility to ten American cities where parity between the numbers of single Black women and men challenged the national trend. Douglas C. Lyons, "US Census Figures Say the Odds Favor Black Women in Some Surprising Places," *Ebony*, July 1993, 30–32, 34.

15. A statistic borrowed from the *Newsweek* article "Too Late for Prince Charming?," which appeared in June 1986.

16. Norman Anderson, Rodolfo Bulatao, and Barney Cohen, eds., *Critical Perspectives on Racial and Ethnic Differences in Health in Late Life* (Washington, DC: National Academies Press, 2004), esp. 53–94; Jerry Kenard, "Health Statistics for Black American Men," *Verywell Health*, June 24, 2019, https://www.verywellhealth.com/black-american-mens-health-2328772; Nana Adjeiwaa-Manu, "Unemployment Data by Race and Ethnicity: Fact Sheet," Center for Global Policy Solutions, August 2017, https://global policysolutions.org/wp-content/uploads/2017/07/Unemployment-Data-by -Race.pdf.

17. Hamilton, Goldsmith, and Darity, "Shedding 'Light' on Marriage," 4; Robert G. Wood, "Marriage Rates and Marriageable Men: A Test of the Wilson Hypothesis," *Journal of Human Resources* 30, no. 1 (1995): 163–193.

18. R. Kelly Raley, Megan Sweeney, and Danielle Wondra, "The Growing Racial and Ethnic Divide in U.S. Marriage Patterns," *Future Child* 25, no. 2 (2015): 89–109, https://www.ncbi.nlm.nih.gov/pmc/articles/PMC 4850739/?report=reader; R. Richard Banks and Su Jin Gatlin, "African American Intimacy: The Racial Gap in Marriage," *Michigan Journal of Race and Law* 11, no. 1 (2005): 115–132, esp. 120–123, https://repository.law .umich.edu/mjrl/vol11/iss1/7.

19. This point is not made to advance in any respect mythologies that conflate criminality with racial Blackness. Extensive studies exist exposing the disparities between police reactions to White and Black criminal suspects. The hyperpolicing of Black communities when compared with the underpolicing of White communities and the criminalization of the crack epidemic within Black communities compared with the sympathetic classification of the methamphetamine epidemic among White communities as a public health crisis have fed stereotypes that racialize criminal behavior as essentially Black. See, for example, research sponsored by the Brennan Center for Justice: Jessica Eaglin and Danyelle Solomon, "Reducing Racial and Ethnic Disparities in Jails: Recommendations for Local Practice," June 25, 2015, www .brennancenter.org/publication/reducing-racial-and-ethnic-disparities-jails -recommendations-local-practice. See also Christopher Mathias, "NYPD Stop and Frisks: 15 Shocking Facts About a Controversial Program," *Huffington Post*, May 15, 2012, www.huffingtonpost.com/2012/05/13/nypd-stop-and-frisks-15-shocking-facts_n_1513362.html; New York Civil Liberties Union, "Stop-and-Frisk 2011," May 9, 2012, www.nyclu.org/files

/publications/NYCLU_2011_Stop-and-Frisk_Report.pdf; Naomi Murakawa, "Electing to Punish: Congress, Race, and the American Criminal Justice State" (PhD diss., Yale University, 2005); and Naomi Murakawa and Katherine Beckett, "The Penology of Racial Innocence: The Erasure of Racism in the Study and Practice of Punishment," *Law & Society Review* 44, nos. 3–4 (2010): 695–730.

20. Wendy Wang, "Interracial Marriage: Who Is 'Marrying Out'?," *Fact Tank: News in the Numbers*, Pew Research Center, June 12, 2015, www.pewresearch.org/fact-tank/2015/06/12/interracial-marriage-who-is -marrying-out/. When Black women do marry, they select Black male partners at high rates. Only 12 percent of newlywed Black women married someone of a different race in 2013. The subjects included in the study were single-raced Black women.

21. Both sibling names are assigned pseudonyms.

22. Although 1619 is the date most Americans associate with the commencement of racial slavery or proto-slavery in the United States, for information on the earliest records of sixteenth-century African captives enslaved in the United States, see Edwin Williams, "Negro Slavery in Florida," *Florida Historical Quarterly* 28, no. 2 (1949): 93–110; and Jane Landers, *Black Society in Spanish Florida* (Urbana: University of Illinois Press, 1999). For information on the last slave ships to smuggle African captives into the United States long after the abolition of the foreign slave trade in 1807, see David Eltis, "The U.S. Transatlantic Slave Trade, 1664–1867: An Assessment," *Civil War History* 54 (2008): 347–378, esp. 353; David Eltis and David Richardson, "A New Assessment of the Transatlantic Slave Trade," in *Extending the Frontiers: Essays on the New Transatlantic Slave Trade Database*, ed. David Eltis and David Richardson (New Haven, CT: Yale University Press, 2008); and David Head, "Slave Smuggling by Foreign Privateers? The Illegal Slave Trade and the Geopolitics of the Early Republic," *Journal of the Early Republic* 33, no. 3 (2013): 433–463.

23. Certainly, instances arose where it was convenient and profitable for slaveholders to encourage the romantic interests and relationships of their human property, but their dissolution of Black love and marriage was a constant feature of racial slavery in America.

24. It might appear repetitive to speak of "colorism" *and* "phenotypic stratification" together, since colorism is a prime example of phenotypic stratification. I risk redundancy with my concept of CPS because "colorism" is a widely used term in Black communities and in scholarly research. However, the term "colorism" does not necessarily signal other forms of phenotypic stratification based on hair texture and color, eye color, or body shape.

25. Ann Zollar and J. Sherwood Williams, "The Contribution of Marriage to the Life Satisfaction of Black Adults," in *Impacts of Incarceration on the African American Family*, ed. Othello Harris and R. Robin Miller (2003; reprint, New Brunswick, NJ: Transaction, 2009), esp. 160–161; Kristen Schultz Lee and Hiroshi Ono, "Marriage, Cohabitation, and Happiness:

A Cross-National Analysis of 27 Countries," *Journal of Marriage and Family* 24, no. 5 (2012): 953–972; Juliana Menasche Horowitz, Nikki Graf, and Gretchen Livingston, "Marriage and Cohabitation in the U.S.," Pew Research Center, November 6, 2019, https://www.pewsocialtrends.org/2019/11/06/marriage-and-cohabitation-in-the-u-s/.

26. W. E. B. Du Bois, *The Souls of Black Folk* (1903; reprint, New York: Pocket Books, 2009), 3.

CHAPTER 1. JUMPING THE BROOM

1. Peggy Garner was born on June 4, 1833, and based on an account from her widower, Robert Garner, died May 14, 1858. See La Vinia Jennings, ed., *Margaret Garner: The Premiere Performances of Toni Morrison's Libretto* (Charlottesville: University of Virginia Press, 2016); Nikki Taylor, *Driven Toward Madness: The Fugitive Slave Margaret Garner and Tragedy on the Ohio* (Athens: Ohio University Press, 2016), 37; Mark Reinhardt, "Who Speaks for Margaret Garner? Slavery, Silence, and the Politics of Ventriloquism," *Critical Inquiry* 29, no. 1 (2002): 115.

2. Taylor, *Driven Toward Madness*, 126.

3. Sylviane Diouf, "Remembering the Women of Slavery," March 27, 2015, www.nypl.org/blog/2015/03/27/remembering-women-slavery.

4. Catherine Adams and Elizabeth Pleck, *Love of Freedom: Black Women in Colonial and Revolutionary New England* (New York: Oxford University Press, 2010), 6–7.

5. Tshilemalema Mukenge, *Culture and Customs of the Congo* (Westport, CT: Greenwood Press, 2002), 117–130; Dixon Mungazi, *Gathering Under the Mango Tree: Values in Traditional Culture in Africa* (Oxford: Peter Lang, 1996), 36–43; Ambe Njoh, *Tradition, Culture and Development in Africa: Historical Lessons for Modern Development Planning* (New York: Routledge, 2016). For more on the absence of cousins in Africa, see Chapter 5, note 38.

6. See *Encyclopedia Virginia: Virginia Humanities* for digitized images of the original legal documents pertaining to the "Parish Tithes (1643)" on African women's labor, ages sixteen and above, https://www.encyclopediavirginia.org/Parishes_and_Tithes_1643. Slave masters were responsible for paying taxes for the African women they held in bondage. Tera Hunter, *Bound in Wedlock: Slave and Free Black Marriage in the Nineteenth Century* (Cambridge, MA: Belknap Press of Harvard University, 2017), 9; Jennifer Morgan, *Laboring Women: Reproduction and Gender in New World Slavery* (Philadelphia: University of Pennsylvania Press, 2004), 72.

7. The term "misogynoir" conveys the intersection of race and gender bias at the heart of misogynistic assaults—discursive, imagistic, physical, ideological, and so on—on Black women. For insight into Moya Bailey's coining of "misogynoir," see her March 14, 2010, article, "They Aren't Talking About Me . . . ," www.crunkfeministcollective.com/2010/03/14/they-arent-talking-about-me/. See also www.thevisibilityproject.com/2014/05/27/on-moya-bailey-misogynoir-and-why-both-are-important/. I sometimes use the

generic phrase "racist-sexism" to refer to misogynoir ideologies and practices. Building on Bailey's neologism, I also introduce the term "misandrynoir" to account for race- and gender-based assaults of Black men later in this book.

8. Although rarely documented, Black girls and women were sexual prey not only for White males who owned and operated around them, but also for some White female slave owners.

9. "Making a way out of no way" is a well-known African American expression whose meaning and significance need no explanation.

10. For historical accounts of Margaret Garner's life, see Taylor, *Driven Toward Madness*; Reinhardt, "Who Speaks for Margaret Garner?"; and Karolyn Smardz Frost et al., eds., *Ontario's African-Canadian Heritage: Collected Writings by Fred Landon, 1918–1967* (Toronto: Natural Heritage Books, 2009), 271–274.

11. *Cincinnati Gazette*, January 30, 1856, www.accessgenealogy.com /black-genealogy/margaret-garner-and-seven-others-fugitive-slave-law.htm. See also Samuel May, *The Fugitive Slave Law and Its Victims* (New York: American Anti-Slavery Society, 1861), 53.

12. Taylor, *Driven Toward Madness*, 72, 80–81.

13. Taylor, *Driven Toward Madness*, 21. Nikki Taylor's argument is very convincing on this point.

14. Mical Darly-Emerson's concept of "reproductive assault" captures an important dimension of enslaved women's sexual exploitation. See "How Sexual Assault Built America," March 14, 2018, www.wellesley.edu/albright /about/blog/4451-how-sexual-assault-built-america.

15. Reverend P. C. Bassett reports Margaret having confessed as much during his interview with her. "She said that when the officers and slave-hunters came to the house in which they were concealed, she caught a shovel and struck two of her children on the head, and then took a knife and cut the throat of the third, and tried to kill the other—that if they had given her time, she would have killed them all—that with regard to herself she cared but little; but she was unwilling to have her children suffer as she had done." See *National Anti-Slavery Standard*, March 15, 1856.

16. Basset's exact words were "I inquired . . . if she were not excited almost to madness when she committed the act?" See May, *Fugitive Slave Law and Its Victims*, 58.

17. May, *Fugitive Slave Law and Its Victims*, 58.

18. Taylor, *Driven Toward Madness*, 99.

19. May, *Fugitive Slave Law and Its Victims*, 59. In actuality, abolitionists were under the belief that Margaret would fare better by returning to Ohio to stand trial instead of returning to a life of bondage in Kentucky. See Taylor, *Driven Toward Madness*, 87.

20. There seems to be no record of the fate of the fifth child Margaret was said to be carrying in 1856. See Taylor, *Driven Toward Madness*, 126.

21. *National Anti-Slavery Standard*, March 15, 1856.

22. Melton McLaurin, *Celia, a Slave: A True Story* (Athens: University of Georgia Press, 1991), 135.

23. McLaurin, *Celia, a Slave*, 121.

24. My account is based on McLaurin's *Celia, a Slave*, the most comprehensive scholarly source that pieces together Celia's narrative. Informed by the limited available court testimonies, McLaurin's portrait of George (29–46) suggests that he did not demonstrate the same depth of loyalty to Celia as she did to him. George's character seems questionable based on the premise that he reportedly told investigators that "he believed the last walking [Newsom] had done was along the path, pointing to the path leading from the house to the Negro Cabin," where Celia resided. George was also drawn into the search for Newsom and purportedly "discovered and turned over to the white members of the search party Newsom's pocketknife." McLaurin's account is certainly reasonable. I am not totally convinced, though, that McLaurin's perspective is the only way to read George's statements and actions while operating under the scrutinizing gaze of White inquisitors and prosecutors. In any event, my narration focuses on *Celia's* emotions and actions, which, from her reported testimony, were clearly unambiguous. For actual documents, including trial testimonies, related to Celia's case, see Douglas Linder, "Celia: A Slave Trial: 1855," University of Missouri–Kansas City School of Law, www .famous-trials.com/celia.

25. The 1662 law was passed in the colony of Virginia. It stated that "all children borne in this country shalbe held bond or free only according to the condition of the mother." See *Encyclopedia Virginia*, "Negro Women's Children to Serve According to the Condition of the Mother" (1662), https://www.encyclopediavirginia.org/_Negro_womens_children_to_serve _according_to_the_condition_of_the_mother_1662; and Sally Kitch, *The Specter of Sex: Gendered Foundations of Racial Formation in the United States* (Albany: State University of New York Press, 2009), 81 (see also 80–81, 161).

26. Alexis Wells-Oghoghomeh, "The Souls of Womenfolk: The Religious Cultures of Enslaved Women in the Lower South" (unpublished manuscript), 87–88.

27. William Geddy will, Virginia Historical Society, Richmond, quoted in Heather Williams, *Help Me to Find My People: The African American Search for Family Lost in Slavery* (Chapel Hill: University of North Carolina Press, 2012), 64.

28. Dorothy Sterling, *We Are Your Sisters: Black Women in the Nineteenth Century* (New York: W. W. Norton, 1997), 13.

29. J. Morgan, *Laboring Women*, 152–163; Emily West, *Enslaved Women in America: From Colonial Time to Emancipation* (Lanham, MD: Rowman & Littlefield, 2017), 36–38.

30. Alexander Garden to Royal Society, April 20, 1755, and John English to Royal Society, November 15, 1760, respectively, in Guard Book I, Royal Society of Arts, London, quoted in Philip Morgan, *Slave Counterpoint: Black*

254 Notes to Chapter 1

Culture in Eighteenth-Century Chesapeake & Lowcountry (Chapel Hill: University of North Carolina Press, 1998), 153.

31. Judith Carney, *Black Rice: The African Origins of Rice Cultivation in the Americas* (Cambridge, MA: Harvard University Press, 2001).

32. J. Morgan, *Laboring Women*, 164.

33. J. Morgan, *Laboring Women*, esp. 12–49; William Bosman, *A New and Accurate Description of the Coast of Guinea: Divided into the Gold, the Slave, and the Ivory Coasts* (1905; reprint, Cambridge: Cambridge University Press, 2011), 199, 344–345, 460. Bosman's first English edition was published in 1704. For an example of how early European male travelers' assessments of women's bodies fed erroneous assumptions and ideas about African women and were cited repeatedly and circulated in the West, see the Church of England's periodical the *Christian Observer* (London: John Hatchard Bookseller, 1804), 3:168.

34. Stephanie Jones-Rogers, *They Were Her Property: White Women as Slave Owners in the American South* (New Haven, CT: Yale University Press, 2019), wrote a groundbreaking text dispelling the myth of White women's indirect and delicate participation in America's system of racial slavery. For a summary of her argument, see Soraya McDonald, "In 'They Were Her Property,' a Historian Shows That White Women Were Deeply Involved in the Slave Economy," *Undefeated*, March 15, 2019, https://theundefeated.com /features/in-they-were-her-property-a-historian-shows-that-white-women -were-deeply-involved-in-the-slave-economy/. In her survey of three thousand bills of sales related to enslaved persons in the state of South Carolina and dating from the 1700s to "pretty recently," Jones-Rogers found that nearly 40 percent "included either a female buyer or a female seller."

35. Countless testimonies from former bondwomen mention experiencing or witnessing others being "[beat] . . . nekked 'til the blood run down [their] back to [their] heels." See Sterling, *We Are Your Sisters*, 25 (see also 13–30); and Deborah Gray White, *Ar'n't I a Woman? Female Slaves in the Plantation South* (New York: W. W. Norton, 1999), 30–34.

36. J. Morgan, *Laboring Women*, 154–165; Alisha Cromwell, "Enslaved Women in the Savannah Marketplace," in *Slavery and Freedom in Savannah*, ed. Leslie Harris and Daina Berry (Athens: University of Georgia Press, 2014), 54–55.

37. Steven Deyle, *Carry Me Back: The Domestic Slave Trade in American Life* (New York: Oxford University Press, 2005), 263–264.

38. Deyle, *Carry Me Back*, 143. See also Edward Baptist, "Cuffy, 'Fancy Maids,' and 'One-Eyed Men': Rape, Commodification, and the Domestic Slave Trade in the United States," in *The Chattel Principle: Internal Slave Trades in the Americas*, ed. Walter Johnson (New Haven, CT: Yale University Press, 2004), 165–202.

39. Harriet Washington, *Medical Apartheid: The Dark History of Medical Experimentation on Black Americans from Colonial Times to the Present* (New York: Harlem Moon, 2006).

40. White, *Ar'n't I a Woman?*, 30–32.

41. By comparison, slaveholdings in the North accounted for only 10 percent of all enslaved persons in the North American colonies on the eve of the Revolutionary War, and the enslaved population never rose above 6 percent of the North's entire population. Heather Williams, *American Slavery: A Short Introduction* (New York: Oxford University Press, 2014), 35; https://eh.net /encyclopedia/slavery-in-the-united-states/.

42. Katherine Franke, *Wedlocked: The Perils of Marriage Equality* (New York: New York University Press, 2015), 66–67. George Washington's seventy-six-hundred-acre estate included farms, gardens, and other landscapes, the size of which he rounded up to eight thousand acres. See "Growth of Mount Vernon," www.mountvernon.org/library/digitalhistory /digital-encyclopedia/article/growth-of-mount-vernon/.

43. Erica Dunbar, *Never Caught: The Washingtons' Relentless Pursuit of Their Runaway Slave, Ona Judge* (New York: Atria/Simon & Schuster, 2017); Ethan Malveaux, *The Colorline: A History* (Bloomington, IN: Xlibris, 2015), 840–843.

44. Charles James McDonald to Dear Cal, December 23, 1854, quoted in Hunter, *Bound in Wedlock*, 49. McDonald served two terms as governor of Georgia between 1839 and 1843.

45. Manda Walker, age eighty, Winnsboro, SC, *Federal Writers' Project: Slave Narrative Project*, vol. 14, South Carolina, pt. 4, Raines-Young, 1936, Manuscript/Mixed Material, www.loc.gov/item/mesn144/.

46. Julia Woodberry, interview prepared by Annie Ruth Davis, November 5, 1937, Marion, SC, *Federal Writers' Project: Slave Narrative Project*, vol. 14, South Carolina, pt. 4, Raines-Young, 1937.

47. Hunter, *Bound in Wedlock*, 26.

48. Spencer Crew, Lonnie Bunch, and Clement Price, eds., *Slave Culture: A Documentary Collection of the Slave Narratives from the Federal Writers' Project* (Westport, CT: Greenwood Press, 2014), 1:357.

49. William Moore, born in 1855 (no age or date of interview given). Moore worked in Selma, Alabama, before moving with his master to Texas during the Civil War. Works Projects Administration, *Slave Narratives: A Folk History of Slavery in the United States from Interviews with Former Slaves*, vol. 16, Texas Narratives, pt. 3 (Washington, DC: Library of Congress, 1941).

50. Opinion of Daniel Dulany, Esquire, December 16, 1767, 1, Thomas Harris Jr. and John McHenry, *Maryland Reports: Being a Series of the Most Important Law Cases, Argued and Determined in the Provincial Court and Court of Appeals of the Then Province of Maryland from the Year 1700 Down to the American Revolution* (New York: L. Riley, 1809), 560 (emphasis in the original), quoted in Hunter, *Bound in Wedlock*, 67.

51. William Moore, Works Projects Administration, *Slave Narratives: A Folk History of Slavery in the United States from Interviews with Former Slaves*.

52. George Bollinger, eighty-four-year-old man, Cape Girardeau, Missouri, *Slave Narratives: A Folk History of Slavery in the United States from*

Interviews with Former Slaves, vol. 10, *Missouri Narratives*, www.gutenberg .org/files/35379/35379-0.txt.

53. Deyle, *Carry Me Back*, 4; Edward Baptist, *The Half Has Never Been Told: Slavery and the Making of American Capitalism* (New York: Basic Books, 2014), xxv.

54. "The end of slavery in the North was propelled more by atrophy of the slave population (through mortality, low fertility, runaways, and the decline of the Atlantic slave trade) than by the efforts of abolitionists." Northern abolition was so protracted that some bondpersons were still alive and functioning in New Jersey by the commencement of the Civil War. See Hunter, *Bound in Wedlock*, 88–89. See also Williams, *American Slavery*, 86–114.

55. Petition for freedom to Massachusetts Governor Thomas Gage, His Majesty's Council, and the House of Representatives, May 25, 1774, Jeremy Belknap Papers, Massachusetts Historical Society, quoted in Adams and Pleck, *Love of Freedom*, 107.

56. "As one former bondwoman explained, they would 'take her by her breasts and pull dem to show how good she was built for raisin' chillum.'" See Deyle, *Carry Me Back*, 264.

57. Deyle, *Carry Me Back*, 126–127.

58. Deyle, *Carry Me Back*, 264. These examinations were typically shielded by screens.

59. Errol Alexander describes, for example, how the "State of Maryland's intelligence and slave rating office" examined bondpersons. Women were "taken behind small screens where there are small sitting stools and stirrups; there, the skin of their private parts is peeled back. Each woman is wiped with a liquid, and then with a hollow three-foot reed, they are sniffed." Alexander also notes, "In some cases, [professional slave testers] will lick the chins of the slaves for the heavy taste of salt, a sure sign of sickness." See his *The Rattling of the Chains: A True Story of an American Family* (Bloomington, IN: Xlibris, 2015), 1:238.

60. Angela Onwuachi-Willig, "The Return of the Ring: Welfare Reform's Marriage Cure as the Revival of Post-bellum Control," *California Law Review* 93, no. 6 (2005): 1655–1656.

61. Mary A. Bell, *Slave Narratives: A Folk History of Slavery in the United States from Interviews with Former Slaves*, vol. 10, *Missouri Narratives*, www .gutenberg.org/files/35379/35379-0.txt.

62. Crew, Bunch, and Price, *Slave Culture*, 1:359, 364, 375.

63. Hunter, *Bound in Wedlock*, 34.

64. Julia Woodberry, interview prepared by Annie Ruth Davis, November 16, 1937, Marion, SC, *Federal Writers' Project: Slave Narrative Project*, vol. 14, South Carolina, pt. 4, Raines-Young, www.loc.gov/resource /mesn.144/?sp=246&st=text.

65. Crew, Bunch, and Price, *Slave Culture*, 1:363.

66. Willie McCullough, sixty-eight years old, Raleigh, NC, October 23, 1937, *Slave Narratives: A Folk History of Slavery in the United States from*

Interviews with Former Slaves, vol. 11, *North Carolina Narratives*, pt. 2, www .gutenberg.org/files/31219/31219-h/31219-h.htm.

67. Works Projects Administration, *Slave Narratives: A Folk History of Slavery in the United States from Interviews with Former Slaves*, vol. 11, *North Carolina Narratives*, pt. 2 (Washington, DC: Library of Congress, 1941), 76.

68. George P. Rawick, *The American Slave: A Composite Autobiography*, supp., ser. 2, vol. 5, *Texas Narratives*, pt. 4 (Westport, CT: Greenwood, 1979), 1445, 1451, 1453.

69. As discussed above, beginning at the age of fourteen, Celia endured five years of repeated rape at the hands of her sixty-year-old White male owner, Robert Newsom, before finally clubbing him to death on June 23, 1855. Celia was hanged for her crime on December 21, 1855, after giving birth to Newsom's (or possibly her lover George's) stillborn child while awaiting execution in prison. See note 82 for information on Jefferson's relationship with his enslaved female property Sally Hemings. James Henry Hammond's sexual exploits will be discussed below.

70. Harriet Jacobs, *Incidents in the Life of a Slave Girl*, 45 (emphasis added), http://docsouth.unc.edu/fpn/jacobs/jacobs.html.

71. Jacobs, *Incidents in the Life of a Slave Girl*, 44–45, 119. Jacobs herself was prey to such advances by her owner, Dr. Flint. The ubiquity of sexual violence against Black girls and women during slavery notwithstanding, it is important to note that slavery also offered unlimited opportunities for the sexual violation of Black boys and men. Scholars are increasingly bringing this buried history to light. See, for example, Thomas Foster, *Rethinking Rufus: Sexual Violations of Enslaved Men* (Athens: University of Georgia Press, 2019).

72. Quoted in Orville Vernon Burton, *In My Father's House Are Many Mansions: Family and Community in Edgefield, South Carolina* (Chapel Hill: University of North Carolina Press, 1985), 187. Hammond admittedly took sexual liberties with four of his teenage nieces as well. See Carol Bleser, ed., *Secret and Sacred: The Diaries of James Henry Hammond, a Southern Slaveholder* (New York: Oxford University Press, 1988), 169–172.

73. Josh Miles, Works Projects Administration, *Slave Narratives: A Folk History of Slavery in the United States from Interviews with Former Slaves*, vol. 16, *Texas Narratives*, pt. 3 (Washington, DC: Library of Congress, 1941), 83. Miles was born in Richmond, Virginia, in 1859. It is also possible that the "old mammy" was the grandmother of the auctioned children.

74. Sojourner Truth, *Narrative of Sojourner Truth: A Bondswoman of Olden Time, Emancipated by the New York Legislature in the Early Part of the Present Century, with a History of Her Labors and Correspondence Drawn from Her "Book of Life"* (1878; reprint, Salem, NH: Ayer, 1990), 82, quoted in Nell Painter, *Sojourner Truth: A Life, a Symbol* (New York: W. W. Norton, 1996), 11–18. For a different theory on the matter, see Margaret Washington's *Sojourner Truth's America* (Urbana: University of Illinois Press, 2009). Washington raises the possibility that Isabella engaged in a noncoercive sexual relationship with John Dumont, who could have been the father of two of her children.

Through updated research, Washington also identifies the "Mrs. Dumont" Isabella "despised" as Elizabeth Dumont, Sally's older sister whom John married after her death. While we may never know for certain who abused Isabella, I find Nell Painter's interpretation extremely compelling.

75. Rachel Feinstein, *When Rape Was Legal: The Untold History of Sexual Violence During Slavery* (New York: Routledge, 2018), 6.

76. Roger Thompson, *Sex in Middlesex: Popular Mores in a Massachusetts County, 1649–1699* (Amherst: University of Massachusetts Press, 1986), 107–108.

77. By law, White men in colonial New England could be charged and prosecuted for raping enslaved Black women. See Adams and Pleck, *Love of Freedom*, 44–45.

78. Adams and Pleck, *Love of Freedom*, 45.

79. Rachel Fairley, Federal Writers' Project interview with S. S. Taylor, Little Rock, AR, June 23, 1938, 4, www.loc.gov/teachers/classroommaterials /connections/narratives-slavery/. Fairley was seventy-five at the time of her interview and was born (1863) during the last years of slavery. For an example of the racial/color-caste category "Yellow" among the prominent nineteenth-century South Carolina senator James Henry Hammond's bills of sale, see Burton, *In My Father's House Are Many Mansions*, 186. Hammond apparently had a penchant for purchasing light-skinned Black females, including a "light complexioned Negro woman" (April 22, 1835), a "mulatto girl" (June 6, 1843), and "a Yellow girl named Lucy" (April 18, 1845).

80. Works Projects Administration, *Slave Narratives: A Folk History of Slavery in the United States from Interviews with Former Slaves*, vol. 16, *Texas Narratives*, pt. 3. Born in Black River, Louisiana, Mary Reynolds was more than one hundred years old at the time of her interview, which took place in Texas.

81. Thomas Jefferson, *Notes on the State of Virginia* (1785; reprint, New York: Penguin Books, 1999), 145. *Notes* was published in French in 1785. The first English translation appeared in 1787.

82. Thomas Jefferson began his long-term sexual relationship with Sally Hemings, an enslaved adolescent he owned, when she was between fourteen and sixteen years old and sired six children with her. See www.monticello.org /site/plantation-and-slavery/thomas-jefferson-and-sally-hemings-brief -account; and www.history.com/topics/sally-hemings. Sally Hemings herself was born of a White father, John Wayles, and a racially mixed enslaved mother, Betty Hemings, whom Wayles owned. "Black" is affixed to "racially mixed" via a dash to indicate the psychosocial complexity of American race-making ideologies. No matter what classifications have been invented to measure degrees of "dilution" from perceived Black or White genealogical purity, the "one-drop" rule that socially classified persons with any degree of African ancestry as Black or Negro has always operated alongside such racial caste social imaginaries, in the first place, to enhance the capital advantages

of White slaveholders who profited from the free labor of any children they sired with Black enslaved women, since such children held the same status as their mothers, and generally speaking to protect the invention of White racial purity.

83. Shavonn Pearce-Doughlin, Arthur Goldsmith, and Darrick Hamilton, "Colorism," in *Encyclopedia of Race and Racism*, ed. Patricia Mason (New York: Macmillan Reference USA), 1:422–428; Jay Scott Smith, "Americans Rank Mixed Raced People Ahead of Blacks Socially," *Grio*, December 21, 2011, http://thegrio.com/2011/12/21/americans -rank-mixed-race-people-ahead-of-blacks-socially/.

84. *Mississippi Digest Annotated: A Complete Digest of all Reported Mississippi Decisions from the Earliest Times to September 2, 1911* (Indianapolis: Bobbs-Merrill, 1912), 3:778. See also James George, *Reports of Cases Argued and Determined in the High Court of Errors and Appeals, for the State of Mississippi* (Philadelphia: T. & J. W. Johnson, 1860), 37:296; Norrece Jones, "Rape in Black and White: Sexual Violence in the Testimony of Enslaved and Free Americans," in Winthrop Jordan, ed., *Slavery and the American South* (Jackson: University Press of Mississippi, 2003), 100; Saidiya Hartman, "Seduction and the Ruse of Power," in "Emerging Women Writers," special issue, *Callaloo* 19, no. 2 (1996): 542; and Anthony Neal, *Unburdened by Conscience: A Black People's Collective Account of America's Ante-bellum South and the Aftermath* (Lanham, MD: University Press of America, 2009), 67.

85. "By Mingo," *Weekly Anglo-African*, August 10, 1861; Lydia Maria Childs, *The Freedmen's Book* (Boston: Tricknor and Fields), 84. According to Childs, Mingo was imprisoned to be sold on account of his "great intelligence," which "only served to make him an object of suspicion." Mingo's wife, Childs adds, "lived to be an aged woman, and was said to have many of his poems in her possession." See also Daina Ramey Berry, *The Price for Their Pound of Flesh: The Value of the Enslaved, from Womb to Grave, in the Building of a Nation* (Boston: Beacon Press, 2017), 196–197.

86. Letter from James Tate, February 4, 1863, Berry Family Collection, Schomburg Center for Research in Black Culture, New York, quoted in Williams, *Help Me to Find My People*, 78–79 (emphasis in the original).

87. Petition of Stephen Lytle to the Tennessee General Assembly, ca. 1832 PAR #11483320, quoted in Loren Schweninger, ed., *The Southern Debate over Slavery*, vol. 1, *Petitions to Southern Legislatures, 1778–1864* (Urbana: University of Illinois Press, 2001), 139–142.

88. Petition of C. A. Featherston, To the Honorable General Assembly of the State of North Carolina, Gaston County, November 1862, PAR #11286203, Proquest.com, *Race and Slavery Petitions Project*, ser. 1, *Petitions to Southern Legislatures*. Beginning with Virginia, between 1856 and 1861 at least seven states ratified laws pertaining to voluntary slavery. See Hunter, *Bound in Wedlock*, 115–120, for more on Featherston's petition and others, including one on behalf of a manumitted man who left Virginia for Ohio,

"forced out by law." He later returned to Virginia, "'anxious to remain'" after "'not being reconciled to live without his wife.' . . . Though a free man, he 'would prefer returning to slavery to losing the society of his wife.'"

89. William Craft and Ellen Craft, *Running a Thousand Miles for Freedom; or, The Escape of William and Ellen Craft from Slavery* (London: William Tweedie, 1860), 27–28.

90. Scholars have found no links between jumping the broom and African wedding rituals. See Tyler Parry, "The Holy Land of Matrimony: The Complex Legacy of the Broomstick Wedding in American History," *American Studies* 55, no. 1 (2016): 86.

91. Some believe the practice was widely known among specific subgroups of British Roma, especially the Northumbrians. Parry, "Holy Land of Matrimony," 86; Tyler Parry, "Married in Slavery Time: Jumping the Broom in Atlantic Perspective," *Journal of Southern History* 81, no. 2 (2015): 281–284; Patrick O'Neil, "Bosses and Broomsticks: Ritual and Authority in Antebellum Slave Weddings," *Journal of Southern History* 75, no. 1 (2009): 39–40. See also Alan Dundes, "'Jumping the Broom': On the Origin and Meaning of an African American Wedding Custom," *Journal of American Folklore* 109, no. 433 (1996): 324–329; and C. W. Sullivan III, "'Jumping the Broom': A Further Consideration of the Origins of an African American Wedding Custom," *Journal of American Folklore* 110, no. 436 (1997): 203–204.

92. During this time, one writer happened upon "a company of Gipsies in Yorkshire, drawn up in two parallel rows, between which the bride and bridegroom passed, jumping over a broomstick that was held across their path about eighteen inches from the ground." See Vernon Morwood, *Our Gipsies in City, Tent, and Van* (London, 1885), 141–142; and T. W. Thompson, "The Ceremonial Customs of the British Gipsies," *Folklore* 24, no. 3 (1913): 336–338. A man of the cloth, Reverend Elias Owen, also recounted how "a parishioner . . . Gwen Williams, told me that she thought no more of marriage in the Registrar's office than of a marriage by jumping over a besom [broom]" because "she had heard that in olden times people could be married by jumping over a broom-stick." Owen soon discovered that "such marriages are spoken of in many parts of North Wales, and, when properly attested, they are supposed to have been considered valid." See Elias Owen, *Old Stone Crosses of the Vale of Clwyd and Neighbouring Parishes* (London: Bernard Quaritch, 1886), 62–63.

93. O'Neil, "Bosses and Broomsticks"; Dundes, "'Jumping the Broom'"; Sullivan, "'Jumping the Broom'"; Parry, "Married in Slavery Time."

94. Patrick O'Neil, "Bosses and Broomsticks," 40. From his study of the practice, Patrick O'Neil argues that "slaves contended . . . with invasive ritualized attempts to degrade them and normalize their subordination. . . . Weddings, and particularly the broomstick ritual, allow us to see the intricate and multifaceted techniques by which masters wedged themselves into their slaves' lives." See O'Neil, "Bosses and Broomsticks," 32.

95. Folklore scholar Tyler Parry scrutinized African American recollections of broomstick weddings under bondage for signs of agency and fulfillment. Parry analyzed 505 narratives of marriage rites among enslaved communities, most occurring around the mid-nineteenth century. Of this number 29 percent mention some sort of broomstick ritual, 34 percent pertain to couples who married without involving any ceremonial rituals, and 37 percent describe either Christian elements or another "matrimonial format." See Parry, "Married in Slavery Time," 292.

96. O'Neil, "Bosses and Broomsticks," 33.

97. During slavery many Whites were curious about the wedding rituals of enslaved communities and would often "steal down and watch when [they] heard that colored folks were going to get married." See Parry, "Holy Land of Matrimony," 91. "A Negro Marriage" was published in at least four papers across the country: *Daily Ohio Statesman* (Columbus), March 29, 1860; *Macon (GA) Daily Telegraph*, April 7, 1860; *Wisconsin Daily Patriot* (Madison), April 9, 1860; and *Columbian Register* (New Haven, CT), September 1, 1860. It is unclear whether both parties were enslaved since only the bridegroom was asked whether he "love her master . . . [and] her mistress."

98. Sullivan, "'Jumping the Broom,'" 203–204.

99. Quoted in Parry, "Married in Slavery Time," 274.

100. Williams, *Help Me to Find My People*, 13, 172–175, 192–197.

101. George Marion McClellan, "The Negro as Writer," in *Twentieth Century Negro Literature; or, A Cyclopedia of Thought on the Vital Topics Relating to the American Negro*, ed. Daniel Wallace Culp (Atlanta: J. L. Nichols, 1902), 284–285. See also Williams, *Help Me to Find My People*, 173.

102. Nettie Henry interview, in *The Unchained: Powerful Life Stories of Former Slaves*, ed. Frederick Douglass et al. (n.p.: Madison & Adams Press, 2018), n.p. See also Williams, *Help Me to Find My People*, 144.

103. Williams, *Help Me to Find My People*, 148.

104. Williams, *Help Me to Find My People*, 154–168. Williams's extensive treatment of dozens of family search ads reveals the tenacity of countless former bondpersons who were determined to achieve reunification with family members.

105. See "Alexander Foley and His Wife Reunited and Remarried After Forty Years," *Maysville (KY) Evening Bulletin*, November 27, 1891. The same newspaper report can be found at "Last Seen: Finding Family After Slavery," http://informationwanted.org/items/show/3289.

106. Quoted in John Thornton, *Africa and Africans in the Making of the Atlantic World, 1400–1800* (Cambridge: Cambridge University Press, 1998), 200; see also 197–199.

107. Ralph Banks, *Is Marriage for White People? How the African American Marriage Decline Affects Everyone* (New York: Penguin Group/Plume, 2011), 1–16.

CHAPTER 2. SLOW VIOLENCE AND WHITE AMERICA'S REIGN OF TERROR

1. Wilma Dunaway, *The African-American Family in Slavery and Emancipation* (Cambridge: Cambridge University Press, 2003), 199–203. See also Ira Berlin and Leslie Rowland, eds., *Families and Freedom: A Documentary History of African-American Kinship in the Civil War Era* (New York: New Press, 1997).

2. Quoted in Dunaway, *African-American Family in Slavery and Emancipation*, 198. Black soldiers who returned to slaveholding properties for their wives and children were often chased away, threatened with lethal violence, and even shot. See Bart Landry, *Black Working Wives: Pioneers of the American Family Revolution* (Berkeley: University of California Press, 2000), 36.

3. Idiosyncratic punctuation and "minuscule/majuscule" lettering are original. Quoted in Berlin and Rowland, *Families and Freedom*, 57.

4. Quoted in Michael Bellesiles, *A People's History of the U.S. Military: Ordinary Soldiers Reflect on Their Experience of War, from the American Revolution to Afghanistan* (New York: New Press, 2012), 115–116.

5. Quoted in Berlin and Rowland, *Families and Freedom*, 60–62.

6. Pauline Schloesser, *The Fair Sex: White Women and Racial Patriarchy in the Early American Republic* (New York: New York University Press, 2002); Robin West, *Marriage, Sexuality, and Gender* (New York: Routledge, 2016), 27–28. The Freedmen's Bureau socialized Black spouses to pursue economic opportunities in alignment with coverture norms when they placed contractual responsibilities for agricultural labor assignments in the hands of husbands, though not without resistance from some Black women. With this arrangement, which individual White Southerners also enforced, Black men were fully authorized to control their wives' employment opportunities and wages. For more on this subject, see Mary Farmer-Kaiser, *Freedwomen and the Freedmen's Bureau: Race, Gender, and Public Policy in the Age of Emancipation* (New York: Fordham University Press, 2010), 64–95, 167–169; and Deirdre Bloome and Christopher Muller, "Tenancy and African American Marriage in the Postbellum South," *Demography* 52, no. 5 (2015): 1409–1430, esp. 1411–1412.

7. Anthony Kaye, *Joining Places: Slave Neighborhoods in the Old South* (Chapel Hill: University of North Carolina Press, 2007), 51–82.

8. Shirley Hill, "Marriage Among African American Women: A Gender Perspective," *Journal of Contemporary Family Studies* 37, no. 3 (2006): 431–433.

9. Lenhardt, "Marriage as Black Citizenship?," 1329 (see also 1327–1328, 1340–1341), http://ir.lawnet.fordham.edu/faculty_scholarship/655. See also Farmer-Kaiser, *Freedwomen and the Freedmen's Bureau*.

10. See Circular No. 5, "Rules and Regulations for Assistant Commissioners," *Freedmen's Record* 1, no. 8 (1865): 131.

11. Quoted in Dunaway, *African-American Family in Slavery and Emancipation*, 261.

12. *Federal Writers' Project: Slave Narrative Project*, vol. 10, Missouri, Abbot-Younger, 1936, Manuscript/Mixed Material, www.loc.gov/item

/mesn100/; Spencer Crew, Lonnie Bunch, and Clement Price, eds., *Slave Culture: A Documentary Collection of the Slave Narratives from the Federal Writers' Project* (Westport, CT: Greenwood Press, 2014), 1:369.

13. Steven Mintz and Sara McNeil, "Spousal Separation Under Slavery," *Digital History*, 2018, www.digitalhistory.uh.edu/disp_textbook .cfm?smtID=3&psid=490.

14. Interview with Emmanuel Elmore, December 23, 1937, in Federal Writers' Project, *Slave Narratives: A Folk History of Slavery in the United States from Interviews with Former Slaves, 1936–1938*, vol. 14, *South Carolina Narratives*, pt. 2, ed. Elmer Turnage (Washington, DC: n.p., 1941), 6–10. Cooper's focus upon her comother rather than cowife status might well indicate that she was a native African, as her son, Emmanuel Elmore, implies several times throughout his interview. For an African feminist theorization of comothering, see Oyèrónkẹ́ Oyěwùmí, *African Women and Feminism: Reflecting on the Politics of Sisterhood* (Trenton, NJ: African World Press, 2004), 1–24. See also Julie Saville, *The Work of Reconstruction: From Slave to Wage Laborer in South Carolina, 1860–1870* (Cambridge: Cambridge University Press, 1996), 102–106, for a relevant historical account of how, in slavery's immediate aftermath, postenslaved women and men sought to reconstitute their households on the basis of kinship rather than antebellum ownership when negotiating sharecropping contracts with former slaveholders.

15. See Chapter 1 for instances of former bondwomen who resisted and accommodated imposed marriages after slavery.

16. Clinton Fisk, *Counsels for Freedmen: In Sixteen Brief Lectures* (Boston: American Tract Society, 1866), 31. Taken together, Fisk's lectures teach the values of patriarchal Christian monogamy and emphasize a male head of household and family provider and female purity, chastity, and domesticity. See also Farmer-Kaiser, *Freedwomen and the Freedmen's Bureau*, 14–38.

17. Elizabeth Regosin, *Freedom's Promise: Ex-Slave Families and Citizenship in the Age of Emancipation* (Charlottesville: University Press of Virginia, 2000), 80–82.

18. American Tract Society, *The Freedman's Spelling-Book* (Boston: American Tract Society, 1865–1866), 127. The hyphenated words were apparently intended to aid those learning how to read to sound out the words. The literacy rate among enslaved persons has not been easy to decipher, but scholars generally agree that no less than 5 percent and perhaps closer to 10 percent of African Americans achieved literacy while in bondage. For a discussion of these figures and wider analysis of African American literacy during and after slavery, see Christopher Hager, *Word by Word: Emancipation and the Act of Writing* (Cambridge, MA: Harvard University Press, 2005), esp. 44–47.

19. Laura Edwards, *Gendered Strife and Confusion: The Political Culture of Reconstruction* (Urbana: University of Illinois Press, 1997), 32.

20. *Acts and Resolutions of the General Assembly of the State of Georgia, Passed in Milledgeville at an Annual Session in December 1865 and January, February,*

and March, 1866 (Milledgeville, GA: Boughton, Nisbet, Barnes, and Moore, State Printers, 1866), 240.

21. Patricia Yamin, *American Marriage: A Political Institution* (Philadelphia: University of Pennsylvania Press, 2012), 35–36.

22. Landry, *Black Working Wives*, 38.

23. Onwuachi-Willig, "The Return of the Ring"; Yamin, *American Marriage*, 32–36; Noralee Frankel, *Freedom's Women: Black Women and Families in Civil War Era Mississippi* (Bloomington: Indiana University Press, 1999), 80–87.

24. Walter Trattner, *From Poor Law to Welfare State: A History of Social Welfare in America* (New York: Free Press, 1994), 77–107; Donald Grant, *The Way It Was in the South: The Black Experience in Georgia* (Athens: University of Georgia Press, 1993), 148–150; Landry, *Black Working Wives*, 36–37.

25. *Decisions of the Department of the Interior in Cases Relating to Pension Claims and the Laws of the United States Granting and Governing Pensions* (Washington, DC: Government Printing Office, 1887), 1:326; Gustavus Weber, *The Bureau of Pensions: Its History, Activities and Organization* (Baltimore: Johns Hopkins University Press, 1923), 4–6. The 1864 act was amended in 1866 to address other issues that emerged for postenslaved persons after emancipation and again in 1873 to clarify and expand acceptable evidence of a claimant's marriage. See Regosin, *Freedom's Promise*, 83–85. With bureaucratic roots going back to the early 1800s, following the Revolutionary War, the US Pension Bureau predated and outlasted the Freedmen's Bureau. The Pension Bureau functioned alongside the Freedmen's Bureau during the latter's years of operation between 1865 and 1869 with continued efforts in educational arenas until 1872. For a comparative analysis of both governmental agencies, see Chad Goldberg, *Citizens and Paupers: Relief, Rights, and Race, from the Freedmen's Bureau to Workfare* (Chicago: University of Chicago Press, 2007). See also Dale Kretz, "Pensions and Protest: Former Slaves and the Reconstructed American State," *Journal of the Civil War Era* 7, no. 3 (2017): 425–445.

26. Two years after issuing *General Instructions*, the new Southern Division of the Pension Bureau was tasked with managing pension cases related to Union troops in the South. As a result, most of the applications filed in connection with veterans of the United States Colored Troops were processed at the Southern Division's offices in Knoxville, Tennessee, beginning in 1883. For more on this subject, see Kretz, "Pensions and Protest," 428.

27. United States Pension Bureau, *General Instructions to Special Examiners of the United States Pension Office* (Washington, DC: Government Printing Office, 1881), 28–29. The *General Instructions* was revised in 1882, 1889, and 1897.

28. Tiffany Player, "'What Are We Going to Do for Ourselves?': African American Women and the Politics of Slavery from the Antebellum Era to the Great Depression" (PhD diss., Washington University, 2018), 24; Larry Logue and Peter Blanck, "Benefit of the Doubt: African-American Civil War

Veterans and Pensions," *Journal of Interdisciplinary History* 38, no. 3 (2008): 383; Kretz, "Pensions and Protest."

29. Brandi Brimmer, "'Her Claim for Pension Is Lawful and Just': Representing Black Union Widows in Late-Nineteenth Century North Carolina," *Journal of the Civil War Era* 1, no. 2 (2011): 211. Even in the North, Black widows could become easy prey for unscrupulous attorneys ready to raid their inheritances. For example, Maria Miller Stewart (1803–1879), the first American woman known to speak publicly to a mixed-gender and -race audience on the plight of Black women, sought legal redress to contest White officials' handling of her deceased husband's estate. Maria Miller's highly public marriage to a free African American independent shipping agent, John Stewart, did nothing to protect her against the vulnerable status of Black widowhood when he died just three years after their union had been sealed before Reverend Thomas Paul, the prominent Baptist pastor of Boston's African Meeting House. Although she is hailed as the mother of Black feminist political thought, Stewart's protracted legal battle to gain access to her husband's estate and her personal plight to surmount a life of deprivation after his untimely death illustrates how unstable widowhood status could be for nineteenth-century Black women beyond the South. See Marilyn Richardson, ed., *Maria Stewart, America's First Black Woman Political Writer: Essays and Speeches* (Bloomington: Indiana University Press, 1987).

30. Brimmer, "'Her Claim for Pension Is Lawful and Just,'" 219.

31. Megan McClintock, "The Impact of the Civil War on Nineteenth-Century Marriages," in *Union Soldiers and the Northern Home Front: Wartime Experiences, Postwar Adjustments*, ed. Paul Cimbala and Randall Miller (Bronx: Fordham University Press, 2002), 409–410.

32. McClintock, "Impact of the Civil War on Nineteenth-Century Marriages," 410.

33. McClintock, "Impact of the Civil War on Nineteenth-Century Marriages," 234; Elizabeth Regosin and Donald Schaffer, *Voices of Emancipation: Understanding Slavery, the Civil War and Reconstruction through the U.S. Pension Bureau Files* (New York: New York University Press, 2008), 199.

34. Brandi Brimmer, "All Her Rights and Privileges: African-American Women and the Politics of Civil War Widows' Pensions" (PhD diss., University of California, Los Angeles, 2006), 14.

35. Kretz, "Pensions and Protest"; Regosin and Schaffer, *Voices of Emancipation*, 3–4; Logue and Blanck, "Benefit of the Doubt."

36. Brimmer, "All Her Rights and Privileges," 15. See also Kretz, "Pensions and Protest."

37. Donald Schaffer, *After the Glory: The Struggles of Black Civil War Veterans* (Lawrence: University Press of Kansas, 2004), 209.

38. Dora Costa, "Pension and Retirement Among Black Union Army Veterans," *Journal of Economic History* 70, no. 3 (2010): 571–573; Regosin and Shaffer, *Voices of Emancipation*, 1–7. An additional nineteen thousand Black men served in the navy.

39. Player, "'What Are We Going to Do for Ourselves?,'" 23–24. Although figures for Black widows are not yet determined, between 1885 and 1893 the total "number of enrolled pensioners" rose from 300,000 to close to 1 million. See Kretz, "Pensions and Protest," 427. See also 434 for his discussion of how the 1890 act impacted Black applicants.

40. Some 46,382 out of 69,341 White applicants were approved in 1889. See Kretz, "Pensions and Protest," 428. See also Costa, "Pensions and Retirement among Black Union Army Veterans," 574. Costa points out that "by 1890 81 percent of whites who had applied for a pension had been approved, compared to only 44 percent of black applicants." Costa further notes that Whites with "tenuous link[s] to service in the war" were often granted pensions, while "black veterans were not granted the same leniency."

41. During the 1868 election season, and across the period of Reconstruction (1865–1877) generally, Southern Blacks attempted to exercise their political rights to assemble, join parties, and vote, many of them Republicans. These civically engaged Blacks and some White Republicans were targeted and murdered by terroristic elements within or aligned with the Southern Democratic Party. A prime example is the September 28, 1868, Opelousas Massacre in St. Landry Parish, Louisiana, where 150–300 politically active Blacks were killed by racist Whites. In Louisiana alone, 2,000 people were killed or brutally wounded as a result of violent politically motivated attacks on the Black electorate and assassinations of Republican Party leaders just weeks before the November 1868 general election. See W. E. B. Du Bois, *Black Reconstruction in America* (1935; reprint, New Brunswick, NJ: Transaction, 2013), 608–610; Stephen Budiansky, *The Bloody Shirt: Terror After Appomattox* (New York: Viking Penguin, 2008); David Williams, *I Freed Myself: African American Self-Emancipation in the Civil War Era* (New York: Cambridge University Press, 2014), 222–229; Michael Perman and Amy Taylor, eds., *Major Problems in the Civil War and Reconstruction: Documents and Essays* (Belmont, CA: Wadsworth, 2010), 455; Gilles Vandal, *Rethinking Southern Violence: Homicides in Post–Civil War Louisiana, 1866–1884* (Columbus: Ohio State University Press, 2000); and Ralph Young, *Dissent: The History of an American Idea* (New York: New York University Press, 2015), 213–233.

42. Equal Justice Initiative, "Lynching in America: Confronting the Legacy of Racial Terror, Report Summary," 2nd ed., 2015, https://eji.org/sites/default/files/lynching-in-america-second-edition-summary.pdf. See also "A Lynching in Georgia: The Living Memorial to America's History of Racist Violence," November 2, 2016, www.theguardian.com/world/2016/nov/02/a-lynching-in-georgia-the-living-memorial-to-americas-history-of-racist-violence; and Mark Berman, "Even More Black People Were Lynched in the U.S. Than Previously Thought, Study Finds," *Washington Post*, February 10, 2015, www.washingtonpost.com/news/post-nation/wp/2015/02/10/even-more-black-people-were-lynched-in-the-u-s-than-previously-thought-study-finds/?utm_term=.0f2802edd145; www.naacp.org/history-of-lynchings/. The NAACP's earlier estimate of 3,959

Black persons lynched between 1877 and 1950 is often cited in a wide range of studies.

43. See "Women and Social Movements in the United States, 1600–2000," http://womhist.alexanderstreet.com/lynch/doc7.htm. See also https://henriettavintondavis.wordpress.com/; and http://memory.loc.gov/ammem/aaohtml/exhibit/aopart6b.html.

44. Mary Turner's age at the time of her death has generally been assumed to be anywhere from eighteen to twenty-one. I find Phillip Williams's research most compelling, which identifies Mary Hattie Graham's birth month and year as December 1884. Williams also determines that Mary's husband, Hayes Turner, was born August 15, 1892, noting that it is also possible he was born in August 1893. See Phillip Williams, "Mary Turner and the Lynching Rampage of 1918 Reexamined," May 18, 2018, https://sites.google.com/view/wiregrassrdhp/mary-turner.

45. For more on Smith's age, see Williams, "Mary Turner and the Lynching Rampage of 1918 Reexamined."

46. According to Vicky Peláez, "From 1870 until 1910, in the state of Georgia, 88% of hired-out convicts were Black. In Alabama, 93% of 'hired-out' miners were Black. In Mississippi, a huge prison farm similar to the old slave plantations replaced the system of hiring out convicts. The notorious Parchman plantation existed until 1972." Peláez, "The Prison Industry in the United States: Big Business or a New Form of Slavery," *Global Research*, February 24, 2019, www.globalresearch.ca/the-prison-industry-in-the-united-states-big-business-or-a-new-form-of-slavery/8289.

47. Christopher Meyers, "Killing Them by the Wholesale: A Lynching Rampage in South Georgia," *Georgia Historical Quarterly* 90, no. 2 (2006): 219–221.

48. Walter White, *Rope and Faggot: A Biography of Judge Lynch* (Notre Dame, IN: University of Notre Dame Press, 2016), 29. See also Kerry Segrave, *Lynchings of Women in the United States: The Recorded Cases, 1851–1946* (Jefferson, NC: McFarland, 2010), 138–140, for a synopsis of the *Chicago Defender*'s report on the series of dramatic disputes between the Smiths and the Turners that led to the grizzly outcome for both couples.

49. Walter White, "The Work of a Mob," *Crisis* 16 (September 1918); Julie Buckner Armstrong, *Mary Turner and the Memory of Lynching* (Athens: University of Georgia Press, 2011), 36; Meyers, "Killing Them by the Wholesale," 214–235; www.blackpast.org/african-american-history/mary-turner-1899-1918/.

50. Carol Anderson, *White Rage: The Unspoken Truth of Our Racial Divide* (New York: Bloomsbury USA, 2016). For other similar examples of the costly impact of White terroristic violence on Black marriage, family life, and wealth building, see Eric Arnesen, *Black Protest and the Great Migration: A Brief History with Documents* (Boston: Bedford/St. Martin's, 2002), 50–53.

51. Patrick Phillips, *Blood at the Root: A Racial Cleansing in America* (New York: W. W. Norton, 2016), 38–39. Phillips provides the most comprehensive

268 Notes to Chapter 2

account of the 1912 lynchings and anti-Black xenophobic events in Forsyth County, Georgia.

52. Phillips, *Blood at the Root*, 42–43.

53. Phillips, *Blood at the Root*, 1. See also John McKay, *It Happened in Atlanta: Events That Shaped History* (Kearney, NE: Morris, 2011), 148.

54. Phillips, *Blood at the Root*, 4, 7; McKay, *It Happened in Atlanta*, 148.

55. Duarte Geraldino, "Column: In Search of the Spot Where Two Black Teens Were Killed," January 16, 2017, *PBS NewsHour*, www.pbs.org /newshour/nation/column-search-spot-two-black-teens-killed; Elliot Jaspin, *Buried in the Bitter Waters: The History of Racial Cleansing in America* (New York: Basic Books, 2007), 129, 135–138; McKay, *It Happened in Atlanta*, 148–149; Phillips, *Blood at the Root*, 45–82.

56. Phillips, *Blood at the Root*, 63, 67. Blacks were driven from five neighboring counties in North Georgia around the same time they were banished from Forsyth County. For example, all Black residents had disappeared from Dawson County by 1920. For an extensive study of towns and counties notorious for expelling Blacks, see James Loewen, *Sundown Towns: A Hidden Dimension of American Racism* (New York: Touchstone, 2006), esp. 178–179, for details about Forsyth, Dawson, and other Georgia counties guilty of racial cleansing.

57. In 1920 twenty-three Blacks were counted among Forsyth County residents in Census data. By 1930 sixteen Blacks were counted in the Census. Subsequently, they dropped from the record. Patrick Phillips surmises that the Stricklands, one of the county's wealthy White families, quietly invited the twenty-three laborers to return to work on their farms after the racial-cleansing campaign had abated. See Phillips, *Blood at the Root*, 68, 186–188, 198. See also Becky Little, "In 1912, This Georgia County Drove Out Every Black Resident," *History*, May 23, 1918, www.history.com/news/georgia -racial-expulsion-stacey-abrams; Michele Cohen, "All-White Forsyth: Quaint, Rural, Racist," *South Florida Sun Sentinel*, January 25, 1987, www.sun -sentinel.com/news/fl-xpm-1987-01-25-8701050886-story.html.

58. Phillips, *Blood at the Root*, 69. See also Grant, *The Way It Was in the South*, 170.

59. Phillips, *Blood at the Root*, 108–110; Ann Short Chirhart, *Torches of Light: Georgia Teachers and the Coming of the Modern South* (Athens: University of Georgia Press, 2005), 35–38.

60. When Oprah Winfrey took her show to Forsyth County in 1987, it still had the reputation of being "a county where no black person had lived for 75 years." Oprah interviewed county residents who brazenly declared their agenda to keep Forsyth County White. Oprah admitted that "she and her producers knew it was dangerous to go down there, but they were smart enough to know to leave town before the sun went down." See "Oprah Visits a County Where No Black Person Had Lived for 75 Years," *The Oprah Winfrey Show*/OWN, January 2, 2015, www.youtube.com/watch?v=WErjPm FulQ0.

61. For more on the relationship between lynchings and Black people's socioeconomic mobility, see Roberto Franzosi, Gianluca De Fazio, and

Stefania Vicari, "Ways of Measuring Agency: An Application of Quantitative Narrative Analysis to Lynchings in Georgia (1875–1930)," *Sociological Methodology* 42 (2012): 1–42; and Stewart Tolnay and Elwood Beck, *A Festival of Violence: An Analysis of Southern Lynchings, 1882–1930* (Urbana: University of Illinois Press, 1995).

62. Unfortunately, one Black minister, Reverend John Dart, would "[travel] through Black communities selling photographs of the Baker family and a written account of the trial, all the while [deceptively] collecting donations and assuring contributors that the family was under his care." See Philip Dray, *At the Hands of Persons Unknown: The Lynching of Black America* (New York: Modern Library/Random House, 2002), 121. William Lloyd Garrison II (son of the celebrated abolitionist) eventually raised funds to purchase a home for the family in Boston. By the time of her death in 1947, Lavinia had outlived all of her remaining children, four of whom died young from tuberculosis. See Terence Finnegan, *A Deed So Accursed: Lynching in Mississippi and South Carolina, 1881–1940* (Charlottesville: University of Virginia Press, 2013), 81–88; Christopher Waldrep, *The Many Faces of Judge Lynch: Extralegal Violence and Punishment in America* (New York: Palgrave Macmillan, 2002), 118; Damon Fordham, *True Stories of Black South Carolina* (Charleston, SC: History Press, 2008); and "'The Dead Father Fell'—Lynching Frazier Baker, a Black Postmaster (1898)," *This Cruel War*, February 21, 2017, www.thiscruelwar.com/lynching-black-postmaster-1898/. Frazier's surviving children in order of age were Rosello, a.k.a. Rosa; Cora; Lincoln; Sarah; and Wille.

63. Some scholars have exposed the spate of race riots and pogroms that occurred across the South immediately after the Civil War. For more information see, for example, Stephen Ash, *A Massacre in Memphis: The Race Riot That Shook the Nation One Year After the Civil War* (New York: Hill and Wang, 2013); John DeSantis, *The Thibodaux Massacre: Racial Violence and the 1887 Sugar Cane Labor Strike* (Charleston, SC: History Press, 2016); and LeeAnna Keith, *The Colfax Massacre: The Untold Story of Black Power, White Terror and the Death of Reconstruction* (New York: Oxford University Press, 2008).

64. The infamous East St. Louis, Illinois, massacre took place during July 1917. See Brian Norman and Piper Kendrix Williams, eds., *Representing Segregation: Toward an Aesthetics of Living Jim Crow, and Other Forms of Racial Division* (Albany: State University of New York Press, 2010), 95.

65. Gunnar Myrdal, *An American Dilemma: The Negro Problem and American Democracy* (New York: Harper & Row, 1944), 566. Émile Durkheim coined the concept of "collective effervescence" to theorize and define religion and its social function in *The Elementary Forms of the Religious Life*, ed. Mark Cladis, trans. Carol Cosman (New York: Oxford University Press, 2001 [1912]).

66. Who could doubt this conclusion? I, for one, can only confess that, under the cloak and comfort of my own professional status, I experienced stress-induced physiological reactions of my own to the stories and historical material I uncovered or revisited while writing this book. See Patti Wigington, "History of the 1923 Rosewood Massacre: Mass Racial Violence in a

Florida Town" *ThoughtCo*, updated December 29, 2017, www.thoughtco.com
/rosewood-florida-massacre-4156825.

67. "History of Lynchings," NAACP, www.naacp.org/history-of
-lynchings/.

68. Isabelle Wilkerson, *The Warmth of Other Suns: The Epic Story of America's Great Migration* (2010; reprint, New York: Vintage Books, 2011), 39.

69. The Tulsa riot occurred May 31–June 1, 1921. Fred Williams, "Black Wall Street: A Legacy of Success," *Ebony*, February 24, 2014, www.ebony.com/black-history/black-wall-street-a-legacy-of-success-798/. See also James Hirsch, *Riot and Remembrance: The Tulsa Race War and Its Legacy* (Boston: Houghton Mifflin, 2002); Scott Ellsworth, *Death in a Promised Land: The Tulsa Race Riot of 1921* (Baton Rouge: Louisiana State University Press, 1982); and Alfred Brophy, *Reconstructing the Dreamland: The Tulsa Riot of 1921* (New York: Oxford University Press, 2002).

70. "A Lynching in Georgia," www.theguardian.com/world/2016/nov/02/a-lynching-in-georgia-the-living-memorial-to-americas-history-of-racist-violence; Equal Justice Initiative, "Moore's Ford Bridge," https://eji.org/reports/online/lynching-in-america-targeting-black-veterans/moores-ford-bridge.

71. Southern Poverty Law Center, "Answers to Last Mass Lynching in U.S. Die When Investigators Close Case After 72 Years," *Hatewatch*, February 7, 2018, www.splcenter.org/hatewatch/2018/02/07/answers-last-mass-lynching-us-die-when-investigators-close-case-after-72-years. See also Orlando Patterson, *Rituals of Blood: Consequences of Slavery in Two American Centuries* (New York: Basic Civitas, 1999), xiii, 188–201. Patterson argues that Southern lynchings fed the senses of White participants and attendees. When Black bodies were roasted to death in bonfires, those present ingested the odor of the burnt Black flesh. For this reason, Patterson describes such violent orgies as acts of "ritual cannibalism." Daina Berry treats pre-emancipation examples of Whites who plundered and made souvenirs of Black flesh and body parts postmortem in her groundbreaking study, *The Price for Their Pound of Flesh: The Value of the Enslaved from Womb to Grave in the Building of a Nation* (Boston: Beacon Press, 2017).

72. Ta-Nehisi Coates, *Between the World and Me* (New York: Spiegel & Grau, 2015). Throughout the book, Coates cites and spins variations of James Baldwin's point that European descendants in America "have brought humanity to the edge of oblivion: because they think they are white." Baldwin originally penned the phrase in a 1984 *Essence* magazine article. It was also published as "On Being White . . . and Other Lies," in *Black on White: Black Writers on What It Means to Be White*, ed. David Roediger (New York: Schocken Books, 1998), 180.

73. Ralph Ginzburg, *100 Years of Lynching* (Baltimore: Black Classic Press, 1962); Amy Louise Wood, *Lynching and Spectacle: Witnessing Racial Violence in America, 1890–1940* (Chapel Hill: University of North Carolina Press, 2009), 71–112, 179–222; Lori Merish, *Sentimental Materialism: Gender,*

Commodity Culture and Nineteenth-Century American Literature (Durham, NC: Duke University Press, 2000), 270–303; Dray, *At the Hands of Persons Unknown*, 13, 94, 218, 349; Frantz Fanon, *Black Skin, White Masks*, trans. Charles Lam Markmann (London: Pluto Press, 1986 [1952]), esp. 155–180; Tommy Curry, *The Man-Not: Race, Class, Genre, and the Dilemmas of Black Manhood* (Philadelphia: Temple University Press, 2017), esp. 34–35.

74. In addition to the gifting of postmortem Black body parts, I have in mind here the common slaveholding practice of gifting an enslaved person to children and extended family as birthday presents and property inheritance without regard for the impact such gifting had upon the severing of Black couples and families.

75. Phillips, *Blood at the Root*, 163.

76. Karlos Hill, *Beyond the Rope: The Impact of Lynching on Black Culture and Memory* (New York: Cambridge University Press, 2016), esp. 83; Wood, *Lynching and Spectacle*, 11, 76, 108; Dray, *At the Hands of Persons Unknown*, 82–83, 168, 181.

77. Wilkerson, *Warmth of Other Suns*, 106–112, 127–138, 150–157.

78. Stewart Tolnay, "The Great Migration and Changes in the Northern Black Family, 1940–1990," *Social Forces* 75, no. 4 (1997): 1213–1238. For older studies, see W. E. B. Du Bois, *The Philadelphia Negro* (1899; reprint, Philadelphia: University of Pennsylvania Press, 1996); E. Franklin Frazier, *The Negro Family in Chicago* (Chicago: University of Chicago Press, 1932); and *The Negro Family in the United States* (Chicago: University of Chicago Press, 1966). See also John Hope Franklin, *From Slavery to Freedom* (New York: Alfred A. Knopf, 1967); and Patterson, *Rituals of Blood*.

79. Thomas Wilson, "Explaining Black Southern Migrants' Advantage in Family Stability: The Role of Selective Migration," *Social Forces* 80, no. 2 (2001): 555–571; Carole Marks, *Farewell We're Good and Gone: The Great Black Migration* (Bloomington: Indiana University Press, 1989).

80. Dylan Penningroth, "African American Divorce in Virginia and Washington D.C., 1865–1930," *Journal of Family History* 33, no. 1 (2008): 21, 27. Dylan also notes, "Between 1865 and 1930, thousands of African Americans got divorced. This was an important part of black life, but it has not attracted very much attention from historians" (22).

81. "St. Louis Blues" was written by W. C. Handy and published in 1914. Bessie Smith recorded her version of the song on January 14, 1925, in New York City with Columbia Records.

82. Rob Nixon, *Slow Violence and the Environmentalism of the Poor* (Cambridge, MA: Harvard University Press, 2011).

83. Annette Gordon-Reed, *Andrew Johnson* (New York: Times Books/Henry Holt, 2011), esp. 118–119.

84. "Into the Fire," on *The African Americans: Many Rivers to Cross*, PBS, November 5, 2013, written and hosted by Henry Louis Gates, directed by Jamila Wignot.

85. Herbert Gutman, *The Black Family in Slavery and Freedom, 1750–1925* (New York: Random House, 1976).

86. Hunter, *Bound in Wedlock*. For more on the Moynihan Report, see Chapter 3.

87. Elaine Pinderhughes, "African American Marriage in the 20th Century," *Family Process* 41, no. 2 (2002): 271.

88. Lenhardt, "Marriage as Black Citizenship?," 1319. See also Amy Stanley, *From Bondage to Contract: Wage Labor, Marriage, and the Market in the Age of Slave Emancipation* (New York: Cambridge University Press, 1998), 45; and Onwuachi-Willig, "Return of the Ring."

89. Hunter, *Bound in Wedlock*, 306.

90. Pinderhughes, "African American Marriage in the 20th Century," 271–272. Pinderhughes specifically identifies the following factors as threats to Black marital occurrence, stability, and longevity after slavery: "the disorganization of the post–Civil War plantation economy, during which there were frequent separations from and desertions by spouses; ongoing economic exploitation; disenfranchisement (maintained by lynching); and other structural inequities affecting employment, housing, and health."

91. See Hunter, *Bound in Wedlock*, 306–307.

92. Raley, Sweeney, and Wondra, "The Growing Racial and Ethnic Divide in the U.S. Marriage Patterns," 89–109. See also Hill, "Marriage Among African American Women," 435; Myrdal, *An American Dilemma*, 359; and Richard Sterner, *The Negro's Share: A Study of Income, Consumption, Housing and Public Assistance* (New York: Harper & Brothers, 1943), 280–281.

93. Donna Franklin and Angela James, *Ensuring Inequality: The Structural Transformation of the African-American Family* (New York: Oxford University Press, 2015), 27–49.

94. John Dittmer, *Local People: The Struggle for Civil Rights in Mississippi* (Urbana: University of Illinois Press, 1995), 15; Michael Newton, *Unsolved Civil Rights Murder Cases, 1934–1970* (Jefferson, NC: McFarland, 2016), 131–132.

95. James Grossman, *Land of Hope: Chicago, Black Southerners, and the Great Migration* (Chicago: University of Chicago Press, 1989), 33–34. The Elaine, Arkansas, massacre of 1919 that left more than two hundred Black farmers dead after making plans to circumvent local capitalist exploitation by unionizing and selling their cotton directly to Boston outlets is another instance of how White patriarchal supremacy undermined Black male ambitions to prosper and build wealth. For more on this massacre and its destruction of Black marriages and families as well as property, see Grif Stockley, *Blood in Their Eyes: The Elaine Race Massacres of 1919* (Fayetteville: University of Arkansas Press, 2001), esp. 50–51, for an example of how, in addition to their Black male rivals, White men even targeted and killed Black women and children.

96. See R. Robin Miller, "Various Implications of the 'Race to Incarcerate' on Incarcerated African American Men and Their Families," in *Impacts of*

Incarceration on the African American Family, ed. Othello Harris and R. Robin Miller (New Brunswick, NJ: Transaction, 2009), 5–6, for a discussion of how incarcerated Black men are particularly excluded from opportunities to fulfill the patriarchal role of "the good provider," even after release from prison.

97. For example, Deirdre Bloome and Christopher Muller cite Martin Ruef's 2012 study that "showed that among all labor contracts collected by Freedmen's Bureau offices in Washington, DC and Alexandria, VA between August 1865 and March 1867, only 18% were signed by women." See their "Tenancy and African American Marriage," 1411. See also Martin Ruef, "Constructing Labor Markets: The Valuation of Black Labor in the U.S. South, 1831 to 1867," *American Sociological Review* 77, no. 6 (2012): 970–998.

98. Bloome and Muller, "Tenancy and African American Marriage," 1414.

99. Hill, "Marriage Among African American Women," 421–440.

100. Stanley, *From Bondage to Contract*, 33–34. See also Hill, "Marriage Among African American Women," 433–435. For more on the formation of Black patriarchy in America and Black women's resistance to it, see Franklin and James, *Ensuring Inequality*, 22–33. For a wider study of postenslaved Black women's entrepreneurial genius, personal agency over their employment within and beyond the homes of former slaveholding mistresses, and their exertion of their rights and power during social interactions with those same mistresses, see Thavolia Glymph, *Out of the House of Bondage: The Transformation of the Plantation Household* (New York: Cambridge University Press, 2008), 63–226.

101. Pinderhughes, "African American Marriage in the 20th Century," 276.

102. Christine Stanik, Susan McHale, and Ann Crouter, "Gender Dynamics Predict Changes in Marital Love Among African American Couples," *Journal of Marriage and Family* 75, no. 4 (2013): 795.

103. Mary A. Bell, *Slave Narratives*, vol. 10, *Missouri Narratives*, www .gutenberg.org/files/35379/35379-0.txt. For my earlier discussion of this testimony, see Chapter 1 of this book.

104. "Ontological" is used here to indicate the reality and essence of *being human*, a reality Black people have never been granted in America without theological debate, cultural contestation, and constitutional and legislative reform.

105. For critical discussions of patriarchy and Black hypermasculinity, see Rudolph Byrd and Beverly Guy-Sheftall, eds., *Traps: African American Men on Gender and Sexuality* (Bloomington: Indiana University Press, 2001).

106. Nixon, *Slow Violence and the Environmentalism of the Poor*, 2–3.

107. Sarah Smalls, *Speeches at the Constitutional Convention by Gen. Robt. Smalls with the Right of Suffrage Passed by the Constitutional Convention* (Charleston, SC: Esquirer Print, 1896), 7, https://archive.org/details /speechesatconsti00smal.

108. John Dollard, *Caste and Class in a Southern Town* (1937; reprint, Garden City, NY: Doubleday, 1957), 359.

109. Bill Steigerwald, *30 Days a Black Man: The Forgotten Story That Exposed the Jim Crow South* (Guilford, CT: Lyons Press, 2017), 142. Steigerwald's book examines the odyssey of Pulitzer Prize–winning journalist Ray Swigle, who passed for a Black man and lived undercover in the Jim Crow South collecting evidence of White racial terror, including the Gilberts' tragic story. For a stunning criticism of Ray and other Whites who have "played Black" in American history, see Alisha Gaines, *Black for a Day: Fantasies of Race and Empathy* (Chapel Hill: University of North Carolina Press, 2017).

110. Robert Johnson, *Returning Home: A Century of African-American Repatriation* (Trenton, NJ: Africa World Press, 2005); Kenneth Barnes, *Journey of Hope: The Back-to-Africa Movement in Arkansas in the Late 1800s* (Chapel Hill: University of North Carolina Press, 2004); Alan Huffman, *Mississippi in Africa: The Saga of the Slaves of Prospect Hill Plantation and Their Legacy in Liberia Today* (Jackson: University Press of Mississippi, 2004).

111. W. E. B. Du Bois, *The Souls of Black Folk* (New York: Oxford University Press, 2007), 13; Billie Holiday, "Strange Fruit," Commodore, April 20, 1939. Abel Meeropol originally composed the lyrics of "Strange Fruit" as a poem.

112. Bessie Smith's recording of "Chicago Bound Blues" was cut on December 4, 1923, in New York. The song was written by Porter Grainger and Bob Ricketts and produced by Columbia Records. Although this book draws on only two blues compositions, it is worth noting that Black women's larger corpus of blues is a powerful source of Black memory that reveals Black women's collective laments about the suppression of Black love in America. For a brilliant treatment of Black women's blues as sites of critical feminist consciousness about race, class, love, and other themes, see Angela Davis's *Blues Legacies and Black Feminism* (New York: Vintage Books, 1998), esp. 19–20, where Davis discusses how women blues singers "did not typically affirm female resignation and powerlessness" as expressed in Bessie Smith's "Chicago Blues."

113. Wilkerson, *Warmth of Other Suns*, 170–172, 185, 292–294, 340–346, 356–361, 398–400, 450–451.

CHAPTER 3. LOVE AND WELFARE

1. Johnnie Tillmon, "Welfare Fraud," in *Welfare Mothers Speak Out: We Ain't Gonna Shuffle Anymore*, ed. Thomas Tarantino and Dismas Becker (New York: W. W. Norton, 1972), 46; Abbie Perry, "The Welfare Rights Movement: Fighting Stereotypes to Gain Equality," *Perspectives: A Journal of Historical Inquiry* 36 (2009): 70, www.calstatela.edu/sites/default/files/groups/Perspectives/Vol36/perry.pdf.

2. Kenneth Neubeck and Noel Cazenave, *Welfare Racism: Playing the Race Card Against America's Poor* (New York: Routledge, 2001), 39.

3. Dorothy E. Roberts, "Welfare and the Problem of Black Citizenship," *Yale Law Journal* 105, no. 1563 (1996): 1570. Cited from Faculty Scholarship, Paper 1283, http://scholarship.law.upenn.edu/faculty_scholarship/1283/.

For more on these programs, which began during the 1920s, see Onwuachi-Willig, "The Return of the Ring," 1665–1670.

4. Neubeck and Cazenave, *Welfare Racism*, 46–50; Robert Lieberman, *Shifting the Color Line: Race and the American Welfare State* (Cambridge, MA: Harvard University Press, 2001).

5. Annelise Orleck, *Storming Caesars Palace* (Boston: Beacon Press, 2005), 99 (emphasis added). Even today, current data reinforce the findings of the earliest welfare commissions and studies that have indicated that White mothers regularly receive more sympathetic treatment and larger welfare payments than Black mothers. See Tracy Jan, "States with More Black People Have Less Generous Welfare Benefits, Study Says," *Washington Post*, June 6, 2017, www.washingtonpost.com/news/wonk/wp/2017/06/06/states-with-more-black-people-have-less-generous-welfare-benefits-study-says/?utm_term=.7d2af135a6e3. See also Neubeck and Cazenave, *Welfare Racism*, esp. 41–65.

6. Neubeck and Cazenave, *Welfare Racism*, 51–54.

7. Based on median annual earnings, by 1970, for every dollar that White men earned, Black men earned 69 cents, White women earned 58 cents, and Black women earned 48 cents, less than half of what White men earned. See "The Wage Gap by Gender and Race," www.infoplease.com/ipa/A0882775.html.

8. Neubeck and Cazenave, *Welfare Racism*, 63.

9. Although the Eisenhower administration relaxed some of the 1935 Social Security Act's punitive welfare regulations, state lawmakers and eventually the federal government resisted and passed new laws that were even more detrimental. See Alison Lefkovitz, "Men in the House: Race, Welfare, and the Regulation of Men's Sexuality in the United States, 1961–1972," *Journal of the History of Sexuality* 20, no. 3 (2011): 597. See also Neubeck and Cazenave, *Welfare Racism*, 59–65; and Roberts, "Welfare and the Problem of Black Citizenship," 1571–1572.

10. *Claudine*, directed by John Berry, written by Lester Pine and Tina Pine (Third World Cinema, 1974).

11. "Mr. Welfare Man" was written and produced by Curtis Mayfield and recorded by Gladys Knight and the Pips on the film's 1974 album, *Claudine*.

12. See, for example, the research of Nicholas Lemann, who cites compelling data for the welfare system's impact upon declining rates of Black marriage in 1960s Chicago in *The Promised Land: The Great Migration and How It Changed America* (New York: Vintage Books, 1992), 282–288.

13. Johnnie Tillmon, "Welfare Is a Women's Issue." *Ms. Magazine*, Spring 1972, www.msmagazine.com/spring2002/tillmon.asp.

14. Brian Lanker, *I Dream a World: Portraits of Women Who Changed America* (1989; reprint, New York: Stewart, Tabori, and Chang, 1999), 96, courtesy of the Brian Lanker Archive; Orleck, *Storming Caesars Palace*, 108.

15. Johnnie Tillmon and Hobart Burch, "Insights of a Welfare Mother: Conversations with Johnnie Tillmon," George Wiley Papers, box 30, folder

5, *Journal* 14 (1970): 14, quoted in Premilla Nadasen, "We Do Whatever Becomes Necessary: Johnnie Tillmon, Welfare Rights and Black Power," in *Want to Start a Revolution? Radical Women in the Black Freedom Struggle*, ed. Jeanne Theoharis and Komozi Woodard (New York: New York University Press, 2009), 321.

16. Sherna Gluck, interview no. 1 with Johnnie Tillmon, February 1984, the Virtual Oral/Aural History Archive, California State University, Long Beach, http://symposia.library.csulb.edu/iii/cpro/DigitalItemViewPage .external;jsessionid=E9AD176910B4FDBCF026CEC0AD5E898E?lang=& sp=1001808&sp=T&sp=1&suite=def.

17. Lanker, *I Dream a World*, 96.

18. For a contemporary discussion of this subject, see Elijah Anderson's chapter "The Nigger Moment" in his book *The Cosmopolitan Canopy: Race and Civility in Everyday Life* (New York: W. W. Norton, 2011), 249–273.

19. M. David Forrest, "Johnnie Tillmon," American National Biography Online, www.anb.org/articles/15/15-01372.html; Nadasen, "We Do Whatever Becomes Necessary," 320.

20. Nadasen, "We Do Whatever Becomes Necessary," 320.

21. Nadasen, "We Do Whatever Becomes Necessary," 320.

22. Nadasen, "We Do Whatever Becomes Necessary," 326.

23. Lanker, *I Dream a World*, 96.

24. Lanker, *I Dream a World*, 96.

25. Tillmon, "Welfare Is a Women's Issue." See also Tillmon's reprinted article, "Welfare Is a Women's Issue," in *Welfare: A Documentary History of U.S. Policy and Politics*, ed. Gwendolyn Mink and Rickie Solinger (New York: New York University Press, 2003), 374.

26. Ellen Reese, *Backlash Against Welfare Mothers: Past and Present* (Berkeley: University of California Press, 2005), 40–41.

27. Sarah Smarsh, *Heartland: A Memoir of Working Hard and Being Broke in the Richest Country* (New York: Scribner, 2018), 131–132.

28. The mother was most likely Black since "the preponderance of Negro families resided" in Wayne County, Detroit. See Winifred Bell, *Aid to Dependent Children* (New York: Columbia University Press, 1965), 47–48.

29. Reese, *Backlash Against Welfare Mothers*; Dána-Ain Davis, *Battered Black Women and Welfare Reform* (Albany: State University of New York Press, 2006); James Patterson, *America's Struggle Against Poverty in the Twentieth Century* (Cambridge, MA: Harvard University Press, 2003).

30. Friels testified before the 1967 US Commission on Civil Rights that was investigating the national problem of impoverishment that welfare recipients tackled daily. See US Commission on Civil Rights, "A Time to Listen . . . a Time to Act: Voices from the Ghettos of the Nation's Cities," Washington, DC, November 1967, 32–33, www2.law.umaryland.edu/marshall /usccr/documents/cr12t48.pdf. See also Mink and Solinger, *Welfare*, 278.

31. Between 1947 and 1970, the unemployment rates for Black males in the civilian labor force regularly doubled that of their White male

counterparts. During these decades, White men had experienced their lowest rates of unemployment—2.5 percent—in the years 1952, 1953, and 1969. The unemployment rates for Black males during those same years were 5.2 percent, 4.8 percent, and 5.3 percent, respectively. White male unemployment reached its highest point of 6.1 percent in 1958. In that same year, the unemployment rate for Black males—also the highest for the designated twenty-three-year period—was 13.8 percent. For Black males who actually were employed, by the year 1970, they were earning only 69 cents on every dollar their White male counterparts holding comparable positions earned (see note 7). US Bureau of the Census, *Historical Statistics of the United States, Colonial Times to 1970*, bicentennial edition, pt. 2 (Washington, DC: Government Printing Office, 1975), 135. The data for Blacks aggregated unemployment percentages for "Negro and other races."

32. Richard Caputo, *U.S. Social Welfare Reform: Policy Transitions from 1981 to the Present* (New York: Springer, 2011), 5; Reese, *Backlash Against Welfare Mothers*, 41.

33. Mink and Solinger, *Welfare*, 218.

34. Lefkovitz, "Men in the House."

35. Alison Lefkovitz, *Strange Bedfellows: Marriage in the Age of Women's Liberation* (Philadelphia: University of Pennsylvania Press, 2018), 103.

36. Lemann, *Promised Land*, 104.

37. Lemann, *Promised Land*, 104–105.

38. Lemann, *Promised Land*, 104–106.

39. Jacquelyn Williams, interview by Chad Freidrichs, *The Pruitt-Igoe Myth*, directed by Chad Freidrichs (2011; Columbia, MO: Unicorn Stencil). For additional stories and documentation of husbands and adult sons who were forced to leave their families due to welfare policies, see US Commission on Civil Rights, "A Time to Listen . . . a Time to Act," 33–34, 108–109.

40. Mink and Solinger, *Welfare*, 169–171.

41. Joyce Ladner, interview by Freidrichs, *The Pruitt-Igoe Myth*.

42. Ladner, interview by Freidrichs, *The Pruitt-Igoe Myth*. See also Lefkovitz, "Men in the House," 606–608.

43. Sylvester Brown, interview by Freidrichs, *The Pruitt-Igoe Myth*.

44. In 1974 Riddick challenged the actual "legality" of the state's coercive strategy, when she sued the state for damages in federal court. After a long fight, Riddick and other North Carolina victims of forced sterilization were awarded $10 million in 2013. See David Zucchino, "Sterilized by North Carolina, She Felt Raped Once More," *Los Angeles Times*, January 25, 2012, www.latimes.com/archives/la-xpm-2012-jan-25-la-na-forced-sterilization-20120126-story.html; Jamie Dean, "Unwanted," *World Magazine*, September 4, 2015, https://world.wng.org/2015/09/unwanted; Associated Press, "Woman Fights for Compensation for Forced Sterilization," *Florida Times-Union*, August 15, 2011, www.jacksonville.com/article/20110815/NEWS/801246149; and Stacey Naggiar, "Victims of Forced Sterilization to Receive $10 Million from North Carolina," *NBC News*,

July 25, 2013, www.nbcnews.com/nightly-news/victims-forced-sterilization
-receive-10-million-north-carolina-flna6C10753957.

45. Joan Railey and Kevin Begos, "'Still Hiding': Woman Sterilized at 14 Still Carrying a Load of Shame," *Winston-Salem (NC) Journal*, December 9, 2002.

46. Elaine Riddick, interviewed by Nancy Snyderman, "State of Shame: NC Sterilization Survivors Fight for Justice," *Rock Center with Brian Williams*, NBC News, November 7, 2011, www.nbcnews.com/video/rockcenter/45201021#45201021.

47. Gluck, interview no. 1 with Tillmon.

48. Allison Puglisi, "Identity, Power, and the California Welfare-Rights Struggle, 1963–1975," *Humanities* 6, no. 14 (2017): 3, www.mdpi.com/journal/humanities.

49. Dee Johnson, interview by Guida West, April 2, 1984, Guida West Papers, Sophia Smith Collection, box 8, folder 9, Smith College, Northampton, MA.

50. Hobart Burch, "Insights of a Welfare Mother: Conversations with Johnnie Tillmon," *Journal* 14 (1970): 13–23; George Wiley Papers, box 30, folder 5, Wisconsin Historical Society, Madison, quoted in Puglisi, "Identity, Power, and the California Welfare-Rights Struggle."

51. Sherna Gluck, interview no. 2 with Johnnie Tillmon, February 1984, the Virtual Oral/Aural History Archive, California State University, Long Beach.

52. Nadasen, "We Do Whatever Becomes Necessary," 324.

53. Lanker, *I Dream a World*, 96.

54. Tillmon, "Welfare Is a Women's Issue"; Mink and Solinger, *Welfare*, 378.

55. Nadasen, "We Do Whatever Becomes Necessary," 328. For more on the history of forced sterilization in America, see Adam Cohen, *Imbeciles: The Supreme Court, American Eugenics, and the Sterilization of Carrie Buck* (New York: Penguin Press, 2016). See also "The Right to Self-Determination: Freedom from Involuntary Sterilization," *Disability Justice*, https://disabilityjustice.org/right-to-self-determination-freedom-from-involuntary-sterilization/.

56. The Tillmon Center's supervisor and central organizer, Mollie Taylor, described these achievements at the time in an interview with a local newspaper journalist. See Carl Coates, "Child Care Center Opens," *Los Angeles Sentinel*, November 7, 1974.

57. Nadasen, "We Do Whatever Becomes Necessary," 329.

58. Gluck, interview no. 2 with Tillmon.

59. Puglisi, "Identity, Power, and the California Welfare-Rights Struggle," 9.

60. Sherna Gluck, interview no. 3 with Johnnie Tillmon, February 1984, the Virtual Oral/Aural History Archive, California State University, Long Beach, quoted in Nadasen, "We Do Whatever Becomes Necessary," 320.

61. Lefkovitz, "Men in the House," 605.

62. *King v. Smith*, 392 U.S. 309 (1968). The case was argued April 23, 1968, and decided June 17, 1968.
63. *King v. Smith*, 392 U.S. 309 (1968).
64. *King v. Smith*, 392 U.S. 309, 315 (1968).
65. *King v. Smith*, 392 U.S. 309, 336 (1968).
66. Tillmon, "Welfare Fraud," 46.
67. Mink and Solinger, *Welfare*, 374. Across the nation today, similar practices continue to victimize Black women on welfare and poor Black men whose children receive public assistance and housing subsidies from the government. These practices will be addressed in Chapter 4.
68. Gluck, interview no. 3 with Tillmon.
69. The unidentified mother resided in Washington, DC, and had received public assistance since 1956. Details of her exchange with an ADC Department of Public Welfare investigator were included in Senator Robert Byrd's 1962 "welfare abuse" studies, which he entered "into the Congressional Record to illustrate the basis of his—and other senators'—outrage about welfare expenditures and fraud in the United States." Mink and Solinger, *Welfare*, 217, 220. Her remark expresses perhaps too a young Black mother's personal sovereignty and, I would hazard, serves as an aperture to the intimate lives of many forgotten Black women since the early twentieth century whom society judged and punished for their "utopian longings," "waywardness," and "refusal to be governed." See Saidiya Hartman's *Wayward Lives, Beautiful Experiments: Intimate Histories of Social Upheaval* (New York: W. W. Norton, 2019), xv.
70. Moynihan's study revealed that nearly 25 percent of Black households were headed by single mothers in 1964. See Daniel Moynihan, "The Negro Family: The Case for National Action" (Washington, DC: Office of Planning and Research, United States Department of Labor, 1965), 1–48. Since its publication, many scholars and activists decried the Moynihan Report's findings as victim blaming, and debates surrounding the impact of the report on popular myths about Black women and Black culture as well as social and public policy are ongoing even today. Precedence, however, for documenting Black "pathology" had been established decades earlier when Karl Gunnar Myrdal's Carnegie-funded 1944 study *An American Dilemma* was released. For a scathing critique of Myrdal's nearly fifteen-hundred-page study, see Ralph Ellison, *"An American Dilemma*: A Review," 1944, http://teaching americanhistory.org/library/document/an-american-dilemma-a-review/. For more information on the Moynihan Report and subsequent debates, see bell hooks, *Ain't I a Woman: Black Women and Feminism* (New York: Routledge, 2015); Ange-Marie Hancock, *The Politics of Disgust: The Public Identity of the Welfare Queen* (New York: New York University Press, 2004); Daniel Gearly, *Beyond Civil Rights: The Moynihan Report and Its Legacy* (Philadelphia: University of Pennsylvania Press, 2015); Susan Greenbaum, *Blaming the Poor: The Long Shadow of the Moynihan Report on Cruel Images About Poverty* (New Brunswick, NJ: Rutgers University Press, 2015); and Dionne Benson Smith, "It's No Longer Just About Race: Social Constructions of American

Citizenship in the Moynihan Report," in *Women's Work Is Never Done: Comparative Studies in Caregiving, Employment and Social Policy Reform*, ed. Sylvia Bashevkin (New York: Routledge, 2002), 41–66.

71. These HUD regulations occurred under President Bill Clinton's administration following his 1996 State of the Union address that included the recommendation that "a 'one-strike-you're out' rule should apply to low-income housing." Under President Obama's administration, HUD changed course and in 2011 began to encourage public housing agencies and owners of federally assisted housing to offer ex-convicts "a second chance." See "Criminal History Policy for Low-Income Housing," http://homeguides .sfgate.com/criminal-history-policy-low-income-housing-8476.html; S.462— 105th Congress (1997–1998), *Public Housing Reform and Responsibility Act of 1997*, www.congress.gov/bill/105th-congress/senate-bill/462; and US Department of Housing and Urban Development/Office of Public and Indian Affairs, "Notice PIH 2015-19," https://portal.hud.gov/hudportal/HUD?src= /program_offices/public_indian_housing/publications/notices/2015. Regarding options for ex-offenders, the Trump administration has not reversed Obama's "a second chance" guidelines for public housing agencies and other proprietors of federally assisted housing. However, Ben Carson, the secretary of Housing and Urban Development, has taken actions that erode Obama administration efforts to enforce fair housing laws. Carson's decision to strike the words "inclusive" and "free from discrimination" from HUD's mission statement, along with other actions that have placed on hold prioritized fair housing investigations from (Obama appointee) Julián Castro's days as HUD secretary, has raised concern among activists and many HUD officials. With $28 billion of hurricane disaster recovery funding at their disposal, many HUD officials lament the lost opportunity to leverage the department's power and resources to address a long legacy of housing discrimination. Trump's administration has also announced austere HUD budget cuts and plans to evict undocumented immigrants residing in public housing. See Glenn Thrush, "Under Ben Carson, HUD Scales Back Fair Housing Enforcement," *New York Times*, March 28, 2018, www.nytimes.com/2018/03/28/us/ben -carson-hud-fair-housing-discrimination.html; Tracy Jan, "HUD Says 55,000 Children Could Be Displaced Under Trump Plan to Evict Undocumented Immigrants," *Washington Post*, May 10, 2019, www.washingtonpost.com /business/2019/05/10/hud-says-children-could-be-displaced-under-trump -plan-evict-undocumented-immigrants/?utm_term=.6762e7451115; and Carmiah Townes, "Ben Carson's HUD Nomination Threatens Ex-prisoners in Search of Housing," *ThinkProgress*, December 14, 2016, https://think progress.org/prisoner-reentry-under-ben-carson-c0cadde1b470/.

CHAPTER 4. BLACK LOVE IN CAPTIVITY

1. By the end of 2014, an estimated 516,900 Black men were serving time in state and federal prisons. See www.bjs.gov/content/pub/pdf/p14.pdf. The number of American women serving time in federal and state prisons in

2014 was approximately 106,232. Black women made up an estimated 21.2 percent of that number. See www.incite-national.org/page/women-color -prisons; www.bjs.gov/content/pub/pdf/p14_Summary.pdf. In 2015, an estimated 501,300 Black men serving sentences in federal and state prisons outnumbered the estimated 21,700 Black women serving sentences in federal and state prisons by 479,600. See "Drug War Facts," https://drugwarfacts .org/table/prison_demographics.

2. David Love, "Behind Bars: 6 Things You Should Know About Black Women in Prison," *Atlanta Black Star*, April 1, 2016, http://atlantablackstar .com/2016/04/01/behind-bars-6-things-you-should-know-about-black -women-in-prison/.

3. Glenn Kessler, "The Stale Statistic That One in Three Black Males 'Born Today' Will End Up in Jail," *Washington Post*, June 16, 2015, www.washingtonpost.com/news/fact-checker/wp/2015/06/16/the-stale -statistic-that-one-in-three-black-males-has-a-chance-of-ending-up-in -jail/?utm_term=.e549280338a5.

4. Ivory A. Toldson, *No BS (Bad Stats): Black People Need People Who Believe in Black People Enough Not to Believe Every Bad Thing They Hear About Black People* (Boston: Brill, 2019), esp. 35–42.

5. The bare numbers in these two statistics, however, do not take into account population fertility outcomes over time and are not adjusted to account for the baseline populations of Black men during these two time periods. There were many more Black men living in 2013 than there were in 1850. The Census Bureau's 2013 estimated Black male population, ages fifteen and above, was 14,656,174, while the Census Bureau's 1850 estimated Black male population, ages fifteen and above, was 999,022. Although around 13 percent of Black men in America were under correctional control in 2013, close to 88 percent of Black men were enslaved in 1850. These figures were calculated from data provided by the US Census Bureau, 2013 American Community Survey, https://factfinder.census.gov/faces/table services/jsf/pages/productview.xhtml?pid=ACS_13_1YR_B01001B&prod Type=table; "Nativities of the Population of the United States, Births, Marriages and Deaths, Classification of Ages," 1850 Census: The Seventh Census of the United States, www.census.gov/library/publications/1853 /dec/1850a.html. In 2013, 1,437,363 Black men were enrolled in college compared to 745,660 Black males in state and federal prisons and local jails at midyear. See Jenée Desmond-Harris, "The Myth That There Are More Black Men in Prison than in College Debunked in One Chart," www.vox .com/2015/2/12/8020959/black-men-prison-college. In 2013, 526,000 Black men were in state and federal correctional institutions. An additional 877,000 were on probation and 280,000 were parolees in 2013. Together 1.68 million Black men were living under state and federal correctional programs. Taking into account the number of Black males serving jail time, this number rises to 1.88 million. See Katie Mulvaney's December 7, 2014, article "Brown U. Student Leader: More African-American Men in Prison System Now Than

Were Enslaved in 1850," www.politifact.com/rhode-island/statements/2014
/dec/07/diego-arene-morley/brown-u-student-leader-more-african-american
-men-p/.

6. Justin Wolfers, David Leonhardt, and Kevin Quealy, "1.5 Million
Missing Black Men," *New York Times*, April 20, 2015, www.nytimes.com
/interactive/2015/04/20/upshot/missing-black-men.html; Kerwin Charles
and Ming Ching Luoh, "Male Incarceration, the Marriage Market and Female Outcomes," *Review of Economics and Statistics* 92, no. 3 (2010): 614–627.

7. Robert Lerman and Steven Martin, "Let's Capture a More Accurate
Picture of America's Missing Black Men," *Urban Wire: Race and Ethnicity, The
Blog of the Urban Institute*, April 28, 2015, www.urban.org/urban-wire/lets
-capture-more-accurate-picture-americas-missing-black-men. Black women
and children have also been undercounted in decennial censuses. For more on
this topic, see Charmaine Runes, "Following a Long History the 2020 Census
Risks Undercounting the Black Population," *Urban Wire: Race and Ethnicity,
The Blog of the Urban Institute*, February 26, 2019, www.urban.org/urban-wire
/following-long-history-2020-census-risks-undercounting-black-population.

8. Marc Mauer, *Race to Incarcerate* (1999; reprint, New York: New Press,
2006).

9. Michelle Alexander, *The New Jim Crow: Mass Incarceration in the Age of
Colorblindness* (New York: New Press, 2012), 18. Although Alexander's point
is well taken, it's important to acknowledge that incarcerated Black men are
still *very* necessary to the new global economy, but as unpaid and underpaid
laborers.

10. Wendy Sawyer and Peter Wagner, "Mass Incarceration: The Whole
Pie, 2019," *Prison Policy Initiative*, March 19, 2019, www.prisonpolicy.org
/reports/pie2019.html.

11. Patricia O'Connor, "The Prison Cage as Home for African American
Men," in *Impacts of Incarceration on the African American Family*, ed. Othello
Harris and R. Robin Miller (2003; reprint, New Brunswick, NJ: Transaction,
2009), 71. Michelle Alexander defines mass incarceration as "the criminal
justice system but also . . . the larger web of laws, rules, policies, and customs
that control those labeled criminals both in and out of prison." She further
explains that "like Jim Crow (and slavery), mass incarceration operates as a
tightly networked system of laws, policies, customs, and institutions that operated collectively to ensure the subordinate status of a group defined largely
by race" (*New Jim Crow*, 13).

12. Black men were being incarcerated at unprecedented rates primarily
for marijuana, which is legal today in many states, and for cocaine, which carried differential sentencing outcomes based on the chemical form and weight
of the substance. Racialized sentencing disparities quickly materialized, as
White drug offenders in possession of powder cocaine were incarcerated at
much lower rates and were given much lighter sentences than Black offenders
who were (most often) in possession of much smaller amounts of crack cocaine. Alexander, *New Jim Crow*, 7, 51–58, 137–139.

13. Mary Balthazar and Lula King, "The Loss of the Protective Effects of Marital and Non-marital Relationships of Incarcerated African American Men: Implications for Social Work," in *Impacts of Incarceration*, ed. Harris and Miller, 33.

14. These figures for 1980 and 2008 include Black men incarcerated in jails and federal and state prisons. It is unclear whether the 1980 figure accounts for Black men under eighteen; however, the 1980 population estimate for Black males fifteen and older was 8,734,964. This means that a likely 1.5 percent of Black men were incarcerated in 1980. The 2008 figure includes Black males under eighteen. Given the estimated Black male population of 13,536,173, for those fifteen years old and above, just over 6 percent of Black men were probably incarcerated in 2013. Justice Policy Institute, "Cellblocks or Classrooms? The Funding of Higher Education and Corrections and Its Impact on African American Men," September 18, 2002, www.justice policy.org/images/upload/02-09_REP_CellblocksClassrooms_BB-AC.pdf; "Population by Age Groups, Race, and Sex for 1960–97," Centers for Disease Control and Prevention, National Center for Health Statistics, www .cdc.gov/nchs/data/statab/pop6097.pdf; Heather West and William Sabol, "Prison Inmates at Midyear 2008—Statistical Tables," Bureau of Justice Statistics, Table 17, p. 17, April 8, 2009, www.bjs.gov/content/pub/pdf/pim08st .pdf.

15. Alexander, *New Jim Crow*, 59–96; Judith Greene, "Entrepreneurial Corrections: Incarceration as a Business Opportunity," in *Invisible Punishment: The Collateral Consequences of Mass Imprisonment*, ed. Marc Mauer and Meda Chesney-Lind (New York: New Press, 2002), 95–113; Corrections Accountability Project at the Urban Justice Center, "The Prison Industrial Complex: Mapping Private Sector Players," April 2018, https:// static1.squarespace.com/static/58e127cb1b10e31ed45b20f4/t/5ade0281f 950b7ab293c86a6/1524499083424/The+Prison+Industrial+Complex +-+Mapping+Private+Sector+Players+%28April+2018%29.pdf.

16. US Department of Justice Fact Sheet, "Violent Crime Control and Law Enforcement Act of 1994," www.ncjrs.gov/txtfiles/billfs.txt.

17. John Clark, James Austin, and D. Alan Henry, "Three Strikes and You're Out: A Review of State Legislation," in *National Institute of Justice: Research in Brief*, US Department of Justice, September 1997, www.ncjrs.gov /pdffiles/165369.pdf.

18. Balthazar and King, "Loss of the Protective Effects," 38.

19. Alexander, *New Jim Crow*, 94.

20. Andra Gillespie, *Race and the Obama Administration: Substance, Symbols, and Hope* (Manchester: Manchester University Press, 2019), 90.

21. US Department of Justice Archives, "The Attorney General's Smart on Crime Initiative," www.justice.gov/archives/ag/attorney-generals -smart-crime-initiative.

22. Melinda Clemmons, "Calling for Reform, President Obama Notes the Impact of Incarceration on Families," July 20, 2015,

https://chronicleofsocialchange.org/news-2/calling-for-reform-president
-obama-notes-the-impact-of-incarceration-on-families.

23. US Department of Justice, "Clemency Statistics," www.justice.gov
/pardon/clemency-statistics; Neil Eggleston, "President Obama Has Now
Granted More Commutations Than Any President in this Nation's History,"
January 17, 2017, https://obamawhitehouse.archives.gov/blog/2017/01/17
/president-obama-has-now-granted-more-commutations-any-president
-nations-history. See also Gillespie, *Race and the Obama Administration*,
90–94.

24. Dave Boyer, "Obama Finalizes Regulation to 'Ban the Box' on Hiring Job Applicants with Criminal Records," *Washington Times*, November
30, 2016, www.washingtontimes.com/news/2016/nov/30/obama-finalizes
-regulation-ban-box-job-applicants/; Angela Hanks, "Ban the Box and Beyond," Center for American Progress, July 27, 2017, www.americanprogress
.org/issues/economy/reports/2017/07/27/436756/ban-box-beyond/. Although the Trump administration has supported the "ban the box" rule, in
February 2019 it proposed a new rule that would require applicants to disclose
information about their involvement with criminal justice programs aimed
to prevent or avoid incarceration. See Jason Tashea, "Trump Administration Seeks to Expand Criminal Background Checks for Federal Job Seekers," *ABA Journal*, April 16, 2019, www.abajournal.com/web/article/trump
-administration-seeks-to-expand-criminal-background-checks-for-federal
-job-seekers.

25. Devah Pager, "The Mark of a Criminal Record," *American Journal of
Sociology* 108, no. 5 (2003): 937–975, esp. 959–962.

26. FIRST STEP is also an acronym for Formerly Incarcerated Reenter Society Transformed Safely Transitioning Every Person Act. Politics might play a role in kicking the teeth out of the First Step Act. For a
practical example of the impact of the First Step Act on a Black male inmate's life, see #FirstStepAct, "David Barren—30 Year Sentence," www
.firststepact.org/david_barren; and C. J. Ciaramella, "This Inmate Received Clemency from Obama. He Might Still Die in Prison," *Reason: Free
Minds and Free Markets*, January 27, 2017, https://reason.com/2017/01/27
/this-inmate-received-clemency-from-obama/.

27. Ames Grawert and Tim Lau, "How the FIRST STEP Act Became
Law—and What Happens Next," January 4, 2019, www.brennancenter.org
/blog/how-first-step-act-became-law-and-what-happens-next.

28. Emily Bazelon, *Charged: The New Movement to Transform
American Prosecution and End Mass Incarceration* (New York: Random
House, 2019), esp. Chapter 8, "The New DAs," 147–173. See also Justin Miller, "The New Reformer DAs," *American Prospect Longform*, January 2, 2018, https://prospect.org/article/new-reformer-das; and David
Garland, "The Road to Ending Mass Incarceration Goes Through the
DA's Office," *American Prospect*, April 8, 2019, https://prospect.org/article
/road-ending-mass-incarceration-goes-through-das-office.

29. Researchers are finding that the incarceration rate for sentenced adult Blacks in the early twenty-first century (2007–2017) decreased (31 percent), a significant decline relative to their White counterparts' (14 percent) and a measurable decline relative to their Hispanic counterparts' (25 percent). See John Gramlich, "The Gap Between the Numbers of Blacks and Whites in Prison Is Shrinking," *Fact Tank: News in the Numbers*, Pew Research Center, April 30, 2019, www.pewresearch.org/fact-tank/2019/04/30/shrinking-gap -between-number-of-blacks-and-whites-in-prison/; and Eli Hager, "A Mass Incarceration Mystery: Why Are Black Imprisonment Rates Going Down? Four Theories," *Marshall Project*, December 15, 2017, www.themarshall project.org/2017/12/15/a-mass-incarceration-mystery. The discussion of the downward trend will continue to be relevant in political discussions on prison reform and abolition. However, the decade of decline in the numbers of Black men serving prison sentences has not changed the reality that Black men are still cripplingly victimized by mass incarceration. I concur with Michelle Alexander's perspective (included in the *Marshall Project* report cited here): "Until we learn the true value of the lives we have wasted, and until we truly reckon with our nation's history . . . and until we muster, as a nation, a willingness to invest heavily in the communities that have suffered the most, we will find ourselves in an endless cycle of reform and retrenchment—periods of apparent progress followed by the creation of new systems of racial and social control."

30. Bruce Western and Betty Pettit, "Incarceration and Social Inequality," *Daedalus: Journal of the American Academy of Arts and Sciences* (Summer 2010): 8–19, esp. 10–11.

31. Robynn Battle et al., "Accessing an Understudied Population in Behavioral HIV/AIDS Research: Low Income African American Women," *Journal of Health and Social Policy* 7, no. 2 (1995): 1–18; Megan Comfort et al., "'You Can't Do Nothing in This Damn Place': Sex and Intimacy Among Couples with an Incarcerated Male Partner," *Journal of Sex Research* 42, no. 1 (2005): 3.

32. Ta-Nehisi Coates, "The Black Family in the Age of Incarceration," *Atlantic*, October 2015, www.theatlantic.com/magazine/archive/2015/10 /the-black-family-in-the-age-of-mass-incarceration/403246/.

33. Peter Kelley, "Nearly Half of African-American Women Know Someone in Prison," *UW Today*, June 11, 2015, www.washington.edu/news/2015 /06/11/nearly-half-of-african-american-women-know-someone-in-prison/.

34. Laura Randolph, "My Husband the Inmate," *Ebony*, August 1993, 120–124. Randolph covers two of these women's stories in her article: Khadijah Abdullah-Fardan, who married her husband, Shukri Fardan, while "in the 10th year of a life sentence for felony murder and armed robbery," and Jackie McPhail, who married her husband, Willard McPhail, during "his 14th year of a life sentence." The two were neighbors and childhood friends and tied the knot ten years after becoming pen pals. See esp. 120, 122. Randolph uses the concept "prisoners of love" to describe the women she interviewed.

35. Mitchell Jackson's *Survival Math: Notes on an All-American Family* (New York: Scribner, 2019) is a riveting memoir that makes a similar point about American identity and values. Jackson shows how some of the most tragic and bewildering circumstances characterizing African American life and struggle don't mark Black folks as deviant Americans but mark them as "all-American."

36. Tayari Jones, *An American Marriage* (Chapel Hill, NC: Algonquin Books of Chapel Hill, 2018), 26, 34–35.

37. Jones, *An American Marriage*, 46.

38. Asha Bandele, *The Prisoner's Wife: A Memoir* (New York: Scribner, 1999), 45–47; Asha Bandele, "Woman Up," in *One Big Happy Family*, ed. Rebecca Walker (New York: Riverhead Books, 2009), 17–28.

39. Bandele, *Prisoner's Wife*, 51.

40. Bandele, *Prisoner's Wife*, 51–52, 153.

41. The phrasing is inspired by Zora Neale Hurston's description of her character Janie after her husband, Joe Starks, physically abuses her for the first time. Hurston writes that Janie "stood there until something fell off the shelf inside her."

42. Bandele, *Prisoner's Wife*, 192–193.

43. Bandele, *Prisoner's Wife*, 131–132.

44. Bandele, *Prisoner's Wife*, 212.

45. Megan Sullivan, "Children of Incarcerated Parents/An Interview by Megan Sullivan, 'Ashe Bandele: One Mother's Perspective,'" *Scholar & Feminist Online* 8, no. 2 (2010): 1, http://sfonline.barnard.edu/children/bandele_02.htm.

46. Bandele, *Prisoner's Wife*, 161; Bandele, "Woman Up," 27.

47. A. Barton and Chalandra Bryant, "Financial Strain and Trajectories of Marital Processes, and African American Newlyweds' Marital Instability," *Journal of Family Psychology* (forthcoming); Carolyn Cutrona et al., "Neighborhood Context and Financial Strain as Predictors of Marital Interaction and Marital Quality in African American Couples," *Journal of Personal Relationships* 10, no. 3 (2003): 389–409; Clifford Broman, "Race Differences in Marital Well-Being," *Journal of Marriage and Family* 55, no. 3 (1993): 724–732.

48. Balthazar and King, "Loss of the Protective Effects," 38.

49. Brad Tripp, "Incarcerated African American Fathers," in *Impacts of Incarceration*, ed. Harris and Miller, 27.

50. Bonnie Carlson and Neil Cervera, *Inmates and Their Wives: Incarceration and Family Life* (Westport, CT: Greenwood Press, 1992), 138–139.

51. Donald Braman, *Doing Time on the Outside: Incarceration and Family Life in Urban America* (Ann Arbor: University of Michigan Press, 2007), 202. All participants in Braman's study were assigned pseudonyms to protect their identities.

52. Sandra Browning, R. Robin Miller, and Lisa Spruance, "Criminal Incarceration Dividing the Ties That Bind: Black Men and Their Families," in *Impacts of Incarceration*, ed. Harris and Miller, 92.

53. Bandele, *Prisoner's Wife*, 120.

54. "S.2520—Inmate Calling Technical Corrections Act," 115th Congress (2017–2018), www.congress.gov/bill/115th-congress/senate-bill/2520 /text; Sam Gustin, "A New Bill Could Finally Ban Predatory Inmate Phone Costs," *The Verge*, March 13, 2018, www.theverge.com/2018/3/13/17113712 /prison-phone-call-bill-reform-senate. For efforts to curtail predatory practices related to telecommunications services in America's prisons under the Obama administration, see www.vice.com/en_us/article/nze8eb /the-fcc-is-voting-to-cap-ridiculous-phone-rates-in-prison.

55. State of Connecticut General Assembly, January Session, 2019, Committee Bill No. 6714, "An Act Concerning the Cost of Telecommunications Services in Correctional Facilities," 2, https://cga.ct.gov/2019/TOB/h /pdf/2019HB-06714-R01-HB.PDF; Worth Rises, "Criminal Justice Advocates, Community Members Celebrate Passage of #PrisonPhoneJustice Bill," April 9, 2019, https://static1.squarespace.com/static/58e127cb1b10e31ed45b 20f4/t/5cb0aba7ee6eb05ebed12440/1555082152282/HB+6714+Press +Release.pdf. In a related case, effective May 1, 2019, New York City became the first city in the nation to provide jail inmates free telephone service for calls placed to numbers in United States. The new law will cost the city approximately $5.5 million collected annually from a system that accumulated around $8 million of revenue per year. See Thomas Tracy and John Annese, "De Blasio: Inmates in NYC Jails Can Now Make Free Phone Calls," *New York Daily News*, May 1, 2019, www.nydailynews.com/new-york/nyc-crime/ny-inmates -free-phone-calls-20190501-okaarqaay5ferjrykwxfhpsrny-story.html.

56. Jenna Carlesso, "Bill That Would Make Prison Phone Calls Free Advances," *Hartford Courant*, April 10, 2019, www.courant.com/politics /hc-pol-prison-phone-calls-20190410-liapt6iowbgptjfgkhhcn6v2xy-story .html. Rachel Cohen also reports that "Connecticut residents pay roughly $15 million annually for prison phone calls, with the state taking 68 percent as a kickback." See her "Free Prison Calls Could Finally Be Coming to Connecticut," *Intercept*, April 2, 2019, https://theintercept.com/2019/04/02 /connecticut-free-prison-calls/.

57. Olga Grinstead et al., "The Financial Cost of Maintaining Relations," in *Impacts of Incarceration*, ed. Harris and Miller, 68–69.

58. Laura Fishman, *Women at the Wall: A Study of Prisoners' Wives Doing Time on the Outside* (Albany: State University of New York Press, 1990), 145.

59. Braman, *Doing Time on the Outside*, 121. See also Megan Comfort, *Doing Time Together: Love and Family in the Shadow of the Prison* (Chicago: University of Chicago Press, 2008), 119; and Comfort et al., "'You Can't Do Nothing in This Damn Place,'" 7.

60. Shanita Hubbard, "Visiting an Inmate You Love Is Its Own Kind of Prison," *Splinter*, June 28, 2017, https://splinternews.com/visiting-an-inmate -you-love-is-its-own-kind-of-prison-1796485834.

61. R. Robin Miller, "Various Implications of the 'Race to Incarcerate' on Incarcerated African American Men and Their Families," in *Impacts of Incarceration*, ed. Harris and Miller, 7.

62. T. K. Cyan-Brock, *Prisoners of Love: A Guide for Anyone Wanting to Cultivate, Maintain and Strengthen Relationships with Loved Ones During Times of Incarceration* (Bloomington, IN: Xlibris, 2011), 102.

63. Fishman, *Women at the Wall*, 163–166; Claudette Spencer-Nurse, *Memoirs of a Prison Lawyer–Prison Wife* (New York: Page, 2018).

64. Comfort, *Doing Time Together*, 119. See also Comfort et al., "'You Can't Do Nothing in This Damn Place,'" 7–8; Lois Girshick, *Soledad Women: Wives of Prisoners Speak Out* (Westport, CT: Praeger, 1996), 3, 70–74; and Fishman, *Women at the Wall*, 164.

65. Fishman, *Women at the Wall*, 160, 165. See also Braman, *Doing Time on the Outside*, 209.

66. Sara Wakefield, Hedwig Lee, and Christopher Wildeman, "Tough on Crime, Tough on Families? Criminal Justice and Family Life in America," *Annals of the American Academy of Political and Social Science* 665, no. 1 (2016): 8–21.

67. Comfort et al., "'You Can't Do Nothing in This Damn Place,'" 3.

68. Braman, *Doing Time on the Outside*, 193–194.

69. Braman, *Doing Time on the Outside*, 198–199.

70. O'Connor, "Prison Cage as Home," 81; Comfort et al., "'You Can't Do Nothing in This Damn Place,'" 8.

71. Comfort et al., "'You Can't Do Nothing in This Damn Place,'" 8. While I cannot be certain that Black women made these remarks, Comfort and her collaborators gathered their data from twenty participants, nine of whom were Black. The other women participants included five Whites, four Hispanics, and two whose racial-ethnic identities were unknown. The study does not specify whether the women were married to their incarcerated partners.

72. Bandele, *Prisoner's Wife*, 212.

73. See Chapter 3, note 71, for a brief summary of the Clinton, Obama, and Trump administrations' HUD regulations and initiatives.

74. NPR, "State-by-State Court Fees," *Guilty and Charged*, May 19, 2014, www.npr.org/2014/05/19/312455680/state-by-state-court-fees; Joseph Shapiro, "Measures Aimed at Keeping People Out of Jail Punish the Poor," *Guilty and Charged*, May 24, 2014, www.npr.org/2014/05/24/314866421/measures-aimed-at-keeping-people-out-of-jail-punish-the-poor.

75. "H.R.5210—Anti-Drug Abuse Act of 1988," 100th Congress (1987–1988), www.congress.gov/bill/100th-congress/house-bill/05210.

76. President William Jefferson Clinton, "State of the Union Address," January 23, 1996, https://clintonwhitehouse4.archives.gov/WH/New/other/sotu.html. See also Gwen Rubenstein and Debbie Mukamal, "Welfare and Housing—Denial of Benefits to Drug Offenders," in *Invisible Punishment*, ed. Mauer and Chesney-Lind, 37–49.

77. Rubenstein and Mukamal, "Welfare and Housing," 47. See also Keesha Middlemass, *Convicted and Condemned: The Politics and Policies of Prisoner Reentry* (New York: New York University Press, 2017), 91–96.

78. Middlemass, *Convicted and Condemned*, 92.
79. Middlemass, *Convicted and Condemned*, 81. "Gavin" is a pseudonym to protect the participant's identity.
80. Middlemass, *Convicted and Condemned*, 92.
81. Miller, "Various Implications of the 'Race to Incarcerate,'" 6; Creasi Hairston and Patricia Lockett, "Parents in Prison: New Directions for Social Services," *Social Work* 32, no. 2 (1987): 162–164; Charles Lanier, "Affective States of Fathers in Prison," *Justice Quarterly* 10, no. 1 (1993): 49–66; Kristin Turney, "Liminal Men: Incarceration and Relationship Dissolution," *Social Problems* 62, no. 4 (2015): 499–528.
82. Sarah Benson, "Beyond the Sentence: Understanding Collateral Consequences," National Institute of Justice, May 2013, www.nij.gov /journals/272/Pages/collateral-consequences.aspx. According to Benson, "Collateral consequences tend to last indefinitely, long after an individual is fully rehabilitated. Many collateral consequences affect a convicted person's employment and business opportunities; others deny access to government benefits and program participation, including student loans, housing, contracting and other forms of participation in civic life." See also various reports on collateral consequences from the Sentencing Project, www.sentencing project.org/issues/collateral-consequences/; Mark Hatzenbuehler et al., "The Collateral Damage of Mass Incarceration: Risk of Psychiatric Morbidity Among Nonincarcerated Residents of High-Incarceration Neighborhoods," *American Journal of Public Health* 105, no. 1 (2015): 138–143; and Abigail Sewell, "Collateral Damage: The Health Effects of Invasive Police Encounters in New York City," *Journal of Urban Health: Bulletin of the New York Academy of Medicine* 93, supp. 1 (2016): 42–67.
83. Pager, "Mark of a Criminal Record."
84. Bruce Western and Christopher Wildeman, "The Black Family and Mass Incarceration," *Annals of the American Academy of Political and Social Science* 621 (January 2009): 234–235.
85. William Sabol and James Lynch, "Assessing the Longer-Run Consequences of Incarceration: Effects on Families and Employment," in *Crime Control and Social Justice: The Delicate Balance*, ed. Darnell Felix Hawkins, Samuel Myers, and Randolph Stone (2003; reprint, Westport, CT: Greenwood Press, 2009), 6–7; Todd Clear, *Imprisoning Communities: How Mass Incarceration Makes Disadvantaged Neighborhoods Worse* (New York: Oxford University Press, 2007), 104–106.
86. One example is Shereé Whitfield of *The Real Housewives of Atlanta*. Whitfield discusses her two-year relationship with Tyrone Gilliams, a Black man serving time in a federal prison who claims he is innocent of the white-collar crime for which he was convicted. Whitfield knew and dated Gilliams before he went to prison. They rekindled their relationship after a four-year hiatus. See her *Essence Now* interview, November 8, 2017, www.youtube.com/watch?v=E3iyBSqNj3I; and Dave Quinn, "*RHOA's* Shereé Whitfield Didn't Know Her Boyfriend Tyrone Gilliams Was

290 Notes to Chapter 4

Going to Jail," *People*, December 3, 2017, https://people.com/tv/rhoas-sheree
-whitfield-didnt-know-her-boyfriend-tyrone-gilliams-was-going-to
-jail/.

87. Shanita Hubbard, "'You're Beautiful, Successful and Educated' and
Waiting on a Man in Prison," *Root*, November 9, 2015, www.theroot.com
/you-re-beautiful-successful-and-educated-and-waiting-1790861683. Hubbard's narrative situates her fiancé's racial identity as Black.

88. Interestingly, Shanita Hubbard actually wrote an article titled
"When It Comes to Co-parenting, Sometimes Love Isn't Enough," *Ebony*,
May 20, 2016, www.ebony.com/life/coparenting-with-ex/. Speaking of her
ex-husband, Hubbard laments, "Our love for each other wasn't enough to
sustain a marriage. Sometimes love isn't enough; it certainly couldn't sustain
the weight of our unhealthy baggage." It is unclear whether the husband she
writes about in the article was her fiancé who had served time in prison.

89. Mary Patillo-McCoy, *Black Picket Fences: Privilege and Peril Among
the Black Middle Class* (Chicago: University of Chicago Press, 1999), 1–5; Alexander, *New Jim Crow*, 97–119.

90. Alexander, *New Jim Crow*, 11.

91. US Department of Health and Human Services, Office of Family Assistance, "Healthy Marriage," April 30, 2019, www.acf.hhs.gov/ofa
/programs/healthy-marriage/healthy-marriage.

92. Daniel Hatcher, "Child Support Harming Children: Subordinating
the Best Interests of Children to the Fiscal Interests of the State," *Wake Forest
Law Review* 42, no. 4 (2007): 1029–1086.

93. Hatcher, "Child Support Harming Children," 1031. See also Lisa
Kelly, "If Anybody Asks You Who I Am: An Outsider's Story of the Duty
to Establish Paternity," *Journal of Gender and the Law* 3, no. 247 (1995): 247–
263. See also Lefkovitz, "Men in the House," 613–614.

94. National Conference of State Legislatures, "Child Support Pass-
Through and Disregard Policies for Public Assistance Recipients," July 18,
2017, www.ncsl.org/research/human-services/state-policy-pass-through
-disregard-child-support.aspx. See also Lenhardt, "Marriage as Black Citizenship?," 1323.

95. Teddy, in discussion with the author, August 23, 2018. "Teddy" is a
pseudonym used to protect the interviewee's identity.

96. Hatcher, "Child Support Harming Children," 1075.

97. Zion, in discussion with the author, May 30, 2019. All subsequent
paraphrased or quoted material pertaining to Zion is derived from the same
discussion. "Zion" is a pseudonym used to protect the interviewee's identity.

98. See discussion of Tillmon's comments in Chapter 3.

99. Pager, "Mark of a Criminal Record."

100. Tamara Gilkes Borr, "How the War on Drugs Kept Black Men
Out of College," *Atlantic*, May 15, 2019, www.theatlantic.com/education
/archive/2019/05/war-drugs-made-it-harder-black-men-attend-college
/588724/. See also Tolani Britton, "Does Locked Up Mean Locked Out? The

Effects of the Anti-Drug Act of 1986 on Black Male Students' College Enrollment," IRLE Working Paper No. 101-19 (April 9, 2019), 1–53, http://irle
.berkeley.edu/files/2019/04/Does-Locked-Up-Mean-Locked-Out.pdf.

101. Alexander, *New Jim Crow*, 16.

102. Sarah Haley, *No Mercy Here: Gender, Punishment, and the Making of
Jim Crow Modernity* (Chapel Hill: University of North Carolina Press, 2016);
Nicole Hahn Rafter, *Partial Justice: Women in State Prisons, 1800–1935* (Boston: New England University Press, 1985); David Oshinsky, *Worse Than Slavery: Parchman Farm and the Ordeal of Jim Crow Justice* (New York: Free Press
Paperbacks, 1997); Kali Gross, "African American Women, Mass Incarceration, and the Politics of Protection," *Journal of American History* 102, no. 1
(2015): 25–33; Kali Gross, *Colored Amazons: Crime, Violence, and Black Women
in the City of Brotherly Love, 1880–1910* (Durham, NC: Duke University
Press, 2006); Barry Godfrey and Steven Soper, "Prison Records from 1800s
Georgia Show Mass Incarceration's Racially Charged Beginnings," *Conversation*, May 22, 2018, http://theconversation.com/prison-records-from-1800s
-georgia-show-mass-incarcerations-racially-charged-beginnings-96612.

103. Drug Policy Alliance, "Women, Prison, and the Drug War," May
2018, www.drugpolicy.org/sites/default/files/women-and-the-drug-war_0
.pdf.

104. Sawyer and Wagner, "Mass Incarceration."

105. Jake Horowitz and Connie Utada, "Community Supervision
Marked by Racial and Gender Disparities," Pew Charitable Trusts, December
6, 2018, www.pewtrusts.org/en/research-and-analysis/articles/2018/12/06
/community-supervision-marked-by-racial-and-gender-disparities.

106. Worth Rises, https://worthrises.org/aboutus.

107. For example, the state of California set a historic precedent when
Governor Gavin Newsom signed a bill on October 11, 2019, that will close
all private prisons and privately run immigrant detention centers by the year
2028. The state will also be prohibited from entering into any new contracts with private entities after January 1, 2020. See Veronica Stracqua-
lursi, "California to Shut Down Private Prisons and Immigrant Detention
Centers," CNN, October 12, 2019, www.cnn.com/2019/10/12/politics
/california-law-ban-private-for-profit-prisons/index.html.

108. See note 29 above.

CHAPTER 5. WILL BLACK WOMEN EVER HAVE IT ALL?

1. Courtney Spradlin, "Benton Couple Celebrates 80 Years of Marriage,"
Shreveport Times, February 12, 2015; WBRZ-2 ABC News, "Meet Louisiana's Longest-Married Couple," February 12, 2018, www.wbrz.com/news
/meet-louisiana-s-longest-married-couple/. Other sources provide different data regarding the number of Player children and grandchildren. Varrie Player died April 17, 2018, two months after her marriage to Lawrence
Player was declared Louisiana's longest. Less than a month after his wife,
Lawrence Player died on May 8, 2018. The couple sealed their marriage vows

on January 27, 1935, when Varrie and Lawrence were sixteen and twenty-one, respectively.

2. KHQ-Q6 News, "North Carolina Couple Celebrate 82 Years of Marriage," www.khq.com/top_video/north-carolina-couple-celebrate-years -of-marriage/video_07fc65fe-5719-11e9-921c-231dcbcb70af.html.

3. "Report: Benton Couple Together 82 Years Officially the Longest Married Couple in Louisiana," *Advocate*, February 12, 2018, www .theadvocate.com/baton_rouge/news/article_5e95f860-f174-11e6-ae93 -af59c7e786e4.html.

4. A few representative articles, commentaries, and digital media featuring the Obamas' love and marriage are Lauren Porter, "All of the Times President Barack Obama Professed His Love for the First Lady," *Essence*, September 21, 2016; "What Michelle Obama Tells Young Couples About Marriage," *The Oprah Winfrey Show*, May 2, 2011, www .oprah.com/own-oprahshow/what-michelle-obama-knows-for-sure-about -marriage; Kathlyn and Gay Hendricks, "The Obama Relationship: A Major Benefit Nobody's Talking About," *Huffington Post*, November 17, 2011, www.huffpost.com/entry/the-obama-relationship-a_b_128896; Jodi Kantor, "The Obamas' Marriage," *New York Times Magazine*, October 26, 2009; and Oretha Winston, "President Barack Obama and First Lady Michelle Obama Quotes of Love," *Elev 8*, https://elev8.hellobeautiful .com/616382/president-barrack-obama-first-lady-michelle-obama-quotes-of -love/.

5. Ralph Banks, *Is Marriage for White People? How the African American Marriage Decline Affects Everyone* (New York: Penguin Group/Plume, 2011), 66.

6. Vanessa Williams, "Dark and Lovely Michelle," *Root*, January 13, 2009, www.theroot.com/dark-and-lovely-michelle-1790868592.

7. I created this neologism to capture Black people's historic structural exclusion from wealth building in America. For more on the financial fragility of the Black middle class relative to the White middle class, see Jermaine Toney et al., "Economic Insecurity in the Family Tree and the Racial Wealth Gap," November 8, 2019, 1–39, *Social Science Research Network*, https:// papers.ssrn.com/sol3/papers.cfm?abstract_id=3397222; Regine Jackson, Darrick Hamilton, and William Darity Jr., "Low Wealth and Economic Insecurity Among Middle Class Blacks in Boston," Community Development Issue Brief No. 3, December 2015, Federal Reserve Bank of Boston, www .bostonfed.org/publications/community-development-issue-briefs/2015/low -wealth-and-economic-insecurity-among-middle-class-blacks-in-boston .aspx. For a concise overview of several principal causes of Black people's inherited wealthlessness, see "Systemic Racism Explained," *ACT TV*, April 16, 2019, www.youtube.com/watch?v=YrHIQIO_bdQ; Lenhardt, "Marriage as Black Citizenship?," 1336; and Ira Katznelson, *When Affirmative Action Was White: An Untold History of Racial Inequality in Twentieth-Century America* (New York: W. W. Norton, 2005).

8. Amber Jamieson, "West Virginia County Worker Fired for Calling Michelle Obama an 'Ape in Heels,'" *The Guardian*, November 15, 2016, www.theguardian.com/us-news/2016/nov/15/michelle-obama-ape-in-heels -post-west-virginia-worker-fired; Nadia Khomami, "Michelle Obama Tells of Being Wounded by Racism as First Lady," July 27, 2017, www.theguardian .com/us-news/2017/jul/27/michelle-obama-wounded-racism-first-lady.

9. For a recent study documenting US citizens' associations of Blacks with apes, see Phillip Goff et al., "Not Yet Human: Implicit Knowledge, Historical Dehumanization, and Contemporary Consequences," *Journal of Personality and Social Psychology* 94, no. 2 (2008): 292–306.

10. Darrick Hamilton, Arthur Goldsmith, and William Darity, "Shedding 'Light' on Marriage: The Influence of Skin Shade on Marriage for Black Females," *Journal of Economic Behavior and Organization* (October 2009): 34.

11. Darrick Hamilton, oral communication with the author, October 6, 2019.

12. Dream McClinton, "Why Dark-Skinned Black Girls Like Me Aren't Getting Married," *Guardian*, April 8, 2019, www.theguardian.com/life andstyle/2019/apr/08/dark-skinned-black-girls-dont-get-married. For reports on corroborating studies about colorism, dating, and marriage among African Americans, see Cedric Herring, Verna Keith, and Hayward Horton, eds., *Skin Deep: How Race and Complexion Matter in the "Color-Blind Era"* (Urbana: University of Illinois Press, 2004).

13. "Race and Attraction, 2009–2014: What's Changed in Five Years?," OkCupid, September 10, 2014, https://theblog.okcupid.com /race-and-attraction-2009-2014-107dcbb4f060.

14. McClinton, "Why Dark-Skinned Black Girls Like Me Aren't Getting Married." See also other articles on CPS in the same weeklong *Guardian* series Shades of Black, which features McClinton's article. https://www .theguardian.com/us-news/series/shades-of-black.

15. The following scholarly works address the impact of our anti-Black (especially anti-dark-skinned Black) social world upon Black females. Lance Hannon, Robert DeFina, and Sarah Bruch, "The Relationship Between Skin Tone and School Suspension for African Americans," *Race and Social Problems* 5, no. 4 (2013): 281–295; Verna Keith, "A Colorstruck World: Skin Tone, Achievement, and Self-Esteem Among African American Women," in *Shades of Difference: Why Skin Color Matters* (Stanford, CA: Stanford University Press, 2009), 25–39; Jill Viglione, Lance Hannon, and Robert DeFina, "The Impact of Light Skin on Prison Time for Black Female Offenders," *Social Science Journal* 48 (2011): 250–258; JeffriAnne Wilder, "Revisiting 'Color Names and Color Notions': A Contemporary Examination of the Language and Attitudes of Skin Color Among Young Black Women," *Journal of Black Studies* 41, no. 1 (2010): 184–206; Diane Brown and Verna Keith, eds., *In and Out of Our Right Minds* (New York: Columbia University Press, 2003). See also Bill Duke and D. Channsin Berry, *Dark Girls* (Oakland, CA: Duke Media/Urban Winter Entertainment, 2011).

16. As discussed in Chapter 1, CPS is a Eurocentric phenomenon that idealizes White, Euro-Western aesthetic and cultural norms. European slave-holding settlers created CPS during the slave period. Their White descendants advanced it, and across the centuries Black communities absorbed it and adjusted to its ubiquitous power over their lives.

17. Veronica Wells, "NFL Player Catches Hell for Toasting to 'More Light-Skinned Babies' with His Fiancée," *Madamenoire*, February 11, 2019, https://madamenoire.com/1060095/nfl-player-catches-hell-for-toasting-to-more -light-skinned-babies-with-his-fiance/. One YouTuber, Paris Milan, claims that Addae's financial adviser (also a dark-complexioned Black man with a White girlfriend) proposed the toast. See her video, "Blk NFL Players Colorist Tweets Exposed After Celebrating Lightskinned Kids," YouTube, February 11, 2019, www.youtube.com/watch?v=USB-prI_8lo.

18. On October 3, 2015, Clark's girlfriend, Salena Manni, used colorful language to explain why she does not deal with Black women. Clark admitted instead that she engages White women because they have resources. For more information, see Hannah Drake, "The Inconvenient Victim: Black Women and Stephon Clark," *WriteSomeShit*, March 30, 2018, https://writesomeshit .com/2018/03/30/the-inconvenient-victim-black-women-stephon-clark/.

19. Kimberly Foster, "Don't Tell Black Women How to Feel About Stephon Clark's Tweets," *Huffington Post*, April 4, 2018, www.huffpost.com/entry /opinion-foster-stephon-clark-misogynoir_n_5ac3dcb7e4b063ce2e56b6ec.

20. Danielle Young, "Stephon Clark and the Hatred of Black Women," *Judge of Characters*, April 6, 2018, www.youtube.com/watch?v=ITlMzg LVDJY. See also Michael Arcenaux, "It's Time to Talk About Stephon Clark's Anti–Black Women Tweets: Do Victims Have to Be Perfect to Garner Our Empathy?," *Essence*, April 10, 2018, www.essence.com/culture /stephon-clark-black-women-tweets/.

21. Drake, "Inconvenient Victim."

22. See Chapter 1 for more information about each of these slaveholders.

23. "Race and Attraction, 2009–2014," https://theblog.okcupid.com /race-and-attraction-2009-2014-107dcbb4f060. The OkCupid study does not show data based on class, so it is yet to be determined whether outcomes would change due to distinctions in participants' educational level, income, and social class.

24. The possibility exists that some Black women who marry Black men might do so not preferentially but due to their constrained options for marrying men of other racial backgrounds. However, these high percentages, coupled with OkCupid's findings on Black women's exclusive preference for dating Black men, suggest that a majority of Black women who marry Black men do so preferentially.

25. The US Census shows that in the year 2009, 87 percent of Black women who were fifty-five and older had been married at least once.

26. Jay Zagorsky, "Marriage and Divorce's Impact on Wealth," *Journal of Sociology* 41, no. 4 (2005): 406–424; Allison Linn, "Why Married

People Tend to Be Wealthier: It's Complicated," *Today*, February 13, 2013, https://www.today.com/money/why-married-people-tend-be-wealthier-its -complicated-1C8364877; Lisa Arnold and Christina Campbell, "The High Price of Being Single in America," *Atlantic*, January 14, 2013, www.the atlantic.com/sexes/archive/2013/01/the-high-price-of-being-single-in-america /267043/. Later in this chapter, I will discuss how, based on income and wealth levels, some Black dual-income households face federal tax penalties and other burdens that can hinder their chances to build wealth as quickly as other Americans.

27. Anthony King and Terrence Allen, "Personal Characteristics of the Ideal African American Marriage Partner: A Survey of Adult Black Men and Women," *Journal of Black Studies* 39, no. 4 (2009): 584.

28. Richard Fry and D'Vera Cohn, "Women, Men, and the New Economics of Marriage," January 19, 2010, www.pewsocialtrends.org/2010/01/19 /women-men-and-the-new-economics-of-marriage/.

29. With his study's focus on heterosexual marriage, Banks argues that middle-class Black men delay marriage or don't marry at all because the marriage market affords them tremendous opportunity to enjoy dating and to selectively capitalize on the large pool of marriageable Black women available to them when they are finally ready to settle down. I think it would be interesting to assess how sexual identity impacts these numbers. If more gay or queer Black men are represented among the highest-paid Black men, then the rates of heterosexual marriage would likely be diminished. Banks, *Is Marriage for White People?*, 9–10. See also Patillo-McCoy, *Black Picket Fences*; Bruce Haynes, *Red Lines, Black Spaces: The Politics of Race and Space in a Black Middle-Class Suburb* (New Haven, CT: Yale University Press, 2001); and Karyn Lacy, *Blue-Chip Black: Race, Class, and Status in the New Black Middle Class* (Berkeley: University of California Press, 2007). For a rare examination of Black upper-class men that addresses the role of marriage in Black men's class status, see Wendy Wang, W. Bradford Wilcox, and Ronald Mincy, "2.5 Million Black Men Are in the Upper Class," Institute for Family Studies, July 23, 2018, https://ifstudies.org/blog/2-5-million-black -men-are-in-the-upper-class. The authors include a link to their related longer report. See W. Bradford Wilcox, Wendy Wang, and Ronald Mincy, "Black Men Making It in America: The Engines of Economic Success for Black Men in America," Institute for Family Studies, 2018, https://www .aei.org/wp-content/uploads/2018/06/BlackMenMakingItInAmerica-Final _062218.pdf.

30. "The Status of Black Women in the United States" (Washington, DC: Institute for Women's Policy Research, 2017). See also Nora Caplan-Bricker, "Black Women in America Really Do Work Harder for Less, New Report Shows," June 7, 2017, https://slate.com/human-interest/2017/06 /black-women-really-do-work-harder-for-less-according-to-a-new-report .html.

31. King and Allen, "Personal Characteristics," 585.

32. US Census Bureau, "Historical Income Tables: People," www.census .gov/data/tables/time-series/demo/income-poverty/historical-income-people .html.

33. Scott Winship, Richard Reeves, and Katherine Guyot, "The Inheritance of Black Poverty: It's All About the Men," March 22, 2018, www.brook ings.edu/research/the-inheritance-of-black-poverty-its-all-about-the-men/.

34. Certainly, more research is needed to make generalizable conclusions.

35. Averil Clarke, *Inequalities of Love: College-Educated Black Women and the Barriers to Romance and Family* (Durham, NC: Duke University Press, 2011), 95.

36. The category of "formerly married" includes those who were separated, divorced, or widowed at the time of the survey. Clarke, *Inequalities of Love*, 95–99, 292.

37. Kim Parker and Renee Stepler, "Americans See Men as the Financial Providers, Even as Women's Contributions Grow," *Fact Tank: News in the Numbers*, Pew Research Center, September 20, 2017, www.pewresearch.org /fact-tank/2017/09/20/americans-see-men-as-the-financial-providers-even -as-womens-contributions-grow/.

38. The word "cousin" does not even exist in many African languages. Instead, terms signifying relationship to senior and junior siblings are salient and indicate how intimate kinship bonds are forged in African families far beyond the boundaries of the Euro-American "nuclear" family. For more on relational kinship terms in African societies, see Ambe Njoh, *Tradition, Culture and Development in Africa: Historical Lessons for Modern Development Planning* (New York: Routledge, 2016), 52–53; and Tshilemalema Mukenge, *Culture and Customs of the Congo* (Westport, CT: Greenwood Press, 2002), 130. For general sources on marriage and kinship in Africa, see Cheikh Anta Diop, *The Cultural Unity of Black Africa: The Domains of Matriarchy and Patriarchy in Classical Antiquity* (London: Karnak House, 1989); Ifi Amadiume, *Male Daughters, Female Husbands: Gender and Sex in an African Society* (1987; reprint, London: Zed Book, 2015); Mary Kolawole, *Womanism and African Consciousness* (Trenton, NJ: Africa World Press, Inc., 1997), esp. 43–71; Ifi Amadiume, *Reinventing Africa: Matriarchy, Religion, and Culture* (London: Zed Book, 1988); and Oyèrónkẹ́ Oyěwùmí, *The Invention of Women: Making an African Sense of Western Gender Discourses* (Minneapolis: University of Minnesota Press, 1997).

39. It's important to remember that contemporary patriarchal traditions in Africa are blended expressions of precolonial patriarchal institutions and patriarchal traditions introduced by Euro-Christian missionaries and colonial settlers as well as Islamic law and social customs. For more information, see sources in note 38.

40. See Chapter 2 for a sustained discussion of this point.

41. For seminal sources on African American traditions of biblical interpretation, see Cain Hope Felder, *Troubling Biblical Waters: Race, Class, and Family* (Maryknoll, NY: Orbis Books, 1989); Allen Callahan, *The Talking*

Book: African Americans and the Bible (New Haven, CT: Yale University Press, 2006); and Mitzi Smith, *Womanist Sass and Talk Back: Social (In)Justice, Intersectionality, and Biblical Interpretation* (Eugene, OR: Cascade, 2018). See also Kelly Brown Douglas, *Sexuality and the Black Church: A Womanist Perspective* (Maryknoll, NY: Orbis Books, 1999); and Anthony Pinn and Dwight Hopkins, eds., *Loving the Body: Black Religious Studies and the Erotic* (New York: Palgrave Macmillan, 2006). These two theological and religious studies texts explore the role of biblical interpretation in Black Christian and popular understandings of love and sex.

42. Stueart adds a link to an article that covers contemporary police killings of Black citizens. See Daniel Funnke and Tina Susman, "From Ferguson to Baton Rouge: Deaths of Black Men and Women at the Hands of Police," *Los Angeles Times*, July 12, 2016, www.latimes.com/nation/la-na-police -deaths-20160707-snap-htmlstory.html.

43. Jerome Stueart, "The Book of Birmingham: Adding Martin Luther King Jr.'s 'Letter from a Birmingham Jail' to the Bible," September 22, 2014, https://talkingdog.wordpress.com/2014/09/22/the-book-of-birmingham -adding-martin-luther-king-jrs-letter-from-a-birmingham-jail-to-the-bible/. Over the years, King's "Letter" has been published under slightly different titles. I use the title as published in James Washington, ed., *A Testament of Hope: The Essential Writings and Speeches of Martin Luther King, Jr.* (New York: Harper and Row, 1986), which appears to be the original title under which it was published in 1963.

44. "Theologians Consider New Black Book Bible Addition," *Jet* 56, no. 22 (August 16, 1979), 52, https://books.google.com/books?id=xEID AAAAMBAJ&pg=PA53&dq=canonize+king%27s+letter+from +birmingham+jail&hl=en&sa=X&ved=0ahUKEwjQqYPTpPfiAhXB c98KHZvIBDMQ6AEIQTAE#v=onepage&q=canonize%20king's%20 letter%20from%2birmingham%20jail&f=false.

45. Among this large and definitive body of scholarship that Black Christians should engage on the topic of patriarchal marriage and gender roles are Shively Smith, *Strangers to Family: Diaspora and 1 Peter's Invention of God's Household* (Waco, TX: Baylor University Press, 2016); Nyasha Junior, *An Introduction to Womanist Biblical Interpretation* (Louisville, KY: Westminster John Knox Press, 2015); Mitzi Smith, ed., *I Found God in Me: A Womanist Biblical Hermeneutics Reader* (Eugene, OR: Cascade Books, 2015); Gaye Byron and Vanessa Lovelace, eds., *Womanist Interpretations of the Bible: Expanding the Discourse* (Atlanta: SBL Press, 2016); Stephanie Crowder, *When Momma Speaks: The Bible and Motherhood from a Womanist Perspective* (Louisville, KY: Westminster John Knox Press, 2016); Delores Williams, *Sisters in the Wilderness: The Challenge of Womanist God-Talk* (1993; reprint, Maryknoll, NY: Orbis Books, 2013); Wilda Gafney, *Womanist Midrash: A Reintroduction to the Women of the Torah and the Throne* (Louisville, KY: Westminster John Knox Press, 2017); and Renita Weems, *Battered Love: Marriage, Sex, and Violence in the Hebrew Prophets* (Minneapolis: Fortress Press, 1995).

46. David Masci, Besheer Mohamed, and Gregory Smith, "Black Americans Are More Likely Than Overall Public to Be Christian, Protestant," *Fact Tank: News in the Numbers*, Pew Research Center, April 23, 2018, www.pewresearch.org/fact-tank/2018/04/23/black-americans-are-more-likely-than-overall-public-to-be-christian-protestant/.

47. Masci, Mohamed, and Smith, "Black Americans Are More Likely Than Overall Public."

48. King and Allen, "Personal Characteristics," 570.

49. Melvin Oliver and Thomas Shapiro, "Disrupting the Racial Wealth Gap," *Contexts* 18, no. 1 (2019): 17–18. See also Dalton Conley, *Being Black, Living in the Red: Race, Wealth, and Social Policy in America* (Berkeley: University of California Press, 1999).

50. Armon Perry, "African American Men's Attitudes Toward Marriage," *Journal of Black Studies* 44, no. 2 (2013): 193. In discussions about "absent" Black fathers, it's important to ask ourselves what we mean by absent in the light of the Centers for Disease Control's 2013 study that revealed that, for data ranging from 2006 to 2010, across a number of measured activities, Black men were more involved with their children on a daily basis than White and Latino men. This was true in many cases for both residential and nonresidential fathers. See Jo Jones and William Mosher, "Fathers' Involvement with Their Children: United States, 2006–2010," December 20, 2013, www.cdc.gov/nchs/data/nhsr/nhsr071.pdf. See also Charles Blow, "Black Dads Are Doing Best of All," *New York Times*, June 8, 2015, www.nytimes.com/2015/06/08/opinion/charles-blow-black-dads-are-doing-the-best-of-all.html.

51. These figures do not account for the fact that unmarried Black women are not necessarily unpartnered. It's not uncommon for unmarried Black mothers to live with their child's father, at least in the early period of the child's life. Thus, it may be misleading to consider their children to be reared exclusively in single-parent homes. Admittedly, cohabitation can be a less stable arrangement than marriage; however, the percentage of Black single-parent homes is significantly smaller when we take into account the prevalence of cohabitation. See Joyce Martin et al., "Births: Final Data for 2017," *National Vital Statistics Reports* 67, no. 8 (2018): 5–6; Annie E. Casey Foundation, Kids Count Data Center, https://datacenter.kidscount.org/data/bar/107-children-in-single-parent-families-by-race?loc=1&loct=1#1/any/false/871/10,11,9,12,1,185,13/431; and Steven Camarota, "Births to Unmarried Mothers by Nativity and Education," Center for Immigration Studies, May 5, 2017, https://cis.org/Camarota/Births-Unmarried-Mothers-Nativity-and-Education. See also Gretchen Livingston, "The Changing Profile of Unmarried Parents," Pew Research Center Social and Demographic Trends, April 25, 2018, www.pewsocialtrends.org/2018/04/25/the-changing-profile-of-unmarried-parents/.

52. See, for example, the fallout from Reverend Jasper Williams's August 31, 2018, comments about single Black mothers and the rearing of sons during

his delivery of Aretha Franklin's eulogy. Paula Rogo cites many responses in her article "Many Were Not Happy with the Eulogy at Aretha Franklin's Funeral," *Essence*, September 2, 2018, www.essence.com/culture/eulogy -aretha-franklin-funeral-reverend-jasper-williams/. See also the African American Policy Forum's *Igniting Change*, "#StandingUpForMom: Resisting the War on Black Single Mothers," hosted by Barbara Arnwine, March 29, 2016, http://aapf.org/black-single-mothers.

53. Asha French, "A 'Daddy-Daughter Date,' Queer Single Mom-Style," *New York Times*, April 26, 2019, www.nytimes.com/2019/04/26/opinion /sunday/daddy-daughter-date.html. For a perspective that addresses Black women who become mothers through adoption, see Nefertiti Austin, *Motherhood So White: A Memoir of Race, Gender, and Parenting in America* (Naperville, IL: Sourcebooks, 2019).

54. For a Black single mother's perspective on marriage that takes into account many of the themes discussed in this chapter, see Tiffanie Drayton, "Marriage Isn't for Black Women," February 15, 2018, *Marie Claire*, www .marieclaire.com/sex-love/a17884845/black-couples-marriage-issues/.

55. Sandra Lane et el., "Marriage Promotion and Missing Men: African American Women in a Demographic Double Bind," *Medical Anthropology Quarterly* 18, no. 4 (2005): 405–428.

56. John Cacioppo and William Patrick, *Loneliness: Human Nature and the Need for Social Connection* (New York: W. W. Norton, 2008), 4. Cacioppo and Patrick also expound upon the link they make between loneliness and health: "Chronic *feelings* of isolation can drive a cascade of physiological events that actually accelerates the aging process. Loneliness not only alters behavior but shows up in measurements of stress hormones, immune function, and cardiovascular function. Over time, these changes in physiology are compounded in ways that may be hastening millions of people to an early grave" (5).

57. Mike Maciag, "Where Have All the Black Men Gone?," *Governing*, February 2019, www.governing.com/topics/public-justice-safety/gov -black-men-gender-imbalance-population.html; "Black Women Students Far Outnumber Black Men at the Nation's Highest-Ranked Universities," *Journal of Blacks in Higher Education* (March 9, 2006), www .jbhe.com/news_views/51_gendergap_universities.html; www.jbhe .com/latest/index030906.html; "The Gender Gap in African American Educational Attainment," March 18, 2019, www.jbhe.com/2019/03 /the-gender-gap-in-african-american-educational-attainment-2/.

58. Banks, *Is Marriage for White People?*, 181.

59. Cheryl Judice, *Interracial Relationships Between Black Women and White Men* (Pennsauken, NJ: BookBaby, 2018), back cover. See also Cheryl Judice, *Interracial Marriages Between Black Women and White Men* (Amherst, MA: Cambria Press, 2008). For a book that addresses Black women's hesitation to date White men, see Karyn Folan, *Don't Bring Home a White Boy: And Other Notions That Keep Black Women from Dating Out* (New York: Gallery Books, 2010).

60. Nicole Cardos, "Why One Sociologist Says It's Time for Black Women to Date White Men," WTTW News, April 17, 2019, https://news .wttw.com/2019/04/17/sociologist-cheryl-judice-interracial-relationships.

61. "Columnist Heidi Stevens in Conversation with Cheryl Judice," *Chicago Tribune*, November 16, 2018, www.youtube.com/watch?v=H7f 2RCf6DLQ.

62. Issa Rae, *The Misadventures of Awkward Black Girl* (2015; reprint, New York: 37 Ink/Atria Paperback, 2016), 137–139; Yesha, "Some People Are Mad Because a Chapter in Issa Rae's 3-Year-Old Book Says Black Women and Asian Men Should Date Each Other," *Root*, April 30, 2018, https://thegrapevine.theroot.com/some-people-are-mad-at-a-3-year-old -passage-in-issa-rae-1825648702; Chantilly Post, "Issa Rae Finally Addresses Comments Made About Asian Men and Black Women Dating," *HotNewHipHop*, August 10, 2018, www.hotnewhiphop.com/issa-rae -finally-addresses-comments-made-about-asian-men-and-black-women -dating-news.57088.html. For a scroll of numerous derisive posts about Issa Rae authored by Black men, see Chrissie, "When Black Men Get a Taste of Their Own Medicine: Issa Rae and Asian Men," May 3, 2018, www.youtube .com/watch?v=_OWEKX1LqNI.

63. Judice, *Interracial Relationships Between Black Women and White Men*, 4.

64. Preamble to the Constitution of the United States: The Bill of Rights and All Amendments, https://constitutionus.com/.

65. For more on the concept of "racial capitalism," see Jodi Melamed, "Racial Capitalism," *Critical Ethnic Studies* 1, no. 1 (2015): 76–85; Nancy Leong, "Racial Capitalism," *Harvard Law Review* 126, no. 8 (June 2013): 2151–2226; and Jordanna Matlon, "Racial Capitalism and the Crisis of Black Masculinity," *American Sociological Review* 81, no. 5 (2016): 1014–1038. See also Cedric Robinson, *Black Marxism: The Making of a Black Radical Tradition* (1983; reprint, Chapel Hill: University of North Carolina Press, 2000), for his pioneering theorization of racial capitalism and its foundations in European feudalism and culture, even before the rise of racial slavery.

66. Danielle McGuire, *At the Dark End of the Street: Black Women, Rape, and Resistance—a New History of the Civil Rights Movement from Rosa Parks to the Rise of Black Power* (New York: Vintage Books, 2011); "New Study Says Black Women Are Least Likely to Get Picked by ANY Race of Men While Online Dating," posted November 15, 2013, https:// tpc.googlesyndication.com/safeframe/1-0-5/html/container.html#xpc =sf-gdn-exp-4&p=https%3A//bossip.com. For an optimistic take on Black women and options for dating outside the race, see Banks, *Is Marriage for White People?*, 115–128.

67. Brittany Slatton, "Deep Frames, White Men's Discourse, and Black Women's Bodies" (PhD diss., Texas A&M University, 2009), iv.

68. Slatton, "Deep Frames, White Men's Discourse, and Black Women's Bodies," 58–61.

69. Brittany Slatton, *Mythologizing Black Women: Unveiling White Men's Deep Frame on Race and Gender* (New York: Routledge, 2014), 48, 65, 101–102. All respondents in Slatton's study were assigned fictional names to protect their identities.

70. Slatton, *Mythologizing Black Women*, 1–36, 107–124.

71. Lillian Singh, "The State of Black Unions: Changing the Color of Love," HuffPost Black Voices, *Huffington Post*, October 12, 2014, www.huffingtonpost.com/lillian-d-singh/the-state-of-black-unions_b_5671579html.

72. Michelle Martin, "Activists Unite for 'No Wedding, No Womb,'" *Tell Me More*, September 22, 2010, www.npr.org/templates/story/story.php?storyId=130047875.

73. Christelyn Karazin and Janice Littlejohn, *Swirling: How to Date, Mate and Relate Mixing Race, Culture and Creed* (New York: Atria Paperback, 2012); Christelyn Karazin, "Beyond Black and White Elite," www.youtube.com/channel/UCcdZS7fxGCG0ZrQNX3EsQLg.

74. *Being Mary Jane*, season 3, episode 10, "Some Things Are Black and White," *BET*, December 14, 2015, www.bet.com/shows/being-mary-jane.html. For a critical take on the new wave of authors and social media influencers who are encouraging Black women to date and marry interracially, see Renee Romano, "Something Old, Something New: Black Women, Interracial Dating, and the Black Marriage Crisis," *Differences: A Journal of Feminist Cultural Studies* 29, no. 2 (2018): 126–153. Karazin and others like her who promote Black women dating outside the race have received growing criticism for messaging to Black women that the ideal non-Black beau is a White one. Some of the critiques are mired in vitriol; however, others are thoughtful and compelling. See, for example, Anita Badejo, "Should Black Women Head to Europe for More Romantic Options?," *For Harriet*, July 11, 2014, www.forharriet.com/2014/07/should-black-women-head-to-europe-for.html; Charing Ball, "When Keeping It Swirl Goes Wrong: Why Are Black People Obsessed with Interracial Dating?," *Madamenoire*, September 5, 2012, https://madamenoire.com/211759/when-keeping-it-swirl-goes-wrong-why-are-black-people-obsessed-with-interracial-dating/; Root Staff, "How an Interracial-Dating Web Series Gets Everything Wrong," *Root*, March 10, 2014, www.theroot.com/how-an-interracial-dating-web-series-gets-everything-wr-1790874880; and Dani, "I'm Not Down with the Swirl (Yeah I Said It)," *OK, Dani: Intentionally Creating a Happier Healthier Life*, February 8, 2016, www.okdani.com/im-in-an-interracial-marriage-and-im-not-down-with-the-swirl/.

75. Armon Perry and Derrick Brooms, "Commitment, Partnership, and Family: African American Men's Concepts of Marriage and Meaning," *Spectrum: A Journal on Black Men* 1, no. 2 (2013): 55.

76. Perry and Brooms, "Commitment, Partnership, and Family," 60–61. All participants in the study were assigned pseudonyms to protect their identities.

77. Perry and Brooms, "Commitment, Partnership, and Family," 61.

78. Perry and Brooms, "Commitment, Partnership, and Family," 66.

79. Perry and Brooms, "Commitment, Partnership, and Family," 69.

80. Perry and Brooms, "Commitment, Partnership, and Family," 72.

81. Some scholars have explained that, despite the views Black couples hold about gendered marital roles, Black couples can find themselves actually adhering to more egalitarian roles in their day-to-day lives. For a recent qualitative study involving close to fifty Black couples that explores among other themes the issue of egalitarian marriage, see Katrina McDonald and Caitlin Cross-Barnet, *Marriage in Black: The Pursuit of Married Life Among American-born and Immigrant Blacks* (New York: Routledge, 2018).

82. Spradlin, "Benton Couple Celebrates 80 Years of Marriage."

83. For sources, see Chapter 2, notes 101–102.

84. Another revealing result was that 52 percent of Blacks (compared with only 27 percent of Whites) said that it was "very important for a woman to be able to provide for a family." This finding suggests to me that the undeniable effects of inherited poverty and wealthlessness upon Black families are impacting Black adults' perceptions of marital responsibilities regarding financial stability. The Pew Research Center's American Trends Panel was used for survey sampling. See Parker and Stepler, "Americans See Men as the Financial Providers."

85. Even in slavery, some scholars argue that Black men's bruised and diminished sense of manhood accounts for the "frequent reports" of violence perpetrated against their wives. See Ann Patton Malone and Angela James, *Sweet Chariot: Slave Family and Household Structure in Nineteenth-Century Louisiana* (Chapel Hill: University of North Carolina Press, 1992), 228–229. See also Jeff Forret, *Slave Against Slave: Plantation Violence in the Old South* (Baton Rouge: Louisiana State University Press, 2015), esp. 236–286; Casey Bond, "Marriages with Female Breadwinners Still Struggle," *Huffington Post*, July 12, 2018, www.huffpost.com/entry/female-breadwinners-marriage_n_5b3ef51fe4b09e4a8b2b780c; and Claire Miller, "When Wives Earn More Than Husbands Neither Partner Likes to Admit It," *New York Times*, July 17, 2018, www.nytimes.com/2018/07/17/upshot/when-wives-earn-more-than-husbands-neither-like-to-admit-it.html.

86. Tamara Harris, "Unfit for the Altar: Black Women Make Their Own Marital Rules," *bitchmedia*, February 28, 2019, www.bitchmedia.org/article/some-us-are-brave/unfit-altar-black-women-make-their-own-marital-rules.

87. Seminal resources for personal and communal reflection on steps toward dismantling patriarchy in Black institutions and affirming healthy modes of Black masculine inhabitance are Rudolph Byrd and Beverly Guy-Sheftall, eds., *Traps: African American Men on Gender and Sexuality* (Bloomington: Indiana University Press, 2001); bell hooks, *The Will to Change: Men, Masculinity, and Love* (New York: Atria Books, 2004); and Johnnetta Cole and Beverly Guy-Sheftall, *Gender Talk: The Struggle for Women's Equality in African American Communities* (New York: Random House, 2003).

88. This number is strikingly low when compared with the 18 percent of "other churches" that offer relationship programs. National Healthy Marriage Resource Center, "Overview and Background of the African American Community," www.healthymarriageinfo.org/research-policy /marriage-facts-and-research/marriage-and-divorce-statistics-by-culture /african-americans-and-black-community/.

89. For a summary of the four major explanatory approaches to African American family structures, see Donna Franklin and Angela James, *Ensuring Inequality: The Structural Transformation of the African-American Family* (New York: Oxford University Press, 2015), xvi–xviii, 3–18. See also Shirley Hill, "Marriage Among African American Women: A Gender Perspective," *Journal of Comparative Family Studies* 37, no. 3 (2006): 421–440.

90. Carol Stack, *All Our Kin: Strategies for Survival in a Black Community* (New York: Basic Books, 1974); Herbert Gutman, *The Black Family in Slavery and Freedom, 1750–1925* (New York: Random House, 1976); Hill, "Marriage Among African American Women," 429–430.

91. Nicholas Lemann, *The Promised Land: The Great Migration and How It Changed America* (New York: Vintage Books, 1992), 31–32. Noralee Frankel's *Freedom's Women* provides a historical account of the cultural and sociopolitical context in which Black Mississippians established Africana marriage and kinship traditions after the Civil War. For more on Africana kinship networks, especially extended family structures, see Stack, *All Our Kin*; Brenda Stevenson, *Life in Black and White: Family and Community in the Slave South* (New York: Oxford University Press, 1996), esp. 325; Tera Hunter, *To 'Joy My Freedom: Southern Black Women's Lives and Labors After the Civil War* (Cambridge, MA: Harvard University Press, 1997), 36–37; Patricia Hill Collins, *Black Feminist Thought: Knowledge, Consciousness, and the Politics of Empowerment* (New York: Routledge, 2000), 53, 179; and Dylan Penningroth, *The Claims of Kinfolk: African American Property and Community in the Nineteenth-Century South* (Chapel Hill: University of North Carolina Press, 2003), 8, 86–89.

92. Franklin and James, *Ensuring Inequality*, 33; Linda Blum and Theresa Deussen, "Negotiating Independent Motherhood: Working-Class African American Women Talk About Marriage and Motherhood," *Gender and Society* 10, no. 2 (1996): 199–211.

93. Scholars posit that living in close proximity to and contact with extended family members (extended family embeddedness) offers Black children nurturance and a social safety net that cushion the blow of divorce/ parental separation. They also hypothesize that because Black children are more commonly exposed to socioeconomic stress, they are not likely to experience divorce/parental separation as a major impediment relative to the other socioeconomic stressors they confront. See Vonnie McLoyd et al., "Marital Processes and Parental Socialization in Families of Color: A Decade Review of Research," *Journal of Marriage and the Family* 62, no. 4 (2000): 1070–1093;

Paul Amato, "Children of Divorce in the 1990s: An Update of the Amato and Keith (1991) Meta-Analysis," *Journal of Family Psychology* 15, no. 3 (2001): 355–370; Paul Amato and Bruce Keith, "Parental Divorce and Adult Well-Being: A Meta-Analysis," *Journal of Marriage and the Family* 53, no. 1 (1991): 43–58; Thomas Smith, "Differences Between Black and White Students in the Effect of Parental Separation on School Grades," *Journal of Divorce and Remarriage* 27, no. 1–2 (1997): 25–42; and Sara McLanahan and Gary Sandefur, *Growing Up with a Single Parent: What Hurts, What Helps* (Cambridge, MA: Harvard University Press, 1994). It is important to acknowledge that even these and many other studies indicate that children reared in homes with both of their biological parents generally experience higher educational attainment than those raised in single-parent homes. For an example of a longitudinal statewide study that showed related results, see Angela Henneberger et al., "Student and School Concentrated Poverty in Maryland: What Are the Long-Term High School, College, and Career Outcomes?," Maryland Longitudinal Data System Center, April 2019, https://mldscenter .maryland.gov/egov/Publications/ResearchReports/MDStudentandSchool ConcentratedPoverty2019.pdf.

94. Christina Cross, "Racial/Ethnic Differences in the Association Between Family Structure and Children's Education," *Journal of Marriage and Family* (2019): 1–22, doi:10.1111/jomf.12625. Although exploring contemporary Africana provillage kinship traditions in the United States is beyond the purview of what I can address in this book, it's important to acknowledge that reports and conversations exist across digital media indicating that some single Black mothers are creating provillage families—kin groups based on the fact that their children share the same father. These kin groups offer incalculable support to one another, especially when their children's father is incarcerated. Other Black women are deliberately entering into plural love relationships and marital unions, and some testify to the pragmatic value of these unions that offer opportunities to pool economic resources and share household responsibilities. I've even heard of two solidly middle-class, young, first-generation families of African continental heritage who created their own provillage kin structure, even investing in a shared home, where two husband-and-wife couples and their children live together under one large roof. Combining their resources allowed them to acquire prized real estate and places four adults at the disposal of the four children in the kin group. For more information, see Patricia Dixon-Spear, *We Want for Our Sisters What We Want for Ourselves: African American Women Who Practice Polygyny by Consent* (Baltimore: Black Classic Press, 2009); and Funlayo Woods-Menzies, "A Look at Polygamy in Black America," *Medium*, February 14, 2019, https:// medium.com/s/story/dating-while-married-an-inside-look-at-poly-gamy-in -black-america-16049c79a96b.

95. Social scientists have discovered, for example, that the government has spent more than $600 million on Healthy Marriage Initiative programs

since 2001, and these programs have yielded negligible outcomes for targeted populations served, including many Black individuals and communities. See Wendy Manning et al., "Healthy Marriage Initiative Spending and U.S. Marriage & Divorce Rates, a State-Level Analysis" (FP-14-02), National Center for Family and Marriage Research, 2014, www.bgsu.edu/content /dam/BGSU/college-of-arts-and-sciences/NCFMR/documents/FP/FP-14 -02_HMIInitiative.pdf; and Matthew Johnson, "Healthy Marriage Initiatives: On the Need for Empiricism in Policy Implementation," *American Psychologist* 67, no. 4 (May–June 2012): 296–308. In "Disrupting the Racial Wealth Gap," 19, sociologists Melvin Oliver and Thomas Shapiro argue that there is no one "big fix" that can remedy Black wealthlessness. Instead, a multipronged, expansive, and inclusive implementation of a wide range of robust policies is essential. To begin, they propose four such policies, including one that I have long championed since I first learned of it some years ago: "Baby Bonds, Universal Basic Income, Reducing or Forgiving Student Debt, and a Federal Job Guarantee."

96. Adrian Florido, "Black, Latino Two-Parent Families Have Half the Wealth of White Single Parents," NPR, February 8, 2017, www.npr.org /sections/codeswitch/2017/02/08/514105689/black-latino-two-parent -families-have-half-the-wealth-of-white-single-parents. See also Hill, "Marriage Among African American Women," 436; and National Center for Education Statistics, "Characteristics of Children's Families," *The Condition of Education, 2019*, updated May 2019, https://nces.ed.gov/programs/coe /indicator_cce.asp.

97. Mary Wood, "Marriage-Penalty Tax Hurts Black Families More, Brown Says," University of Virginia School of Law, *News and Media*, February 2, 2004, www.law.virginia.edu/news/2004_spr/brown_tax.htm. See also Dorothy Brown, "The Marriage Penalty/Bonus Debate: Legislative Issues in Black and White," *New York Law School Journal of Human Rights* 16 (1999): 287–302, esp. 292–299; and Drayton, "Marriage Isn't for Black Women."

98. Alisha Gaines, *Black for a Day: Fantasies of Race and Empathy* (Chapel Hill: University of North Carolina Press, 2017). Building on her book's central argument, Gaines lectured on her concept of "empathy plus"—real risk taking and sacrifice on the part of Whites who profess to care about the structural oppression of Black people. Alisha Gaines, "Black for a Day: White Fantasies of Race and Empathy," UNCF/Mellon Mays 2019 Undergraduate Fellowship Summer Institute Rudolph Byrd Distinguished Lecture, Emory University, June 6, 2019.

99. Tommy Curry, *The Man-Not*.

100. Winship, Reeves, and Guyot, "Inheritance of Black Poverty."

101. When comparing across gender and race, Black women actually have the highest economic fragility. Researchers found that Black women are at the highest risk for remaining in poverty (62 percent), followed by Black

men (50 percent), White women (33 percent), and White men (28 percent), when considering mobility within the context of adult family incomes. See Winship, Reeves, and Guyot, "Inheritance of Black Poverty."

102. Melamed, "Racial Capitalism," 77.

103. Wang, Wilcox, and Mincy, "2.5 Million Black Men Are in the Upper Class."

104. Darrick Hamilton, "How 'Baby Bonds' Could Help Close the Wealth Gap," TED Talk, January 15, 2019, www.youtube.com/watch?v=qlz johcBkmg; Lynn Parramore, "Baby Bonds: A Plan for Black/White Wealth Equality Conservatives Could Love?," October 25, 2016, www.inet economics.org/perspectives/blog/baby-bonds-a-plan-for-black-white-wealth -equality-conservatives-could-love-1; Heather Long, "There's a Serious Proposal to Give Babies Born in the United States $20,000 (or More)," *Washington Post*, January 8, 2019, www.washingtonpost.com/news/wonk /wp/2018/01/08/theres-a-serious-proposal-to-give-every-baby-born-in -america-20000-or-more/?utm_term=.d2463a0e425b; Matthew Boesler, "'Baby Bonds' Could Help the U.S. Wealth Gap," *Bloomberg*, April 5, 2019, www.bloomberg.com/news/articles/2019-04-05/-baby-bonds-could-help -the-u-s-wealth-gap; Paul Solman, "Can Baby Bonds Help the U.S. Close Its Staggering Racial Wealth Gap?," *PBS NewsHour*, June 13, 2019; Darrick Hamilton and William Darity Jr., "Can 'Baby Bonds' Eliminate the Racial Wealth Gap in Putative Post-racial America?," *Review of Black Political Economy* 37, nos. 3–4 (2010): 207–216.

105. "Cory Booker Shares His Big Idea for 'Baby Bonds,'" *Nightly News*, NBC, June 17, 2019, www.nbcnews.com/nightly-news/video/cory -booker-shares-his-big-idea-for-baby-bonds-62122053719. For more on how America's "bigoted policies" created race-based "differentials in wealth," see "Systemic Racism Explained," www.youtube.com/watch?v=YrHIQIO_bdQ.

106. Sydney Combs, "What Is Juneteenth—and What Does It Celebrate?," *National Geographic*, June 19, 2019, www.nationalgeographic.com /culture/holidays/reference/juneteenth/.

107. Ta-Nehisi Coates, "The Case for Reparations," *Atlantic*, June 2014, www.theatlantic.com/magazine/archive/2014/06/the-case-for -reparations/361631/.

108. The National African American Reparations Committee (NAARC) proposes a comprehensive ten-point "Preliminary Reparations Program." My suggestions concerning Black women's reproductive and maternal health should be considered as part of a larger agenda aimed at dismantling "medical apartheid" and racial disparities in health care and health care outcomes. They already align with and could be encompassed under point five: "Resources for the Health, Wealth and Healing of Black Families and Communities." For the full program, see National African American Reparations Committee, "Preliminary Reparations Program: A Document for Review, Revision and Adoption as a Platform to Guide the Struggle for Reparations for People of African Descent in the U.S.," https://ibw21.org/docs/naarc/NAARC

_Preliminary_Reparations_Program.pdf. For sources on the perils and disadvantages Black women face pertaining to reproductive and maternal health, see Clarke, *Inequalities of Love*; Washington, *Medical Apartheid*; Richard Behrman and Adrienne Butler, eds., *Preterm Birth: Causes, Consequences, and Prevention* (Washington, DC: National Academies Press, 2007); and Arden Handler, Joan Kennelly, and Nadine Peacock, eds., *Reducing Racial/ Ethnic Disparities in Reproductive and Perinatal Outcomes: The Evidence from Population-Based Interventions* (New York: Springer Science+Business Media, 2011). See also George Halvorson, *Ending Racial, Ethnic, and Cultural Disparities in Healthcare* (North Charleston, SC: CreateSpace, 2013); and the Black Women's Health Imperative website, https://bwhi.org/. For a compelling perspective that complements the substantive focus on women and family that I believe is necessary in any reparations deliberations pertaining to African descendants in America, see Susan Oiken, *Justice, Gender, and the Family* (New York: Basic Books, 1989). Oiken argues that family is a central component of imagining and expanding justice because of pervasive gender inequalities in America.

109. Tara John and Swati Gupta, "Miss India Finalists Photograph Stirs Debate over Fair Skin Obsession," CNN, May 31, 2019, www.msn.com /en-us/news/world/miss-india-finalists-photograph-stirs-debate-over-fair -skin-obsession/ar-AACbBi4?ocid=spartanntp. According to this report, "Cosmetic brands globally have profited from the insecurity [over skin color], cashing in on a multi-million dollar industry of creams, skin bleaches and invasive procedures that promise to lighten skin. The demand for whiteners is projected to reach $31 billion by 2024, up from $18 billion in 2017, especially in Asia, the Middle East and Africa, according to market intelligence firm Global Industry Analysts. Routine skin whitener use ranges from 25 percent in Mali to 77 percent in Nigeria, and it's 40 percent in China, Malaysia, the Philippines, and South Korea, according to the World Health Organization." See also Elizabeth Hordge-Freeman, *The Color of Love: Racial Features, Stigma, and Socialization in Black Brazilian Families* (Austin: University of Texas Press, 2015); Obiora Anekwe, "Global Colorism: An Ethical Issue and Challenge in Bioethics," *Voices in Bioethics*, September 9, 2014, www.voicesinbioethics.net/features/2014/09/09 /global-colorism-an-ethical-issue-and-challenge-in-bioethics.

110. Sarah Webb, "Recognizing and Addressing Colorism in Schools," *Teaching Tolerance*, January 25, 2016, www.tolerance.org/magazine /recognizing-and-addressing-colorism-in-schools; Hannon, DeFina, and Bruch, "Relationship Between Skin Tone and School Suspension"; Ed Gordon, "Does Darker Skin Equal More Prison Time?," NPR, June 7, 2006, www.npr.org/templates/story/story.php?storyId=5457607; Traci Burch, "Skin Color and the Criminal Justice System: Beyond Black-White Disparities in Sentencing," *Journal of Empirical Legal Studies* 12, no. 3 (2015): 395–420; Ryan King and Brian Johnson, "A Punishing Look: Skin Tone and Afrocentric Features in the Halls of Justice," *American Journal of Sociology* 122,

no. 1 (2016): 90–124; Arthur Goldsmith, Darrick Hamilton, and William Darity Jr., "Shades of Discrimination: Skin Tone and Wages," *American Economic Review* 96, no. 2 (2006): 242–245; Matthew Harrison, "Colorism: The Often Un-discussed '-ism' in America's Workforce," in *The Jury Expert: The Art and Science of Litigation Advocacy*, American Society of Trial Experts, January 2010, 67–72, www.thejuryexpert.com/wp-content /uploads/HarrisonTJEJan2010.pdf; Kimberly Norwood, ed., *Color Matters: Skin Tone Bias and the Myth of a Post-racial America* (New York: Routledge, 2014); Kaitlyn Greenidge, "Why Black People Discriminate Among Ourselves: The Toxic Legacy of Colorism," *Guardian*, April 9, 2019, www .theguardian.com/lifeandstyle/2019/apr/09/colorism-racism-why-black -people-discriminate-among-ourselves; Michael Dyson, "The Color Line: Stephen Curry's Prominence Resurfaces Issues of Colorism Among Blacks," *Undefeated*, June 1, 2016, https://theundefeated.com/features/light -skinned-vs-dark-skinned/.

111. For example, see Chrissie, "Black Girl in Paris ft. Spirited Pursuit," April 18, 2019, www.youtube.com/watch?v=ytttFFP7_hU&list=PLo2p 3iEfGb37Fp59O2nkAc7s1BDQo1WBa; "Beautiful Older Black Woman, No Stereotypes: Corrective Promotion for Dark Skinned Women," April 4, 2019, www.youtube.com/watch?v=DJ6868B3fnM&list=PLo2p3iEfGb37F p59O2nkAc7s1BDQo1WBa&index=3.

112. "Flexin' in Her Complexion," *Steve TV Show*, October 8, 2017, www .youtube.com/watch?v=Qz26iwRox9Y; Jamie Yuccas, "'Flexin' in My Complexion': Girl Turns Bullying Experience into a Booming Business," *CBS This Morning*, July 31, 2018, www.cbsnews.com/news/flexin-in-my-complexion -how-a-girl-turned-her-bullying-experience-into-a-booming-business/. "This Tween Launched Flexin' in My Complexion After Being Bullied," *Make It*, produced by Andrea Kramar, CNBC, July 13, 2018, www.youtube .com/watch?v=Yb5Kv2YyQ3o.

113. Alice Walker is among the first three women of African descent to coin and develop the concept of "womanism," during the late 1970s and early 1980s, based on Black women's culturally and spiritually rich ways of caring for self, family, and community in a world marred by anti-Black intersectional violence and oppression. Womanism "is rooted in the lived experience of survival, community building, intimacy with the natural environment, health, healing and personal growth among everyday people from all walks of life," and it's "Black women's gift to the world," writes womanist scholar Layli Maparyan. See her volume *The Womanist Idea* (New York: Routledge, 2012), 31, 33.

114. Yuccas, "'Flexin' in My Complexion.'"

115. "Fox Refers to Michelle Obama as 'Baby Mama,'" *Today*, June 12, 2008, www.today.com/popculture/fox-refers-michelle-obama-baby-mama -wbna25129598; David Bauder, "Fox News: Michelle Obama Is 'Obama's Baby Mama,'" *Fox News*, www.youtube.com/watch?v=TvZEZL2LmA8.

116. Hillary Clinton, *It Takes a Village: And Other Lessons Children Teach Us* (New York: Simon & Schuster, 1996).

117. My phrasing here is inspired by Aretha Franklin's recording of "Wholly Holy," on her album *Amazing Grace* (Atlantic Records, June 1, 1972). The song was cowritten by Al Cleveland, Marvin Gaye, and Renaldo Benson and originally released by Marvin Gaye on his *What's Going On* album (Tamia Records, May 21, 1971).

118. Among the numerous organizations and sodalities that promote Black sisterhood are Black Girls Travel Too, www.blackgirlstraveltoo.com/; Black Girls Run, https://blackgirlsrun.com/; Black Girls Rock, https://blackgirlsrock.com/; and Well-Read Black Girl, www.wellreadblackgirl.com/.

Afterword

1. *Being Mary Jane*, season 5, episode 1, "Becoming Pauletta," *BET*, April 23, 2019, https://www.bet.com/shows/being-mary-jane.html.

Index

About the Author

Credit: Heather LaShun

Dianne Marie Stewart is an associate professor of religion and African American Studies at Emory University specializing in African heritage religious cultures in the Caribbean and the Americas. She obtained her BA degree from Colgate University in English and African American Studies, her MDiv degree from Harvard Divinity School, and her PhD degree in systematic theology from Union Theological Seminary in New York City, where she studied with well-known scholars such as Delores Williams, James Washington, and her adviser, James Cone. Stewart joined Emory's faculty of Arts and Sciences in 2001 and teaches courses in the graduate and undergraduate programs.

Stewart has won several awards and fellowships, including the Emory Williams Distinguished Undergraduate Teaching Award, Emory College of Arts and Sciences' Distinguished Advising Award, Emory University Laney Graduate School's Eleanor Main Graduate Faculty Mentor Award, a Fulbright Scholar award, and a senior fellowship at the Bill and Carol Fox Center for Humanistic Inquiry. Stewart has also served on several committees within the American Academy of Religion, and she is a founding coeditor, with Jacob Olupona and Terrence Johnson, of the Religious Cultures of African and African Diaspora People series at Duke University Press.